Lecture Notes in Computer Science

Edited by G. Goos, J. Hartmanis, and J. van Lee

Springer

Berlin
Heidelberg
New York
Barcelona
Hong Kong
London
Milan
Paris
Tokyo

Maria Marinaro   Roberto Tagliaferri (Eds.)

Neural Nets

13th Italian Workshop on Neural Nets, WIRN VIETRI 2002
Vietri sul Mare, Italy, May 30 – June 1, 2002
Revised Papers

Springer

Series Editors

Gerhard Goos, Karlsruhe University, Germany
Juris Hartmanis, Cornell University, NY, USA
Jan van Leeuwen, Utrecht University, The Netherlands

Volume Editors

Maria Marinaro
Dipartimento di Fisica, "E.R. Caianiello"
Via S. Allende, Baronissi (Salerno), Italy
and
International Institute for Advanced Scientific Studies
"E.R. Caianiello", IIASS
Via G. Pellegrino, 19, 84019 Vietri Sul Mare (Salerno), Italy
E-mail: iiass.vietri@tin.it

Roberto Tagliaferri
Dipartimento di Matematica ed Informatica
Via S. Allende, Baronissi (Salerno), Italy
E-mail: robtag@unisa.it

Cataloging-in-Publication Data applied for

Die Deutsche Bibliothek - CIP-Einheitsaufnahme

Neural nets : revised papers / 13th Italian Workshop on Neural Nets, WIRN
VIETRI 2002, Vietri sul Mare, Italy, May 30 - June 1, 2002. Maria Marinaro ;
Roberto Tagliaferri (ed.). - Berlin ; Heidelberg ; New York ; Hong Kong ;
London ; Milan ; Paris ; Tokyo : Springer, 2002
   (Lecture notes in computer science ; Vol. 2486)
   ISBN 3-540-44265-0

CR Subject Classification (1998): F.1.1, I.2.6, B.6.1., C.1, J.3

ISSN 0302-9743
ISBN 3-540-44265-0 Springer-Verlag Berlin Heidelberg New York

Springer-Verlag Berlin Heidelberg New York,
a member of BertelsmannSpringer Science+Business Media GmbH

http://www.springer.de

© Springer-Verlag Berlin Heidelberg 2002
Printed in Germany

Typesetting: Camera-ready by author, data conversion by DA-TeX Gerd Blumenstein
Printed on acid-free paper   SPIN: 10870619   06/3142   5 4 3 2 1 0

Preface

This volume contains the proceedings of the 13th Italian Workshop on Neural Nets WIRN VIETRI 2002, jointly organized by the International Institute for Advanced Scientific Studies "Eduardo R. Caianiello" (IIASS), the Società Italiana Reti Neuroniche (SIREN), the IEEE NNC Italian RIG, and the Italian SIG of the INNS.

In this book a review talk, dealing with a very up-to-date topic "Ensembles of Learning Machines", and original contributions, approved by the referee committee as oral or poster presentations, have been collected. The contributions have been assembled, for reading convenience, into sections.

The last section, devoted to "Learning in Neural Networks: Limitations and Future Trends", was organized by Prof. M. Gori and also contains the invited lecture "Mathematical Modeling of Generalization" given by Dr. Martin Anthony. The first and second sections are dedicated, respectively, to the memory of two scientists who were friends in life, Professors Francesco Lauria and Eduardo R. Caianiello.

The editors thank all the participants for their qualified contributions, while special thanks go to Prof. M. Gori for his help in the organization, and to the referees for their accurate work.

July 2002

Maria Marinaro
Roberto Tagliaferri

Table of Contents

Image and Signal Processing

Special Session on "Learning in Neural Networks: Limitations and Future Trends" Chaired by Marco Gori

Part I

Review Papers

Ensembles of Learning Machines

Giorgio Valentini[1,2] and Francesco Masulli[1,3]

[1] INFM, Istituto Nazionale per la Fisica della Materia
16146 Genova, Italy
[2] DISI, Università di Genova
16146 Genova, Italy
valenti@disi.unige.it
[3] Dipartimento di Informatica, Università di Pisa
56125 Pisa, Italy
masulli@di.unipi.it

Abstract. Ensembles of learning machines constitute one of the main current directions in machine learning research, and have been applied to a wide range of real problems. Despite of the absence of an unified theory on ensembles, there are many theoretical reasons for combining multiple learners, and an empirical evidence of the effectiveness of this approach. In this paper we present a brief overview of ensemble methods, explaining the main reasons why they are able to outperform any single classifier within the ensemble, and proposing a taxonomy based on the main ways base classifiers can be generated or combined together.

Keywords: Ensemble methods, Combining Multiple Learners.

1 Introduction

Ensembles are sets of learning machines whose decisions are combined to improve the performance of the overall system. In this last decade one of the main research areas in machine learning has been represented by methods for constructing ensembles of learning machines. Although in the literature [86, 129, 130, 69, 61, 23, 33, 12, 7, 37] a plethora of terms, such as committee, classifier fusion, combination, aggregation and others are used to indicate sets of learning machines that work together to solve a machine learning problem, in this paper we shall use the term *ensemble* in its widest meaning, in order to include the whole range of combining methods. This variety of terms and specifications reflects the absence of an unified theory on ensemble methods and the youngness of this research area. However, the great effort of the researchers, reflected by the amount of the literature [118, 70, 71] dedicated to this emerging discipline, achieved meaningful and encouraging results.

Empirical studies showed that both classification and regression problem ensembles are often much more accurate than the individual base learner that make them up [8, 29, 40], and recently different theoretical explanations have been proposed to justify the effectiveness of some commonly used ensemble methods [69, 112, 75, 3].

M. Marinaro and R. Tagliaferri (Eds.): WIRN VIETRI 2002, LNCS 2486, pp. 3–20, 2002.
© Springer-Verlag Berlin Heidelberg 2002

The interest in this research area is motivated also by the availability of very fast computers and networks of workstations at a relatively low cost that allow the implementation and the experimentation of complex ensemble methods using off-the-shelf computer platforms. However, as explained in Sect. 2 of this paper there are deeper reasons to use ensembles of learning machines. motivated by the intrinsic characteristics of the ensemble methods.

This work presents a brief overview of the main areas of research, without pretending to be exhaustive or to explain the detailed characteristics of each ensemble method.

The paper is organized as follows. In the next section the main reasons for combining multiple learners are depicted. Sect. 3 presents an overview of the main ensemble methods reported in the literature, distinguishing between *generative* and *non-generative* methods, while Sect. 4 outlines some open problems not covered in this paper.

2   Reasons for Combining Multiple Learners

Both empirical observations and specific machine learning applications confirm that a given learning algorithm outperforms all others for a specific problem or for a specific subset of the input data, but it is unusual to find a single expert achieving the best results on the overall problem domain. As a consequence multiple learner systems try to exploit the local different behavior of the base learners to enhance the accuracy and the reliability of the overall inductive learning system. There are also hopes that if some learner fails, the overall system can recover the error. Employing multiple learners can derive from the application context, such as when multiple sensor data are available, inducing a natural decomposition of the problem. In more general cases we can dispose of different training sets, collected at different times, having eventually different features and we can use different specialized learning machine for each different item.

However, there are deeper reasons why ensembles can improve performances with respect to a single learning machine. As an example, consider the following one given by Tom Dietterich in [28]. If we have a dichotomic classification problem and L hypotheses whose error is lower than 0.5, then the resulting majority voting ensemble has an error lower than the single classifier, as long as the error of the base learners are uncorrelated. In fact, if we have 21 classifiers, and the error rates of each base learner are all equal to $p = 0.3$ and the errors are independent, the overall error of the majority voting ensemble will be given by the area under the binomial distribution where more than $L/2$ hypotheses are wrong:

$$P_{error} = \sum_{(i=\lceil L/2 \rceil)}^{L} \binom{L}{i} p^i (1-p)^{L-i} \quad \Rightarrow P_{error} = 0.026 \ll p = 0.3$$

This result has been studied by mathematicians since the end of the XVIII century in the context of social sciences: in fact the *Condorcet Jury Theorem* [26]) proved that the judgment of a committee is superior to those of individuals, provided the individuals have reasonable competence (that is, a probability of being correct higher than 0.5). As noted in [85], this theorem theoretically justifies recent research on multiple "weak" classifiers [63, 51, 74], representing an interesting research direction diametrically opposite to the development of highly accurate and specific classifiers.

This simple example shows also an important issue in the design of ensembles of learning machines: the effectiveness of ensemble methods relies on the independence of the error committed by the component base learner. In this example, if the independence assumption does not hold, we have no assurance that the ensemble will lower the error, and we know that in many cases the errors are correlated. From a general standpoint we know that the effectiveness of ensemble methods depends on the *accuracy* and the *diversity* of the base learners, that is if they exhibit low error rates and if they produce different errors [49, 123, 92]. The correlated concept of independence between the base learners has been commonly regarded as a requirement for effective classifier combinations, but recent works have shown that not always independent classifiers outperform dependent ones [84]. In fact there is a trade-off between accuracy and independence: more accurate are the base learners, less independent they are.

Learning algorithms try to find an hypothesis in a given space $\mathcal{H}$ of hypotheses, and in many cases if we have sufficient data they can find the optimal one for a given problem. But in real cases we have only limited data sets and sometimes only few examples are available. In these cases the learning algorithm can find different hypotheses that appear equally accurate with respect to the available training data, and although we can sometimes select among them the simplest or the one with the lowest capacity, we can avoid the problem averaging or combining them to get a good approximation of the unknown true hypothesis.

Another reason for combining multiple learners arises from the limited representational capability of learning algorithms. In many cases the unknown function to be approximated is not present in $\mathcal{H}$, but a combination of hypotheses drawn from $\mathcal{H}$ can expand the space of representable functions, embracing also the true one. Although many learning algorithms present universal approximation properties [55, 100], with finite data sets these asymptotic features do not hold: the effective space of hypotheses explored by the learning algorithm is a function of the available data and it can be significantly smaller than the virtual $\mathcal{H}$ considered in the asymptotic case. From this standpoint ensembles can enlarge the effective hypotheses coverage, expanding the space of representable functions.

Many learning algorithms apply local optimization techniques that may get stuck in local optima. For instance inductive decision trees employ a greedy local optimization approach, and neural networks apply gradient descent techniques to minimize an error function over the training data. Moreover optimal training with finite data both for neural networks and decision trees is NP-hard [13, 57]. As a consequence even if the learning algorithm can in principle find the best hypothesis, we actually may not be able to find it. Building an ensemble using, for instance, different starting points may achieve a better approximation, even if no assurance of this is given.

Another way to look at the need for ensembles is represented by the classical bias–variance analysis of the error [45, 78]: different works have shown that several ensemble methods reduce variance [15, 87] or both bias and variance [15, 39, 77]. Recently the improved generalization capabilities of different ensemble methods have also been interpreted in the framework of the theory of large margin classifiers [89, 113, 3], showing that methods such as boosting and ECOC enlarge the margins of the examples.

3   Ensemble Methods Overview

A large number of combination schemes and ensemble methods have been proposed in literature. Combination techniques can be grouped and analysed in different ways, depending on the main classification criterion adopted. If we consider the representation of the input patterns as the main criterion, we can identify two distinct large groups, one that uses the same and one that uses different representations of the inputs [68, 69].

Assuming the architecture of the ensemble as the main criterion, we can distinguish between serial, parallel and hierarchical schemes [85], and if the base learners are selected or not by the ensemble algorithm we can separate selection-oriented and combiner-oriented ensemble methods [61, 81]. In this brief overview we adopt an approach similar to the one cited above, in order to distinguish between *non-generative* and *generative* ensemble methods. Non-generative ensemble methods confine theirselves to combine a set of given possibly well-designed base learners: they do not actively generate new base learners but try to combine in a suitable way a set of existing base classifiers. Generative ensemble methods generate sets of base learners acting on the base learning algorithm or on the structure of the data set and try to actively improve diversity and accuracy of the base learners.

3.1   Non-generative Ensembles

This large group of ensemble methods embraces a large set of different approaches to combine learning machines. They share the very general common property of using a predetermined set of learning machines previously trained with suitable algorithms. The base learners are then put together by a combiner module that may vary depending on its adaptivity to the input patterns and on the requirement of the output of the individual learning machines.

The type of combination may depend on the type of output. If only labels are available or if continuous outputs are hardened, then *majority voting*, that is the class most represented among the base classifiers, is used [67, 104, 87].

This approach can be refined assigning different weights to each classifier to optimize the performance of the combined classifier on the training set [86], or, assuming mutual independence between classifiers, a *Bayesian decision rule* selects the class with the highest posterior probability computed through the estimated class conditional probabilities and the Bayes' formula [130, 122]. A Bayesian approach has also been used in *Consensus based classification* of multisource remote sensing data [10, 9, 19], outperforming conventional multivariate methods for classification. To overcome the problem of the independence assumption (that is unrealistic in most cases), the Behavior-Knowledge Space (BKS) method [56] considers each possible combination of class labels, filling a look-up table using the available data set, but this technique requires a huge volume of training data.

Where we interpret the classifier outputs as the support for the classes, fuzzy aggregation methods can be applied, such as simple connectives between fuzzy sets or the fuzzy integral [23, 22, 66, 128]; if the classifier outputs are possibilistic, *Dempster-Schafer* combination rules can be applied [108]. Statistical methods and similarity measures to estimate classifier correlation have also been used to evaluate expert system combination for a proper design of multi-expert systems [58].

The base learners can also be aggregated using simple operators as *Minimum*, *Maximum*, *Average* and *Product* and *Ordered Weight Averaging* [111, 18, 80]. In particular, on the basis of a common bayesian framework, Josef Kittler provided a theoretical underpinning of many existing classifier combination schemes based on the product and the sum rule, showing also that the sum rule is less sensitive to the errors of subsets of base classifiers [69].

Recently Ljudmila Kuncheva has developed a global combination scheme that takes into account the decision profiles of all the ensemble classifiers with respect to all the classes, designing *Decision templates* that summarize in matrix format the average decision profiles of the training set examples. Different similarity measures can be used to evaluate the matching between the matrix of classifier outputs for an input x, that is the decision profiles referred to x, and the matrix templates (one for each class) found as the class means of the classifier outputs [81]. This general fuzzy approach produce soft class labels that can be seen as a generalization of the conventional crisp and probabilistic combination schemes.

Another general approach consists in explicitly *training combining rules*, using second-level learning machines on top of the set of the base learners [34]. This stacked structure makes use of the outputs of the base learners as features in the intermediate space: the outputs are fed into a second-level machine to perform a trained combination of the base learners.

3.2 Generative Ensembles

Generative ensemble methods try to improve the overall accuracy of the ensemble by directly boosting the accuracy and the diversity of the base learner. They can modify the structure and the characteristics of the available input data, as in *resampling* methods or in *feature selection* methods, they can manipulate the aggregation of the classes (*Output Coding* methods), can select base learners specialized for a specific input region (*mixture of experts* methods), can select a proper set of base learners evaluating the performance and the characteristics of the component base learners (*test-and-select* methods) or can randomly modify the base learning algorithm (*randomized* methods).

Resampling Methods Resampling techniques can be used to generate different hypotheses. For instance, bootstrapping techniques [35] may be used to generate different training sets and a learning algorithm can be applied to the obtained subsets of data in order to produce multiple hypotheses. These techniques are effective especially with unstable learning algorithms, which are algorithms very sensitive to small changes in the training data, such as neural-networks and decision trees.

In *bagging* [15] the ensemble is formed by making bootstrap replicates of the training sets, and then multiple generated hypotheses are used to get an aggregated predictor. The aggregation can be performed averaging the outputs in regression or by majority or weighted voting in classification problems [120, 121].

While in bagging the samples are drawn with replacement using a uniform probability distribution, in *boosting* methods the learning algorithm is called at each iteration using a different distribution or weighting over the training examples [111, 40, 112, 39, 115, 110, 32, 38, 33, 32, 16, 17, 42, 41]. This technique places the highest weight on the examples most often misclassified by the previous base learner: in this way the base learner focuses its attention on the hardest examples. Then the boosting algorithm combines the base rules taking a weighted majority vote of the base rules. Schapire and Singer showed that the training error exponentially drops down with the number of iterations [114] and Schapire et al. [113] proved that boosting enlarges the margins of the training examples, showing also that this fact translates into a superior upper bound on the generalization error. Experimental work showed that bagging is effective with noisy data, while boosting, concentrating its efforts on noisy data seems to be very sensitive to noise [107, 29].

Another training set sampling method consists in constructing training sets by leaving out disjoint subsets of the training data as in *cross-validated committees* [101, 102] or sampling without replacement [116].

Another general approach, named *Stochastic Discrimination* [73, 74, 75, 72], is based on randomly sampling from a space of subsets of the feature space underlying a given problem, then combining these subsets to form a final classifier, using a set-theoretic abstraction to remove all the algorithmic details of classifiers and training procedures. By this approach the classifiers' decision regions are considered only in form of point sets, and the set of classifiers is just a sample into the power set of the feature space. A rigorous mathematical treatment starting from the "representativeness" of the examples used in machine learning problems leads to the design of ensemble of weak classifiers, whose accuracy is governed by the law of large numbers [20].

Feature Selection Methods This approach consists in reducing the number of input features of the base learners, a simple method to fight the effects of the classical curse of dimensionality problem [43]. For instance, in the *Random Subspace Method* [51, 82], a subset of features is randomly selected and assigned to an arbitrary learning algorithm. This way, one obtains a random subspace of the original feature space, and constructs classifiers inside this reduced subspace. The aggregation is usually performed using weighted voting on the basis of the base classifiers accuracy. It has been shown that this method is effective for classifiers having a decreasing learning curve constructed on small and critical training sample sizes [119]

The *Input Decimation* approach [124, 98] reduces the correlation among the errors of the base classifiers, decoupling the base classifiers by training them with different subsets of the input features. It differs from the previous Random Subspace Method as for each class the correlation between each feature and the output of the class is explicitly computed, and the base classifier is trained only on the most correlated subset of features.

Feature subspace methods performed by partitioning the set of features, where each subset is used by one classifier in the team, are proposed in [130, 99, 18]. Other methods for combining different feature sets using genetic algorithms are proposed in [81, 79]. Different approaches consider feature sets obtained by using different operators on the original feature space, such as Principal Component Analysis, Fourier coefficients, Karhunen-Loewe coefficients, or other [21, 34]. An experiment with a systematic partition of the feature space, using nine different combination schemes is performed in [83], showing that there are no "best" combinations for all situations and that there is no assurance that in all cases a classifier team will outperform the single best individual.

Mixtures of Experts Methods The recombination of the base learners can be governed by a supervisor learning machine, that selects the most appropriate element of the ensemble on the basis of the available input data. This idea led to the *mixture of experts* methods [60, 59], where a gating network performs the division of the input space and small neural networks perform the effective calculation at each assigned region separately. An extension of this approach is the *hierarchical mixture of experts* method, where the outputs of the different experts are non-linearly combined by different supervisor gating networks hierarchically organized [64, 65, 59].

Cohen and Intrator extended the idea of constructing local simple base learners for different regions of input space, searching for appropriate architectures that should be locally used and for a criterion to select a proper unit for each region of input space [24, 25]. They proposed a hybrid MLP/RBF network by combining RBF and Perceptron units in the same hidden layer and using a forward selection [36] to add units until an error goal is reached. Although the resulting *Hybrid Perceptron/Radial Network* is not in a strict sense an ensemble, the way by which the regions of the input space and the computational units are selected and tested could be in principle extended to ensembles of learning machines.

Output Coding Decomposition Methods *Output Coding* (OC) methods decompose a multiclass–classification problem in a set of two-class subproblems, and then recompose the original problem combining them to achieve the class label [94, 90, 28]. An equivalent way of thinking about these methods consists in encoding each class as a bit string (named codeword), and in training a different two-class base learner (dichotomizer) in order to separately learn each codeword bit. When the dichotomizers are applied to classify new points, a suitable misure of similarity between the codeword computed by the ensemble and the codeword classes is used to predict the class.

Different *decomposition schemes* have been proposed in literature: In the One-Per-Class (OPC) decomposition [5], each dichotomizer f_i has to separate a single class from all others; in the *PairWise Coupling* (PWC) decomposition [50], the task of each dichotomizer f_i consists in separating a class C_i form class C_j, ignoring all other classes; the *Correcting Classifiers* (CC) and the *PairWise Coupling Correcting Classifiers* (PWC-CC) are variants of the PWC decomposition scheme, that reduce the noise originated in the PWC scheme due to the processing of non pertinent information performed by the PWC dichotomizers [96].

Error Correcting Output Coding [30, 31] is the most studied OC method, and has been successfully applied to several classification problems [1, 11, 46, 6, 126, 131]. Thisdecomposition method tries to improve the error correcting capabilities of the codes generated by the decomposition through the maximization of the minimum distance between each couple of codewords [77, 90]. This goal is achieved by means of the redundancy of the coding scheme [127].

ECOC methods present several open problems. The tradeoff between error recovering capabilities and complexity/learnability of the dichotomies induced by the decomposition scheme has been tackled in several works [3, 125], but an extensive experimental evaluation of the tradeoff has to be performed in order to achieve a better understanding of this phenomenon. A related problem is the analysis of the relationship between codeword length and performances: some preliminary results seem to show that long codewords improve performance [46]. Another open problem, not sufficiently investigated in literature [46, 91, 11], is the selection of optimal dichotomic learning machines for the decomposition unit. Several methods for generating ECOC codes have been proposed: exhaustive codes, randomized hill climbing [31], random codes [62], and Hadamard and BCH codes [14, 105]. An open problems is still the joint maximization of distances between rows and columns in the decomposition matrix. Another open problem consists in designing codes for a given multiclass problem. An interesting greedy approach is proposed in [94], and a method based on soft weight sharing to learn error correcting codes from data is presented in [4]. In [27] it is shown that given a set of dichotomizers the problem of finding an optimal decomposition matrix is NP-complete: by introducing continuous codes and casting the design problem of continuous codes as a constrained optimization problem, we can achieve an optimal continuous decomposition using standard optimization methods.

The work in [91] highlights that the effectiveness of ECOC decomposition methods depends mainly on the design of the learning machines implementing the decision units, on the similarity of the ECOC codewords, on the accuracy of the dichotomizers, on the complexity of the multiclass learning problem and on the correlation of the codeword bits. In particular, Peterson and Weldon [105] showed that if errors on different code bits are dependent, the effectiveness of error correcting code is reduced. Consequently, if a decomposition matrix contains very similar rows (dichotomies), each error of an assigned dichotomizer will be likely to appear in the most correlated dichotomizers, thus reducing the effectiveness of ECOC. These hypotheses have been experimentally supported by a quantitative evaluation of the dependency among output errors of the decomposition unit of ECOC learning machines using mutual information based measures [92, 93].

Test and Select Methods The *test and select* methodology relies on the idea of selection in ensemble creation [117]. The simplest approach is a greedy one [104], where a new learner is added to the ensemble only if the resulting squared error is reduced, but in principle any optimization technique can be used to select the "best" component of the ensemble, including genetic algorithms [97].

It should be noted that the time complexity of the selection of optimal subsets of classifiers is exponential with respect to the number of base learners used. From this point of view heuristic rules, as the "choose the best" or the "choose the best in the class", using classifiers of different types strongly reduce the computational complexity of the selected phase, as the evaluation of different classifier subsets is not required [103]. Moreover test and select methods implicitly include a "production stage", by which a set of classifiers must be generated.

Different selection methods based on different search algorithm mututated from feature selection methods (forward and backward search) or for the solution of complex optimization tasks (tabu search) are proposed in [109]. Another interesting approach uses clustering methods and a misure of diversity to generate sets of diverse classifiers combined by majority voting, selecting the ensemble with the highest performance [48]. Finally, *Dynamic Classifier Selection* methods [54, 129, 47] are based on the definition of a function selecting for each pattern the classifier which is probably the most accurate, estimating, for instance the accuracy of each classifier in a local region of the feature space surrounding an unknown test pattern [47].

Randomized Ensemble Methods Injecting randomness into the learning algorithm is another general method to generate ensembles of learning machines. For instance, if we initialize with random values the initial weights in the backpropagation algorithm, we can obtain different learning machines that can be combined into an ensemble [76, 101].

Several experimental results showed that randomized learning algorithms used to generate base elements of ensembles improve the performances of single non-randomized classifiers. For instance in [29] randomized decision tree ensembles outperform single C4.5 decision trees [106], and adding gaussian noise to the data inputs, together with bootstrap and weight regularization can achieve large improvements in classification accuracy [107].

4   Conclusions

Ensemble methods have shown to be effective in many applicative domains and can be considered as one of the main current directions in machine learning research. We presented an overview of the ensemble methods, showing the main areas of research in this discipline, and the fundamental reasons why ensemble methods are able to outperform any single classifier within the ensemble. A general taxonomy, distinguishing between *generative* and *non–generative* ensemble methods, has been proposed, considering the different ways base learners can be generated or combined together.

Several important issues have not been discussed in this paper. In particular the theoretical problems behind ensemble methods need to be reviewed and discussed more in detail, even if a general theoretical framework for ensemble methods has not been developed. Other open problems not covered in this work are the relationships between ensemble methods and data complexity [52, 53, 88], a systematic research of hidden commonalities among all the combination approaches despite their superficial differences, and a general analysis of the relationships between ensemble methods and the characteristics of the base learners used in the ensemble itself.

Acknowledgments

This work has been partially funded by INFM.

References

[1] D. Aha and R. Bankert. Cloud classification using error-correcting output codes. In *Artificial Intelligence Applications: Natural Science, Agriculture and Environmental Science*, volume 11, pages 13–28. 1997.   10

[2] K. M. Ali and M. J. Pazzani. Error reduction through learning multiple descriptions. *Machine Learning*, 24(3):173–202, 1996.

[3] E. L. Allwein, R. E. Schapire, and Y. Singer. Reducing multiclass to binary: a unifying approach for margin classifiers. *Journal of Machine Learning Research*, 1:113–141, 2000.   3, 6, 10

[4] E. Alpaydin and E. Mayoraz. Learning error-correcting output codes from data. In *ICANN'99*, pages 743–748, Edinburgh, UK, 1999.   10

[5] R. Anand, G. Mehrotra, C. K. Mohan, and S. Ranka. Efficient classification for multiclass problems using modular neural networks. *IEEE Transactions on Neural Networks*, 6:117–124, 1995.   10

[6] G. Bakiri and T. G. Dietterich. Achieving high accuracy text-to-speech with machine learning. In *Data mining in speech synthesis*. 1999.   10

[7] R. Battiti and A. M. Colla. Democracy in neural nets: Voting schemes for classification. *Neural Networks*, 7:691–707, 1994.   3

[8] E. Bauer and R.. Kohavi. An empirical comparison of voting classification algorithms: Bagging, boosting and variants. *Machine Learning*, 36(1/2):525–536, 1999. 3

[9] J. Benediktsson, J. Sveinsson, O. Ersoy, and P. Swain. Parallel consensual neural networks. *IEEE Transactions on Neural Networks*, 8:54–65, 1997. 7

[10] J. Benediktsson and P. Swain. Consensus theoretic classification methods. *IEEE Transactions on Systems, Man and Cybernetics*, 22:688–704, 1992. 7

[11] A. Berger. Error correcting output coding for text classification. In *IJCAI'99: Workshop on machine learning for information filtering*, 1999. 10

[12] C. M. Bishop. *Neural Networks for Pattern Recognition*. Clarendon Press, Oxford, 1995. 3

[13] A. Blum and R. L. Rivest. Training a 3-node neural network is NP-complete. In *Proc. of the 1988 Workshop ob Computational Learning Learning Theory*, pages 9–18, San Francisco, CA, 1988. Morgan Kaufmann. 5

[14] R. C. Bose and D. K. Ray-Chauduri. On a class of error correcting binary group codes. *Information and Control*, (3):68–79, 1960. 10

[15] L. Breiman. Bagging predictors. *Machine Learning*, 24(2):123–140, 1996. 6, 8

[16] L. Breiman. Arcing classifiers. *The Annals of Statistics*, 26(3):801–849, 1998. 8

[17] L. Breiman. Prediction games and arcing classifiers. *Neural Computation*, 11(7):1493–1517, 1999. 8

[18] M. Breukelen van, R. P. W. Duin, D. Tax, and J. E. Hartog den. Combining classifiers fir the recognition of handwritten digits. In *Ist IAPR TC1 Workshop on Statistical Techniques in Pattern Recognition*, pages 13–18, Prague, Czech republic, 1997. 7, 9

[19] G. J. Briem, J. A. Benediktsson, and J. R. Sveinsson. Boosting. Bagging and Consensus Based Classification of Multisource Remote Sensing Data. In J. Kittler and F. Roli, editors, *Multiple Classifier Systems. Second International Workshop, MCS 2001, Cambridge, UK*, volume 2096 of *Lecture Notes in Computer Science*, pages 279–288. Springer-Verlag, 2001. 7

[20] D.. Chen. *Statistical estimates for Kleinberg's method of Stochastic Discrimination*. PhD thesis, The State University of New York, Buffalo, USA, 1998. 8

[21] K. J. Cherkauker. Human expert-level performance on a scientific image analysis task by a system using combined artificial neural networks. In Chan P., editor, *Working notes of the AAAI Workshop on Integrating Multiple Learned Models*, pages 15–21. 1996. 9

[22] S. Cho and J. Kim. Combining multiple neural networks by fuzzy integral and robust classification. *IEEE Transactions on Systems, Man and Cybernetics*, 25:380–384, 1995. 7

[23] S. Cho and J. Kim. Multiple network fusion using fuzzy logic. *IEEE Transactions on Neural Networks*, 6:497–501, 1995. 3, 7

[24] S. Cohen and N. Intrator. A Hybrid Projection Based and Radial Basis Function Architecture. In J. Kittler and F. Roli, editors, *Multiple Classifier Systems. First International Workshop, MCS 2000, Cagliari, Italy*, volume 1857 of *Lecture Notes in Computer Science*, pages 147–156. Springer-Verlag, 2000. 9

[25] S. Cohen and N. Intrator. Automatic Model Selection in a Hybrid Perceptron/Radial Network. In *Multiple Classifier Systems. Second International Workshop, MCS 2001, Cambridge, UK*, volume 2096 of *Lecture Notes in Computer Science*, pages 349–358. Springer-Verlag, 2001. 9

[26] N. C. de Condorcet. *Essai sur l' application de l' analyse à la probabilité des decisions rendues à la pluralité des voix*. Imprimerie Royale, Paris, 1785. 4

[27] K. Crammer and Y. Singer. On the learnability and design of output codes for multiclass problems. In *Proceedings of the Thirteenth Annual Conference on Computational Learning Theory*, pages 35–46, 2000. 10

[28] T. G. Dietterich. Ensemble methods in machine learning. In J. Kittler and F. Roli, editors, *Multiple Classifier Systems. First International Workshop, MCS 2000, Cagliari, Italy*, volume 1857 of *Lecture Notes in Computer Science*, pages 1–15. Springer-Verlag, 2000. 4, 10

[29] T. G. Dietterich. An experimental comparison of three methods for constructing ensembles of decision tress: Bagging, boosting and randomization. *Machine Learning*, 40(2):139–158, 2000. 3, 8, 11

[30] T. G. Dietterich and G. Bakiri. Error - correcting output codes: A general method for improving multiclass inductive learning programs. In *Proceedings of AAAI-91*, pages 572–577. AAAI Press / MIT Press, 1991. 10

[31] T. G. Dietterich and G. Bakiri. Solving multiclass learning problems via error-correcting output codes. *Journal of Artificial Intelligence Research*, (2):263–286, 1995. 10

[32] H. Drucker and C. Cortes. Boosting decision trees. In *Advances in Neural Information Processing Systems*, volume 8. 1996. 8

[33] H. Drucker, C. Cortes, L. Jackel, Y. LeCun, and V. Vapnik. Boosting and other ensemble methods. *Neural Computation*, 6(6):1289–1301, 1994. 3, 8

[34] R. P. W. Duin and D. M. J. Tax. Experiments with Classifier Combination Rules. In J. Kittler and F. Roli, editors, *Multiple Classifier Systems. First International Workshop, MCS 2000, Cagliari, Italy*, volume 1857 of *Lecture Notes in Computer Science*, pages 16–29. Springer-Verlag, 2000. 7, 9

[35] B. Efron and R. Tibshirani. *An introduction to the Bootstrap*. Chapman and Hall, New York, 1993. 8

[36] S. E. Fahlman and C. Lebiere. The cascade-correlation learning architecture. In D. S. Touretzky, editor, *Advances in Neural Information Processing Systems*, volume 2, pages 524–532. Morgan Kauffman, San Mateo, CA, 1990. 9

[37] E. Filippi, M. Costa, and E. Pasero. Multi-layer perceptron ensembles for increased performance and fault-tolerance in pattern recognition tasks. In *IEEE International Conference on Neural Networks*, pages 2901–2906, Orlando, Florida, 1994. 3

[38] Y. Freund. Boosting a weak learning algorithm by majority. *Information and Computation*, 121(2):256–285, 1995. 8

[39] Y. Freund and R. Schapire. A decision-theoretic generalization of on-line learning and an application to boosting. *Journal of Computer and Systems Sciences*, 55(1):119–139, 1997. 6, 8

[40] Y. Freund and R. E. Schapire. Experiments with a new boosting algorithm. In *Proceedings of the 13th International Conference on Machine Learning*, pages 148–156. Morgan Kauffman, 1996. 3, 8

[41] J. Friedman. Greedy function approximation: A gradient boosting machine. *The Annals of Statistics*, 39(5), 2001. 8

[42] J. Friedman, T. Hastie, and R. Tibshirani. Additive logistic regression: A statistical view of boosting. *The Annals of Statistics*, 38(2):337–374, 2000. 8

[43] J. H. Friedman. On bias, variance, 0/1 loss and the curse of dimensionality. *Data Mining and Knowledge Discovery*, 1:55–77, 1997. 9

[44] C. Furlanello and S. Merler. Boosting of Tree-based Classifiers for Predictive Risk Modeling in GIS. In J. Kittler and F. Roli, editors, *Multiple Classifier Systems. First International Workshop, MCS 2000, Cagliari, Italy*, volume 1857 of *Lecture Notes in Computer Science*, pages 220–229. Springer-Verlag, 2000.

[45] S. Geman, E. Bienenstock, and R. Doursat. Neural networks and the bias-variance dilemma. *Neural Computation*, 4(1):1–58, 1992. 6

[46] R. Ghani. Using error correcting output codes for text classification. In *ICML 2000: Proceedings of the 17th International Conference on Machine Learning*, pages 303–310, San Francisco, US, 2000. Morgan Kaufmann Publishers. 10

[47] G. Giacinto and F. Roli. Dynamic Classifier Fusion. In J. Kittler and F. Roli, editors, *Multiple Classifier Systems. First International Workshop, MCS 2000, Cagliari, Italy*, volume 1857 of *Lecture Notes in Computer Science*, pages 177–189. Springer-Verlag, 2000. 11

[48] G. Giacinto and F. Roli. An approach to automatic design of multiple classifier systems. *Pattern Recognition Letters*, 22:25–33, 2001. 11

[49] T. Hastie and R. Tibshirani. *Generalized Additive Models*. Chapman and Hall, London, 1990. 5

[50] T. Hastie and R. Tibshirani. Classification by pairwise coupling. *The Annals of Statistics*, 26(1):451–471, 1998. 10

[51] T. K. Ho. The random subspace method for constructing decision forests. *IEEE Transactions on Pattern Analysis and Machine Intelligence*, 20(8):832–844, 1998. 5, 9

[52] T. K. Ho. Complexity of Classification Problems ans Comparative Advantages of Combined Classifiers. In J. Kittler and F. Roli, editors, *Multiple Classifier Systems. First International Workshop, MCS 2000, Cagliari, Italy*, volume 1857 of *Lecture Notes in Computer Science*, pages 97–106. Springer-Verlag, 2000. 12

[53] T. K. Ho. Data Complexity Analysis for Classifiers Combination. In J. Kittler and F. Roli, editors, *Multiple Classifier Systems. Second International Workshop, MCS 2001, Cambridge, UK*, volume 2096 of *Lecture Notes in Computer Science*, pages 53–67, Berlin, 2001. Springer-Verlag. 12

[54] T. K. Ho, J. J. Hull, and S. N. Srihari. Decision combination in multiple classifiers. *IEEE Trans. on Pattern Analysis and Machine Intelligence*, 19(4):405–410, 1997. 11

[55] K. Hornik. Approximation capabilities of multilayer feedforward networks. *Neural Networks*, 4:251–257, 1991. 5

[56] Y. S. Huang and Suen. C. Y. Combination of multiple experts for the recognition of unconstrained handwritten numerals. *IEEE Trans. on Pattern Analysis and Machine Intelligence*, 17:90–94, 1995. 7

[57] L. Hyafil and R. L. Rivest. Constructing optimal binary decision tree is np-complete. *Information Processing Letters*, 5(1):15–17, 1976. 5

[58] S. Impedovo and A. Salzo. A New Evaluation Method for Expert Combination in Multi-expert System Designing. In J. Kittler and F. Roli, editors, *Multiple Classifier Systems. First International Workshop, MCS 2000, Cagliari, Italy*, volume 1857 of *Lecture Notes in Computer Science*, pages 230–239. Springer-Verlag, 2000. 7

[59] R. A. Jacobs. Methods for combining experts probability assessment. *Neural Computation*, 7:867–888, 1995. 9

[60] R. A. Jacobs, M. I. Jordan, S. J. Nowlan, and G. E. Hinton. Adaptive mixtures of local experts. *Neural Computation*, 3(1):125–130, 1991. 9

[61] A. Jain, R. Duin, and J. Mao. Statistical pattern recognition: a review. *IEEE Transactions on Pattern Analysis and Machine Intelligence*, 22:4–37, 2000. 3, 6

[62] G. James. *Majority vote classifiers: theory and applications*. PhD thesis, Department of Statistics - Stanford University, Stanford, CA, 1998. 10

[63] C. Ji and S. Ma. Combinination of weak classifiers. *IEEE Trans. Neural Networks*, 8(1):32–42, 1997. 5

[64] M. Jordan and R. Jacobs. Hierarchies of adaptive experts. In *Advances in Neural Information Processing Systems*, volume 4, pages 985–992. Morgan Kauffman, San Mateo, CA, 1992. 9

[65] M. I. Jordan and R. A. Jacobs. Hierarchical mixture of experts and the em algorithm. *Neural Computation*, 6:181–214, 1994. 9

[66] J. M. Keller, P. Gader, H. Tahani, J. Chiang, and M. Mohamed. Advances in fuzzy integratiopn for pattern recognition. *Fuzzy Sets and Systems*, 65:273–283, 1994. 7

[67] F. Kimura and M. Shridar. Handwritten Numerical Recognition Based on Multiple Algorithms. *Pattern Recognition*, 24(10):969–983, 1991. 6

[68] J. Kittler. Combining classifiers: a theoretical framework. *Pattern Analysis and Applications*, (1):18–27, 1998. 6

[69] J. Kittler, M. Hatef, R. P. W. Duin, and Matas J. On combining classifiers. *IEEE Trans. on Pattern Analysis and Machine Intelligence*, 20(3):226–239, 1998. 3, 6, 7

[70] J. Kittler and F. (editors) Roli. *Multiple Classifier Systems, Proc. of 1st International Workshop, MCS 2000, Cagliari, Italy*, volume 1857 of *Lecture Notes in Computer Science*. Springer-Verlag, Berlin, 2000. 3

[71] J. Kittler and F. (editors) Roli. *Multiple Classifier Systems, Proc. of 2nd International Workshop, MCS2001, Cambridge, UK*. Springer-Verlag, Berlin, 2001. 3

[72] E. M. Kleinberg. On the Algorithmic Implementation of Stochastic Discrimination. *IEEE Transactions on Pattern Analysis and Machine Intelligence*. 8

[73] E. M. Kleinberg. Stochastic Discrimination. *Annals of Mathematics and Artificial Intelligence*, pages 207–239, 1990. 8

[74] E. M. Kleinberg. An overtraining-resistant stochastic modeling method for pattern recognition. *Annals of Statistics*, 4(6):2319–2349, 1996. 5, 8

[75] E. M. Kleinberg. A Mathematically Rigorous Foundation for Supervised Learning. In J. Kittler and F. Roli, editors, *Multiple Classifier Systems. First International Workshop, MCS 2000, Cagliari, Italy*, volume 1857 of *Lecture Notes in Computer Science*, pages 67–76. Springer-Verlag, 2000. 3, 8

[76] J. Kolen and Pollack J. Back propagation is sensitive to initial conditions. In *Advances in Neural Information Processing Systems*, volume 3, pages 860–867. Morgan Kauffman, San Francisco, CA, 1991. 11

[77] E. Kong and T. G. Dietterich. Error - correcting output coding correct bias and variance. In *The XII International Conference on Machine Learning*, pages 313–321, San Francisco, CA, 1995. Morgan Kauffman. 6, 10

[78] A. Krogh and J. Vedelsby. Neural networks ensembles, cross validation and active learning. In D. S. Touretzky, G. Tesauro, and T. K. Leen, editors, *Advances in Neural Information Processing Systems*, volume 7, pages 107–115. MIT Press, Cambridge, MA, 1995. 6

[79] L. I. Kuncheva. Genetic algorithm for feature selection for parallel classifiers. *Information Processing Letters*, 46:163–168, 1993. 9

[80] L. I. Kuncheva. An application of OWA operators to the aggregation of multiple classification decisions. In *The Ordered Weighted Averaging operators. Theory and Applciations*, pages 330–343. Kluwer Academic Publisher, USA, 1997. 7

[81] L. I. Kuncheva, J. C. Bezdek, and R. P. W. Duin. Decision templates for multiple classifier fusion: an experimental comparison. *Pattern Recognition*, 34(2):299–314, 2001. 6, 7, 9

[82] L. I. Kuncheva, F. Roli, G. L. Marcialis, and C. A. Shipp. Complexity of Data Subsets Generated by the Random Subspace Method: An Experimental Investigation. In J. Kittler and F. Roli, editors, *Multiple Classifier Systems. Second International Workshop, MCS 2001, Cambridge, UK*, volume 2096 of *Lecture Notes in Computer Science*, pages 349–358. Springer-Verlag, 2001. 9

[83] L. I. Kuncheva and C. J. Whitaker. Feature Subsets for Classifier Combination: An Enumerative Experiment. In J. Kittler and F. Roli, editors, *Multiple Classifier Systems. Second International Workshop, MCS 2001, Cambridge, UK*, volume 2096 of *Lecture Notes in Computer Science*, pages 228–237. Springer-Verlag, 2001. 9

[84] L. I. Kuncheva et al. Is independence good for combining classifiers? In *Proc. of 15th Int. Conf. on Pattern Recognition*, Barcelona, Spain, 2000. 5

[85] L. Lam. Classifier combinations: Implementations and theoretical issues. In *Multiple Classifier Systems. First International Workshop, MCS 2000, Cagliari, Italy*, volume 1857 of *Lecture Notes in Computer Science*, pages 77–86. Springer-Verlag, 2000. 5, 6

[86] L. Lam and C. Sue. Optimal combination of pattern classifiers. *Pattern Recognition Letters*, 16:945–954, 1995. 3, 6

[87] L. Lam and C. Sue. Application of majority voting to pattern recognition: an analysis of its behavior and performance. *IEEE Transactions on Systems, Man and Cybernetics*, 27(5):553–568, 1997. 6

[88] M. Li and P Vitanyi. *An Introduction to Kolmogorov Complexity and Its Applications*. Springer-Verlag, Berlin, 1993. 12

[89] L. Mason, P. Bartlett, and J. Baxter. Improved generalization through explicit optimization of margins. *Machine Learning*, 2000. 6

[90] F. Masulli and G. Valentini. Comparing decomposition methods for classification. In R. J. Howlett and L. C. Jain, editors, *KES'2000, Fourth International Conference on Knowledge-Based Intelligent Engineering Systems & Allied Technologies*, pages 788–791, Piscataway, NJ, 2000. IEEE. 10

[91] F. Masulli and G. Valentini. Effectiveness of error correcting output codes in multiclass learning problems. In *Lecture Notes in Computer Science*, volume 1857, pages 107–116. Springer-Verlag, Berlin, Heidelberg, 2000. 10

[92] F. Masulli and G. Valentini. Dependence among Codeword Bits Errors in ECOC Learning Machines: an Experimental Analysis. In *Lecture Notes in Computer Science*, volume 2096, pages 158–167. Springer-Verlag, Berlin, 2001. 5, 11

[93] F. Masulli and G. Valentini. Quantitative Evaluation of Dependence among Outputs in ECOC Classifiers Using Mutual Information Based Measures. In K. Marko and P. Webos, editors, *Proceedings of the International Joint Conference on Neural Networks IJCNN'01*, volume 2, pages 784–789, Piscataway, NJ, USA, 2001. IEEE. 11

[94] E. Mayoraz and M. Moreira. On the decomposition of polychotomies into dichotomies. In *The XIV International Conference on Machine Learning*, pages 219–226, Nashville, TN, July 1997. 10

[95] S. Merler, C. Furlanello, B. Larcher, and A. Sboner. Tuning Cost-Sensitive Boosting and its Application to Melanoma Diagnosis. In J. Kittler and F. Roli, editors, *Multiple Classifier Systems. Second International Workshop, MCS 2001, Cambridge, UK*, volume 2096 of *Lecture Notes in Computer Science*, pages 32–42. Springer-Verlag, 2001.

[96] M. Moreira and E. Mayoraz. Improved pairwise coupling classifiers with correcting classifiers. In C. Nedellec and C. Rouveirol, editors, *Lecture Notes in Artificial Intelligence, Vol. 1398*, pages 160–171, Berlin, Heidelberg, New York, 1998. 10

[97] D. W. Opitz and J. W. Shavlik. Actively searching for an effective neural network ensemble. *Connection Science*, 8(3/4):337–353, 1996. 11

[98] N. C. Oza and K. Tumer. Input Decimation Ensembles: Decorrelation through Dimensionality Reduction. In J. Kittler and F. Roli, editors, *Multiple Classifier Systems. Second International Workshop, MCS 2001, Cambridge, UK*, volume 2096 of *Lecture Notes in Computer Science*, pages 238–247. Springer-Verlag, 2001. 9

[99] H. S. Park and S. W. Lee. Off-line recognition of large sets handwritten characters with multiple Hidden-Markov models. *Pattern Recognition*, 29(2):231–244, 1996. 9

[100] J. Park and I. W. Sandberg. Approximation and radial basis function networks. *Neural Computation*, 5(2):305–316, 1993. 5

[101] B. Parmanto, P. Munro, and H. Doyle. Improving committe diagnosis with resampling techniques. In D. S. Touretzky, M. Mozer, and M. Hesselmo, editors, *Advances in Neural Information Processing Systems*, volume 8, pages 882–888. MIT Press, Cambridge, MA, 1996. 8, 11

[102] B. Parmanto, P. Munro, and H. Doyle. Reducing variance of committee predition with resampling techniques. *Connection Science*, 8(3/4):405–416, 1996. 8

[103] D. Partridge and W. B. Yates. Engineering multiversion neural-net systems. *Neural Computation*, 8:869–893, 1996. 11

[104] M. P. Perrone and L. N. Cooper. When networks disagree: ensemble methods for hybrid neural networks. In Mammone R. J., editor, *Artificial Neural Networks for Speech and Vision*, pages 126–142. Chapman & Hall, London, 1993. 6, 11

[105] W. W. Peterson and E. J.Jr. Weldon. *Error correcting codes*. MIT Press, Cambridge, MA, 1972. 10, 11

[106] J. R. Quinlan. *C4.5 Programs for Machine Learning*. Morgan Kauffman, 1993. 11

[107] Y. Raviv and N. Intrator. Bootstrapping with noise: An effective regularization technique. *Connection Science*, 8(3/4):355–372, 1996. 8, 12

[108] G. Rogova. Combining the results of several neural neetworks classifiers. *Neural Networks*, 7:777–781, 1994. 7

[109] F. Roli, G. Giacinto, and G. Vernazza. Methods for Designing Multiple Classifier Systems. In J. Kittler and F. Roli, editors, *Multiple Classifier Systems. Second International Workshop, MCS 2001, Cambridge, UK*, volume 2096 of *Lecture Notes in Computer Science*, pages 78–87. Springer-Verlag, 2001. 11

[110] R. Schapire and Y. Singer. Boostexter: A boosting-based system for text categorization. *Machine Learning*, 39(2/3):135–168, 2000. 8

[111] R. E. Schapire. The strenght of weak learnability. *Machine Learning*, 5(2):197–227, 1990. 7, 8

[112] R. E. Schapire. A brief introduction to boosting. In Thomas Dean, editor, *16th International Joint Conference on Artificial Intelligence*, pages 1401–1406. Morgan Kauffman, 1999. 3, 8

[113] R. E. Schapire, Y. Freund, P. Bartlett, and W. Lee. Boosting the margin: A new explanation for the effectiveness of voting methods. *The Annals of Statistics*, 26(5):1651–1686, 1998. 6, 8

[114] R. E. Schapire and Y. Singer. Improved boosting algorithms using confidence-rated predictions. *Machine Learning*, 37(3):297–336, 1999. 8

[115] H. Schwenk and Y. Bengio. Training methods for adaptive boosting of neural networks. In *Advances in Neural Information Processing Systems*, volume 10, pages 647–653. 1998. 8

[116] A. Sharkey, N. Sharkey, and G. Chandroth. Diverse neural net solutions to a fault diagnosis problem. *Neural Computing and Applications*, 4:218–227, 1996. 8

[117] A Sharkey, N. Sharkey, U. Gerecke, and G. Chandroth. The test and select approach to ensemble combination. In J. Kittler and F. Roli, editors, *Multiple Classifier Systems. First International Workshop, MCS 2000, Cagliari, Italy*, volume 1857 of *Lecture Notes in Computer Science*, pages 30–44. Springer-Verlag, 2000. 11

[118] A. Sharkey (editor). *Combining Artificial Neural Nets: Ensemble and Modular Multi-Net Systems*. Springer-Verlag, London, 1999. 3

[119] M. Skurichina and R. P. W. Duin. Bagging, boosting and the randon subspace method for linear classifiers. *Pattern Analysis and Applications*. (in press). 9

[120] M. Skurichina and R. P. W. Duin. Bagging for linear classifiers. *Pattern Recognition*, 31(7):909–930, 1998. 8

[121] M. Skurichina and R. P. W. Duin. Bagging and the Random Subspace Method for Redundant Feature Spaces. In *Multiple Classifier Systems. Second International Workshop, MCS 2001, Cambridge, UK*, volume 2096 of *Lecture Notes in Computer Science*, pages 1–10. Springer-Verlag, 2001. 8

[122] C. Suen and L. Lam. Multiple classifier combination methodologies for different output levels. In *Multiple Classifier Systems. First International Workshop, MCS 2000, Cagliari, Italy*, volume 1857 of *Lecture Notes in Computer Science*, pages 52–66. Springer-Verlag, 2000. 7

[123] K. Tumer and J. Ghosh. Error correlation and error reduction in ensemble classifiers. *Connection Science*, 8(3/4):385–404, 1996. 5

[124] K. Tumer and N. C. Oza. Decimated input ensembles for improved generalization. In *IJCNN-99, The IEEE-INNS-ENNS International Joint Conference on Neural Networks*, 1999. 9

[125] G. Valentini. Upper bounds on the training error of ECOC-SVM ensembles. Technical Report TR-00-17, DISI - Dipartimento di Informatica e Scienze dell' Informazione - Università di Genova, 2000. ftp://ftp.disi.unige.it/person/ValentiniG/papers/TR-00-17.ps.gz. 10

[126] G. Valentini. Gene expression data analysis of human lymphoma using Support Vector Machines and Output Coding ensembles. *Artificial Intelligence in Medicine* (to appear). 10

[127] J. Van Lint. *Coding theory*. Spriger Verlag, Berlin, 1971. 10

[128] D. Wang, J. M. Keller, C. A. Carson, K. K. McAdoo-Edwards, and C. W. Bailey. Use of fuzzy logic inspired features to improve bacterial recognition through classifier fusion. *IEEE Transactions on Systems, Man and Cybernetics*, 28B(4):583–591, 1998. 7

[129] K. Woods, W. P. Kegelmeyer, and K. Bowyer. Combination of multiple classifiers using local accuracy estimates. *IEEE Trans. on Pattern Analysis and Machine Intelligence*, 19(4):405–410, 1997. 3, 11

[130] L Xu, C Krzyzak, and C. Suen. Methods of combining multiple classifiers and their applications to handwritting recognition. *IEEE Transactions on Systems, Man and Cybernetics*, 22(3):418–435, 1992. 3, 7, 9

[131] C. Yeang et al. Molecular classification of multiple tumor types. In *ISMB 2001, Proceedings of the 9th International Conference on Intelligent Systems for*

Molecular Biology, pages 316–322, Copenaghen, Denmark, 2001. Oxford University Press. 10

Part II

Eduardo R. Caianiello
Lecture

Learning Preference Relations from Data

Theodoros Evgniou[1] and Massimiliano Pontil[2]

[1] Dipartimento di Ingegneria dell'Informazione
Via Roma 56, 53100 Siena, Italy
pontil@dii.unisi.it
[2] INSEAD, Technology Management Department
Fontainebleau, France
theodoros.evgeniou@insead.fr

Abstract. A number of learning tasks can be solved robustly using key concepts from statistical learning theory. In this paper we first summarize the main concepts of statistical learning theory, a framework in which certain learning from examples problems, namely classification, regression, and density estimation, have been studied in a principled way. We then show how the key concepts of the theory can be used not only for these standard learning from examples problems, but also for many others. In particular we discuss how to learn functions which model a preference relation. The goal is to illustrate the value of statistical learning theory beyond the standard framework it has been used until now.

Keywords: Statistical learning theory, Preference relations.

1 Introduction

With the explosion of the amount of data gathered in recent years, largely due to new technologies such as Internet related ones, a large number of data mining problems have appeared. Developing ad hoc techniques for these problems leads only to suboptimal systems. There is therefore a need for rigorous solutions to the variety of data mining problems based on fundamental principles. Statistical learning theory [17, 18] has set the foundations for general theories to solve certain problems of model development from data: the standard problems approached within this theory have been classification, regression, and density estimation [17, 6].

The goal of this paper is to show that the key principles of statistical learning theory can be used to solve a wide variety of problems beyond these standard ones. The paper is organized as follows: first we give a brief overview of the key ideas of statistical learning theory. We also discuss how these ideas have been used to solve the standard problems of classification and regression. Then in 3 we discuss how the key ideas of the theory can be used to solve other types of problems by illustrating this through an example.

M. Marinaro and R. Tagliaferri (Eds.): WIRN VIETRI 2002, LNCS 2486, pp. 23–32, 2002.

2   Statistical Learning Theory

The basic idea of Statistical Learning Theory [17] can be phrased as follows: for
a finite set of training examples (data) the search for the best model (typically
an approximating function) has to be constrained to an appropriately "small"
hypothesis space (which can also be thought of as a space of machines or models
or network architectures). If the space is too large, models can be found which
will fit exactly the data but will have a poor generalization performance, that is
poor predictive capability on new data. The theory characterizes and formalizes
these concepts in terms of the *capacity* of a set of functions and *capacity control*
depending on the training data: for instance, for a small training set the capacity
of the function space in which a model is sought has to be small whereas it can
increase with a larger training set. A key part of the theory is to define and
bound the capacity of a set of functions. We now discuss more formally the
theory mainly within the standard setup if finding a function either for the
classification or the regression problem.

We consider two sets of random variables $\mathbf{x} \in X \subseteq R^d$ and $y \in Y \subseteq R$
related by a probabilistic relationship. The relationship is probabilistic because
generally an element of X does not determine uniquely an element of Y, but
rather a probability distribution on Y. This can be formalized assuming that
an unknown probability distribution $P(\mathbf{x}, y)$ is defined over the set $X \times Y$. We
are provided with *examples* of this probabilistic relationship, that is with a data
set $D_\ell \equiv \{(\mathbf{x}_i, y_i) \in X \times Y\}_{i=1}^\ell$ called *training set*, obtained by sampling ℓ times
the set $X \times Y$ according to $P(\mathbf{x}, y)$. The "problem of learning" consists in, given
the data set D_ℓ, providing an *estimator*, that is a function $f : X \to Y$, that can
be used, given any value of $\mathbf{x} \in X$, to predict a value y.

In SLT, the standard way to solve the learning problem consists in defining
a *risk functional*, which measures the average amount of error or risk associated
with an estimator, and then looking for the estimator with the lowest risk. If
$V(y, f(\mathbf{x}))$ is the loss function measuring the error we make when we predict y
by $f(\mathbf{x})$, then the average error, the so called *expected risk*, is:

$$I[f] \equiv \int_{X,Y} V(y, f(\mathbf{x}))P(\mathbf{x}, y) \, d\mathbf{x}dy$$

We assume that the expected risk is defined on a "large" class of functions $\mathcal{F}$
and we will denote by f_0 the function which minimizes the expected risk in $\mathcal{F}$.
The function f_0 is our ideal estimator, and it is often called the *target* function.
This function cannot be found in practice, because the probability distribution
$P(\mathbf{x}, y)$ that defines the expected risk is unknown, and only a sample of it, the
data set D_ℓ, is available. To overcome this shortcoming we need an *induction
principle* that we can use to "learn" from the limited number of training data
we have. SLT, as developed by Vapnik [17], builds on the so-called *empirical risk
minimization (ERM)* induction principle. The ERM method consists in using
the data set D_ℓ to build a stochastic approximation of the expected risk, which

is usually called the *empirical risk*, defined as

$$I_{\text{emp}}[f;\ell] = \frac{1}{\ell}\sum_{i=1}^{\ell} V(y_i, f(\mathbf{x}_i)).$$

Straight minimization of the empirical risk in $\mathcal{F}$ can be problematic. First, it is usually an *ill-posed* problem [16], in the sense that there might be many, possibly infinitely many, functions minimizing the empirical risk. Second, it can lead to *overfitting*, meaning that although the minimum of the empirical risk can be very close to zero, the expected risk – which is what we are really interested in – can be very large.

SLT provides probabilistic bounds on the distance between the empirical and expected risk of any function (therefore including the minimizer of the empirical risk in a function space that can be used to control overfitting). The bounds involve the number of examples ℓ and the *capacity* h of the function space, a quantity measuring the "complexity" of the space. Appropriate capacity quantities are defined in the theory, the most popular one being the VC-dimension [18] or scale sensitive versions of it [10, 2]. The bounds have the following general form: with probability at least η

$$I[f] < I_{emp}[f] + \Phi(\sqrt{\frac{h}{\ell}}, \eta). \tag{1}$$

where h is the capacity, and Φ an increasing function of $\frac{h}{\ell}$ and η. For more information and for exact forms of function Φ we refer the reader to [18, 17, 2]. Intuitively, if the capacity of the function space in which we perform empirical risk minimization is very large and the number of examples is small, then the distance between the empirical and expected risk can be large and overfitting is very likely to occur.

Since the space $\mathcal{F}$ is usually very large (e.g. $\mathcal{F}$ could be the space of square integrable functions), one typically considers smaller hypothesis spaces $\mathcal{H}$. Moreover, inequality (1) suggests an alternative method for achieving good generalization: instead of minimizing the empirical risk, find the best trade off between the empirical risk and the *complexity of the hypothesis space* measured by the second term in the r.h.s. of inequality (1). This observation leads to the method of *Structural Risk Minimization (SRM)*.

The idea of SRM is to define a nested sequence of hypothesis spaces $H_1 \subset H_2 \subset \ldots \subset H_M$, where each hypothesis space H_m has finite capacity h_m and larger than that of all previous sets, that is: $h_1 \leq h_2, \ldots, \leq h_M$. For example H_m could be the set of polynomials of degree m, or a set of splines with m nodes, or some more complicated nonlinear parameterization. Using such a nested sequence of more and more complex hypothesis spaces, SRM consists of choosing the minimizer of the empirical risk in the space H_{m^*} for which the bound on the *structural risk*, as measured by the right hand side of inequality (1), is minimized. Further information about the statistical properties of SRM can be found in [5, 17].

To summarize, in SLT the problem of learning from examples is solved in three steps: (a) we define a loss function $V(y, f(\mathbf{x}))$ measuring the error of predicting the output of input $\mathbf{x}$ with $f(\mathbf{x})$ when the actual output is y; (b) we define a nested sequence of hypothesis spaces $H_m, m = 1, \ldots, M$ whose capacity is an increasing function of m; (c) we minimize the empirical risk in each of H_m and choose, among the solutions found, the one with the best trade off between the empirical risk and the capacity as given by the right hand side of inequality (1).

2.1   Classification and Regression

In the case of classification problems, the output Y is the set $\{-1, 1\}$ for binary classification, and the function $f(\mathbf{x})$ is an *indicator function* which specifies whether data $\mathbf{x}$ belongs to class 1 ($y = 1$), or not ($y = -1$). In the case of regression the output Y is a continuous variable and $f(\mathbf{x})$ is a regression function which maps input data $\mathbf{x}$ to the output y. Both these cases have been extensively studied and a number of methods for solving, many of them based on the principles of SLT outlined above, have been developed.

It is important to notice that the key principles of SLT, namely the idea that a trade off must be found between the complexity of a model and the error of a model on the existing training data, is a general one although it has been developed mainly having classification and regression in mind. Therefore in general one should be able to develop models from data for any other problem as long as the following are defined:

1. The type of the possible models is defined, that is a "hypothesis space" is decided.
2. A loss function measuring the error of any given model on a set of data must be defined.
3. A measure of complexity of the model must be defined and a way to control it must be found.
4. The development of the model can be done in a computationally efficient way through finding a trade off between the training error defined according to the loss function and the complexity of the model defined.

We now discuss a particular problem for which by following these steps motivated by statistical learning theory one can develop robust models.

3   Learning from Examples: Beyond Classification, Regression, and Density Estimation

We saw that the key idea of statistical learning theory is to develop models from the data (observations) that are "balanced" between fitting the existing data and keeping a low "complexity". We now discuss how this idea can be used for other problems of developing models from data. The goal is to illustrate that the concepts of statistical learning theory can be used in a variety of contexts.

3.1   Learning Preferences

We consider here a particular problem, namely that of estimating a utility function from a set of examples of past choices. Formally we have a list of n past transactions $T_1, T_2, \ldots T_n$, where each transaction T_i is a pair of a set of k_i multi-attribute options (i.e. products, bids, etc) $\{\mathbf{x}_i^1, \mathbf{x}_i^2, \ldots, \mathbf{x}_i^{k_i}\}$, and of the option chosen, index $c_i \in \{1, 2, \ldots, k_i\}$. We assume that for all transactions, all options are fully characterized by m-dimensional vectors, where m is the number of attributes describing the options. Missing or different dimensional attributes can be handled for example by adding dummy attribute values. We represent the jth option of transaction T_i as $\mathbf{x}_i^j = \{x_i^j(1), x_i^j(2), \ldots x_i^j(m)\}$ (notice that we note vectors using bold letters). So the i transaction T_i is a set of k_i such m-dimensional vectors and the index c_i of the chosen option.

Without loss of generality, from each past recorded transaction, the useful information that is used is that a single bid (the selected one) was more preferable to the rest of the offered bids. For example, for transaction T_i we have that k_i bids were received and that bid $\mathbf{x}_i^{c_i}$ was selected, so the useful information is that bid c_i was considered better than bids 1, 2,... k_i. So we are looking for a utility function that is in agreement with this information. Clearly variations of this setup (i.e. cases where we know pairwise relative preferences with intensities) can be modeled in a similar way.

The problem of modeling preference is a very important one in the field of marketing research. One of the main methods for modeling preferences from data is conjoint analysis [3, 8]. A number of conjoint analysis methods have been proposed – see for example [12]. Since the early 1970s conjoint analysis continues to be a very popular approach with hundreds of commercial applications per year [20]. In conjoint analysis a methodology involving the generation of a questionnaire is also included in the process of preference modeling. The central part is the choice of questions or product profiles presented to the subjects [11], whether it is self-explicated ones or full profile [3]. Another approach is within the Discrete Choice Analysis field, where typically users' preferences are modeled as random variables of logit models, under the assumption that every attribute is substitutable to some extend, by a combination of the other attributes available to the decision makers [1]. Like in the case of conjoint analysis, discrete choice empiricists have always faced the trade off between model (multinomial logit models) complexity and ease of model estimation. For the case of nonparametric utility models, this trade off is linked to the well known "curse of dimensionality" [15]: as the number of dimensions increases, an exponential increase in sample size is needed to maintain reliable model estimation. Here we illustrate how to use the key ideas from statistical learning theory discussed above to develop models that do not suffer from these problems and are robust.

We first consider a very simple model where we make the standard assumption [1, 14] that the utility function is a linear function of the values (or logarithms of the values, without loss of generality) of the attributes describing the options. In other words we first assume that for an option $\mathbf{x} = \{x(1), x(2), \ldots, x(m)\}$ the utility is $U(\mathbf{x}) = w_1 x(1) + w_2 x(2) + \ldots + w_m x(m)$.

We are then looking for parameters $w_1, w_2, \ldots w_m$ that give a utility function that agrees with the information from the past transactions. Because the utility function can be defined only up to a scaling factor – and anyway we care about the relative utility and not the actual values – we impose a scaling constraint so that $w_1^2 + w_2^2 + \ldots w_m^2 = 1$. So in the simplest case we are looking for parameters $w_1, \ldots w_m$ that belong in the feasible area defined by the following constraints:

$$w_1 x_i^{c_i}(1) + w_2 x_i^{c_i}(2) + \ldots + w_m x_i^{c_i}(m) \geq$$
$$\geq w_1 x_i^j(1) + w_2 x_i^j(2) + \ldots + w_m x_i^j(m)$$

for $\forall i \in \{1, \ldots n\}$ and $\forall j \in \{1, \ldots k_i\}$ for each i with $j \neq c_i$, and

$$w_1^2 + w_2^2 + \ldots w_m^2 = 1$$

There are $(k_1 - 1) + (k_2 - 1) + \ldots + (k_n - 1) + 1$ constraints.

To allow for errors/inconsistencies we introduce slack variables to the simple model above. So for each of the $(k_1 - 1) + (k_2 - 1) + \ldots + (k_n - 1)$ inequality constraints corresponding to the choices made for each of the n transactions we introduce a positive slack variable ξ_{ij} which effectively measures how much inconsistency/error there is. So we are now looking for a set of parameters $w_1, w_2, \ldots, w_m$ so that we minimize this error. This corresponds to the following optimization problem:

Problem1 :   minimize $_{w_1, \ldots w_m, \xi_{ij}}$ $\sum_{i=1..n, j=1..k_i} \xi_{ij}$

Subject to:

$w_1^2 + w_2^2 + \ldots w_m^2 = 1$

$w_1(x_i^{c_i}(1) - x_i^j(1)) + w_2(x_i^{c_i}(2) - x_i^j(2)) + \ldots + w_m(x_i^{c_i}(m) - x_i^j(m)) \geq 0$

$\xi_{ij} \geq 0$

for all $i \in \{1, 2, \ldots, n\}, j \in \{1, 2, \ldots, k_i\}, j \neq c_i$

Notice that one may require to minimize the L_0 norm of the slack variables ξ_{ij} so that what is penalized is the number of errors/inconsistencies and not the "amount" of it. However in that case the problem becomes an integer programming problem which is hard to solve. Also notice that if the comparisons define a feasible area, then $\xi_{ij} = 0$ for all comparison inequalities so the solution is a solution in the feasible area as before. In the general case we have some ξ_{ij}'s nonzeros – these correspond to "training errors" in the sense that the corresponding comparisons are not satisfied by the computed utility function.

So we are looking for a utility function of the predefined (linear) form that minimizes the amount of error/inconsistencies among the observations we have. In a sense this is a simple empirical error minimization formulation within the framework of statistical learning theory outlined above. This, however, potentially leads to utility function models that over-fit [17] the past example transactions and can suffer from the curse of dimensionality as we discussed in the introduction. It is therefore important to augment this model in a way that some control to avoid over-fitting is included. Statistical learning theory suggests that this can be done by controlling the *complexity* of the model developed. Appropriate measures of complexity that are *not* necessarily related to the dimensionality of the space where the function is estimated have been defined in the past [18, 2, 17, 6]. We now present a way to do this that turns out to be very similar to that for support vector machines, an advanced method for learning from data [17, 6] developed within the framework of statistical learning theory.

3.2 Robust Preference Modeling Methods

Choosing the appropriate complexity control is an important subject of ongoing research. The main question is *what are the characteristics of a utility function that make it complex?* For example, in the standard case of learning functions from examples, that is the case of regression, a standard measure of complexity of a model/function is how "smooth" the function is - formally the integral of its first derivative [19, 16, 17, 7]. This is in a sense a "natural" measure of complexity for regression. However it is not clear if having a "smooth" utility function is necessarily "natural". And clearly, in either case the dimensionality of the space where a function is estimated (i.e. the dimensionality of the data) can be but does not *need to be* a measure of complexity – for example in the case of regression a highly non-smooth function is a small dimensional space is more complex than a very smooth function in a high dimensional space.

As a first step towards developing utility function estimation models we augmented the simple models above with a model complexity control that is standard in other learning from examples situations [17, 19, 6, 7]. Instead of scaling the function using the constraint $w_1^2 + w_2^2 + \ldots + w_m^2 = 1$, we scale the function by requiring that the constraints defined by the choices (constraints with the slack variables in Problem 1) hold with a "margin" 1 as indicated in the system below – we will explain the motivation behind this below. This is the way complexity is controlled in the case of Support Vector Machines [17]. Constraints on the estimated function have also been used in the past for conjoint analysis [13, 14]. However in our case the constraints are motivated through statistical learning theory, and lead to a family of methods that are related to the well known method of support vector machines and have similar useful characteristics as we discuss below – namely the estimation involves fast quadratic programming optimization, the generalization to highly nonlinear utility functions is easy, the estimated utility function turns out to depend only on certain data – the "hard choices" – that are automatically detected, and guarantees on the future performance of the estimated model can be given. Furthermore we use the L_2 norm of the parameter vector as a measure of complexity – see below for an intuitive explanation of what this implies. We are therefore looking for a utility function – parameters $w_1, w_2, \ldots, w_m$ in the simple linear case – that solves the following optimization problem:

Problem2 :   minimize $_{w_1, \ldots w_m, \xi_{ij}}$ $\sum_{i=1..n, j=1..k_i} \xi_{ij} + \lambda \sum_{i=1...m} w_i^2$

Subject to:

$$w_1(x_i^{c_i}(1) - x_i^j(1)) + w_2(x_i^{c_i}(2) - x_i^j(2)) + \ldots$$

$$\ldots + w_m(x_i^{c_i}(m) - x_i^j(m)) \geq 1 - \xi_{ij}$$

$$\xi_{ij} \geq 0$$

for all $i \in \{1, 2, \ldots, n\}, j \in \{1, 2, \ldots, k_i\}, j \neq c_i$

Parameter λ controls the trade off between fitting the data (empirical error) and the complexity of the model. There are a number of ways to choose this parameter [19, 17]. For example it can be chosen so that the prediction error in a small validation set is minimized. Notice the role of the constant 1 at the constraints: for constraints for which the slack variable is zero – meaning that the utility function is consistent with the corresponding ranking of the options – we need to effectively "scale" the utility function so that the difference of utility is at least 1. This is a standard scaling method that is used, for example, in Support Vector Machines and is important for the intuitive motivation of the complexity control that we now discuss.

An Intuitive Interpretation of the Complexity Control The control of the complexity $\sum_{i=1}^m w_i^2$ given the scaling achieved by using the constant 1 in the constraints has an intuitive natural interpretation. Consider the case where the feasible area defined by the comparison constraints without the slack variables is non-empty. If we look only among functions that have zero empirical error in this case – as the simple model does - then any solution w in the feasible area will be good according to the simplest model. However the function among the ones in the feasible area that has the smallest L_2 norm, which is what we get if we also control the complexity the way it is done in Problem 2, is a specific function in the feasible area. If we represent each constraint as a hyperplane in the space of parameters w_i, then the feasible area is a polyhedron in that space. The solution with the smallest L_2 norm (smallest $\|w\|^2$ in Problem 2), given the normalization achieved by the use of the constant 1 at the constraints, is then the point in the feasible area that is the center of the largest inscribed sphere in this polyhedron. In a sense this is the point the "furthest" from the constraints: the solution that satisfies the "worst" comparison constraints "the most". In this sense it is the most robust solution in the feasible space [17]. This can be used as a justification of the particular form of the complexity control in Problem 2, namely $\|w\|^2$.

In the case that empirical errors exist (there are non-zero slack variables) the intuition is similar: we want to minimize the amount of error while satisfying the correct comparisons "as much as possible". Although this is not a rigorous justification of the particular choice of the complexity control, it can lead to some insights as to what other complexity controls can be used. It also turns out that, as we will see below, under some assumptions the robustness of this solution, measured in terms of the distance of the solution point from the closest "constraint" (hyperplane defined by the constraint), influences the quality of the preference model in the sense of how well the model can predict future choices: the more robust – that is the larger the distance - the better the predictive ability of the model. Furthermore, but controlling the estimation of the utility function in this way, it turns out that we can estimate highly nonlinear utility functions and deal with very high numbers of attributes (high dimensional **w**) without overfitting or suffering from the curse of dimensionality [17, 6].

4 Conclusion

Statistical Learning Theory sets the foundations on which a number of data mining problems can be approached. Traditionally the theory has been used for solving certain problems of modeling from data, namely classification, regression, and density estimation. In this paper we argue that the key ideas of the theory can be used to approach many other problems of developing models from data. The theory offers a framework within which robust models from data can be developed. In this paper we have simply focused on the key ideas of the theory and illustrated its use for a problem different from the standard ones solved in machines learning. A lot of work can be done in applying the key ideas of the theory to a number of new problems, and we are currently working towards this direction.

References

[1] Ben-Akiva, M. E. and S. R. Lerman. Discrete Choice Analysis: Theory and Application to Travel Demand. MIT Press, Cambridge, Ma., 1995. 27

[2] Alon, N., S. Ben-David, N. Cesa-Bianchi, and D. Haussler. 'Scale-sensitive dimensions, uniform convergence, and learnability'. *Symposium on Foundations of Computer Science*, 1993. 25, 29

[3] Carroll, J. D. and P. Green. " Psychometric Methods in Marketing Research: Part I, Conjoint Analysis". *Journal of Marketing Research*, 32, November 1995, p. 385-391. 27

[4] Cortes, C. and V. Vapnik. "Support Vector Networks'. *Machine Learning* **20**, 1–25, 1995.

[5] Devroye, L., L. Györfi, and G. Lugosi. *A Probabilistic Theory of Pattern Recognition*, No. 31 in Applications of mathematics. New York: Springer, 1996. 25

[6] Evgeniou, T., M. Pontil, and T. Poggio. "Regularization Networks and Support Vector Machines'. Adv. In Computational Mathematics, 13, pp 1–50, 2000. 23, 29, 31

[7] Girosi, F., M. Jones, and T. Poggio. "Regularization theory and neural networks architectures". *Neural Computation* **7**, 219–269, 1995. 29

[8] Green, P. and V. Srinivasan. "Conjoint Analysis in Marketing: New Developments with Implications for Research and Practice" *Journal of Marketing*, 54, 4, p. 3-19, 1990. 27

[9] Jaakkola, T. and D. Haussler. "Probabilistic Kernel Regression Models". In: *Proc. of Neural Information Processing Conference*, 1998.

[10] Kearns, M. and R. Shapire "Efficient distribution-free learning of probabilistic concepts" *Journal of Computer and Systems Sciences* **48**(3), 464–497, 1994. 25

[11] Oppewal, H., J. Louviere, and H. Timmermans. "Modeling Hierarchical Conjoint Processes with Integrated Choice Experiments" *Journal of Marketing Research*, 31, p. 92-105, 1994. 27

[12] Sawtooth Software, 'HB-Reg: Hierarchical Bayes Regression'. *URL: http://www.sawtoothsoftware.com/hbreg.shtml* 27

[13] Srinivasan, V., A. Jain, and N. Malhotra. "Improving the Predictive Power of Conjoint Analysis by Constrained Parameter Estimation" *Journal of Marketing Research*, 20,(November), p. 433-438, 1983. 29

[14] Srinivasan, V. and A. Shocker. "Linear Programming Techniques for Multidimensional Analysis of Preferences" *Psychometrica*, 38,3, p. 337-369, 1973. 27, 29

[15] Stone, C. J.. "Additive Regression and Other Nonparametric Models" *Annals of Statistics*, 13, p. 689-705, 1985. 27

[16] Tikhonov, A. N. and V. Y. Arsenin. *Solutions of Ill-posed Problems*. Washington, D. C.: W. H. Winston, 1977. 25, 29

[17] Vapnik, V. N.. *Statistical Learning Theory*. New York: Wiley, 1998. 23, 24, 25, 29, 30, 31

[18] Vapnik, V. N. and A. Y. Chervonenkis. " On the Uniform Convergence of Relative Frequencies of events to their probabilities". *Th. Prob. and its Applications* **17**(2), 264–280, 1971. 23, 25, 29

[19] Wahba, G. *Splines Models for Observational Data*. Philadelphia: Series in Applied Mathematics, Vol. 59, SIAM, 1990. 29, 30

[20] Wittink, D. and P. Cattin. "Commercial Use of Conjoint Analysis: An Update" *Journal of Marketing*, 53, 3, p. 91-96, 1989. 27

Part III

Francesco E. Lauria Lecture

Increasing the Biological Inspiration of Neural Networks

Francesco E. Lauria

Dipartimento di Scienze Fisiche, Universit gravea di Napoli Federico II
& INFM Complesso Universitario di Monte Sant'Angelo
Via Vicinale Cupa Cintia 16, I-80126 Napoli, Italy (EU)
`lauria@na.infn.it`

Abstract. Starting from a nerve cell functional characterization, we define formally *the autonomous learning to concatenate sequences* and prove it to be a possible solution for the problem that faces the, eg vertebrate, nervous systems: ie, to choose and to store, without outside help, the instructions to compute the actual sensor/effector correspondences they have to control. In our formal system we assign the initial connection matrix elements so that the rules, namely the Caianiello relation iterated application, autonomously and deterministically control the meta-rule, namely the Hebbian rule, application.

Keywords: Autonomus learning, Concatenate sequences, Caianiello model, Hebbian rule.

1 Introduction

Whereas it is useless to transmit to the progeny the information needed to pack the cells in an organ like the liver or a bone, as it is irrelevant which cell is in contact to which, the nervous system very raison d' être is the web of contacts between different neurons, ie, the parents must transmit genetically to the progeny the nervous system blueprint. A nervous system controls either an inflexible, ie, a rigidly predeterminate behavior, as eg in an insect, or a flexible, ie, an adaptable behavior, as eg in a vertebrate. In the former case the information needed to implement the finite set of sensors/effectors correspondences is genetically transmitted from the parents to the offsprings and the nervous system works as a special purpose control system. In the latter case the genetically transmitted blueprint must ensure, also, the proper functioning of the very same nervous system controlling the flexible behavior: actually, an adaptable nervous system is an auto-programming general purpose control system. Among the many synergies induced by the interactions of the various components in a system as complex as a nervous system there is *learning*, a gestalt expression. Nevertheless *learning* has been characterized also as a functional phenomenon, ie, it has been defined by means of the properties of the nervous system components, namely as a consequence of some of the nerve cells functional facets. Whereas in the inflexible behavior case all the instructions to compute a number

M. Marinaro and R. Tagliaferri (Eds.): WIRN VIETRI 2002, LNCS 2486, pp. 35–43, 2002.

of input/output correspondences must be transmitted to the progeny nervous system, at birth, in the flexible behavior case it seems more suitable to transmit the instructions to select and to control, autonomously, the eventual storing and the proper execution of the particular input/output correspondences needed to survive notwithstanding the vagaries of an impredictable and unknown evolving environment. To sum it up, if a flexible behavior is the goal, either a number of sensory/effector correspondences have to be transmitted, more or less expensively, to the progeny nervous system so that, depending on the environment events, it is always possible to compute the appropriate one or, instead of all the possible correspondences, the rules must be transmitted to *learn*, ie, both to program and eventually to store, autonomously in any case, only the particular input/output correspondences to compute. In order to characterize *the autonomous learning of the sequence concatenation* as a consequence of the nerve cells functional aspects, we begin with the Caianiello algebraic formalization and the Hebbian rule.

2   The Caianiello Transform and the Hebbian Rule

2.1   The Caianiello Formal Model

To obtain a nerve cell formal model, let us consider an $N \times N$ matrix $||C||$, the *connection matrix* or CM, and an N component vector F, the *state vector* or SV. Let us call CME the generic $||C||$ element: *facilitatory* is a positive CME $c_{h,k}$. We call *absolutely inhibitory*, or simply *inhibitory*, a negative CME if its absolute value is greater than the sum of all the positive CMEs in the same row. We call *relatively inhibitory* a negative CME, if its absolute value is no greater than the sum of all the positive CMEs in the same row. Unless explicitly stated, from now on we shall consider only facilitatory or inhibitory CMEs, ie, we shall not consider relatively inhibitory CMEs. We compute the *state* function $f_h[t]$, at the *iterartion* t, by means of the *Caianiello transform*, see [1]:

$f_h[t] = \Theta[\Sigma_k c_{h,k} f_k[t-1] - T]$,

where: $T > 0$ is the *threshold*, $\Theta[x] = 1$ for $x \geq 0$ and $\Theta[x] = 0$ for $x < 0$. Once given the CM $||C||$ and the *initial* SV $||F[1]||$, the Caianiello transform enable us to compute iteratively the SV succession.

As illustrative examples, we give the CMEs relative to the SVCs computing the *conjunction* and the *inclusive disjunction*. We say the component h, computes the *conjunction* of i and j, if:

$T/2 < c_{h,i} < T$, $T/2 < c_{h,j} < T$ and $\forall k \neq i, j :: c_{h,k} = 0$.

We say the component h computes the *inclusive disjunction*, or the *disjunction*, of i and j, if:

$c_{h,i} \geq T$, $c_{h,j} \geq T$ and $\forall k \neq i, j :: c_{h,k} = 0$.

From now on we shall give only the CMEs different from zero $c_{h,k} \neq 0$, ie, we give no longer, explicitly, the CMEs equal to zero $c_{h,k} = 0$.

We leave to the reader to prove the possibility *to compute any given finite number of combinations of logical connectives in a finite number of iterations by suitably choosing the CMEs*.

Actually, for some ganglia we can distinguish two subsets of nerve cells: the input subset and the output subset, respectively. E. g., in the mammalian cerebral cortex, a ganglion usually referred to by the layman as 'the brain', there are the sensory, or input, and the motor, or output, areas. Accordingly, we define two proper subsets of the SVCs: let us call *input set* the set of the first n SVCs and *output set* the set of the last m SVCs, with $0 < n + m < N$. We represent as $I[t]$ the input set and as $O[t]$ the output set.

As each SVC is either one or zero, there is a one-to-one correspondence between the state of the input, output, set elements and the n, m, digit binary numerals. Besides the SV succession, we consider the n, m, digit binary numeral successions as the representative of the successions of the first n, last m, SVCs: we call them the *input* and *output successions*.

Let us consider an input set state $I[t]$ characterized by the $n^* < n$ SVCs $f_i[t] = \ldots = f_j[t] = 1$, and the remaining $n - n^*$ SVCs equal zero. We say the input set state $I[t]$ *identifies the SVC h*, either if $T > c_{h,i} > T/n^*$ and $\ldots$ and $T > c_{h,j} > T/n^*$ or if $c_{h,i} > T$ and $\ldots$ and $c_{h,j} > T$. We say the SVC k *identifies the component h with a delay one*, or a *unitary delay*, if $c_{h,k} > T$. We say the SVC k *identifies the component h with a delay d*, if there are $d - 1$ sorted components such that the component k is the first of them and each of them identifies the next one, with a unitary delay, and the last of them identifies h, with a unitary delay.

2.2   The Iteration Dependent Matrix Elements

Up to now, we have considered the positive CMEs $c_{h,k}$ as iteration independent, or II, constants, ie, as positive rational numbers initially given once for all. For a discussion of the negative iteration dependent CMEs see [4,5]. Now we are going to introduce a rule, the *Hebbian rule*, see [2,3,4,5], to change the value of a CME as a function both of the SVC k value, at the iteration $t - 1$, and of the SVC h value, at the iteration t, namely we shall consider the iteration dependent CME, or IDME, $c_{h,k}[t]$: initially, we shall set $0 < c_{h,k}[1] < T$. Unfortunately the name "Hebbian rule" is a misnomer: whereas the Caianiello relation is the rule to compute the next SV an Hebbian rule is, actually, a meta-rule to adjourn the latter computation. However, we shall continue to call it a rule because of the consuetude.

We represent as $c_{h,k'}[t]$ an IDME such that the SVC h has the value one at the iteration t and the SVCs k' have the value one at the iteration $t - 1$. We represent as $c_{h,k''}[t]$ an IDME such that the SVC h has the value one at the iteration $t + 1$ and the SVCs k'' have the value zero at the iteration t. That is, for all the IDMEs with the first index h representing a SVC having the value one at the iteration t, we call k', k'', the second index if it represents a SVC having the value one, zero, at the iteration $t - 1$.

Let us call *Hebbian parameters* the four positive constants a, b, e, g: to implement the Hebbian rule we compute the IDME values at every iteration by applying the algorithm:

if $f_h[t + 1] = f_k[t] = 0$ and $0 \leq c_{h,k}[t] - a$ then $c_{h,k}[t + 1] = c_{h,k}[t] - a$, if $f_h[t+1] = f_k[t] = 0$ and $c_{h,k}[t] - a\ < 0$ then $c_{h,k}[t+1] = -[c_{h,k}[t] - a]$,

if $f_h[t+1] = 1 - f_k[t] = 1$ and $\Sigma_k c_{h,k}[t]f_k[t] < T$ and $c_{h,k}[t] - e \geq 0$ then $c_{h,k}[t+1] = c_{h,k}[t] - e$,

if $f_h[t+1] = 1 - f_k[t] = 1$ and $\Sigma_k c_{h,k}[t]f_k[t] < T$ and $c_{h,k}[t] - e < 0$ then $c_{h,k}[t+1] = -[c_{h,k}[t] - e]$,

if $f_h[t+1] = 1 - f_k[t] = 0$ and $0 \leq c_{h,k}[t] - b$ then $c_{h,k}[t+1] = c_{h,k}[t] - b$,

if $f_h[t+1] = 1 - f_k[t] = 0$ and $c_{h,k}[t] - b < 0$ then $c_{h,k}[t+1] = -[c_{h,k}[t] - b]$,

if $f_h[t+1] = f_k[t] = 1$ and $\Sigma_k c_{h,k}[t]f_k[t] < T$ then $c_{h,k}[t+1] = c_{h,k}[t] + g$,

if $f_h[t+1] = f_k[t] = 1$ and $\Sigma_k c_{h,k}[t]f_k[t] \geq T$ then both $c_{h,k''}[t+1] = c_{h,k''}[1]$ and $c_{h,k'}[t+1] = c_{h,k'}[t] = c_{h,k'}$, namely they have been *frozen*.

The Hebbian parameter values determine the *cadence*, that is, the number of times, within the iteration interval under consideration, for both the component h, at the iteration $t+1$, and the component k, at the iteration t, have to assume the value one so that the $c_{h,k}[t]$ becomes *frozen*. Actually, if we choose a sufficiently high value for the Hebbian parameter g, relative to the values we choose for a and b and e, the $c_{h,k}[t]$ can be frozen in as little as two iterations.

To distinguish the II CMEs, or IICMEs, from the IDMEs we shall insert an H among the variable k arguments. That is, if the SVC h computes the function $B[k[1], k[2], \ldots, k[i, H], \ldots, k[p]]$, then whereas $c_{h,k[1]}, c_{h,k[2]}, \ldots, c_{h,k[p]}$ are II $c_{h,k[i,H]}$ is iteration dependent.

The Hebbian rule leads naturally to a succession of matrices: ie, besides the SV succession generated by the Caianiello transform iterated application, there is a CM succession, generated by the Hebbian rule iterated application. As the Caianiello transform and the Hebbian rule have to be applied in the order, for short we call them the *CH transform*, the two successions elements are in a one-to-one correspondence. For short we call MVS the CM and the SV successions generated by the CH transform.

3   The Hebbian Rule and the MVS

Whereas it is possible for a ganglion to be given with a sufficient number of nerve cells to compute a correspondence defined on all the possible $I[t]$ values, it does not come cheap. E. g., just one human optic nerve is a bundle of something like $10^{**}6$ fibers and, as a fiber is either active or not, the human optic nerve has $2^{**}[10^{**}6]$ different states. Because the number of elementary particle in the universe is many order of magnitude smaller, the complete classification of just one optic nerve states is only a theoretical possibility. A possible alternative is to consider only a subset of all the possible $I[t]$ values. However both solutions imply the ability, at manufacturing time, to decide which particular correspondences have to be implemented in the initial CM. That is, the parents should have to know which subset of the offspring sensory configurations shall represent the ganglion actual input in the offspring lifetime and the particular motor response each sensory configuration has to correspond to. As there is no telling which input subsets shall be the ganglion actual inputs, and the corresponding motor responses, neither solution can be the natural selection choice. However, once we have both introduced the IDMEs and set some of the CMEs so that the SV last O components are identified, respectively, by the first O components, ie, so that the primitive correspondences are defined, there is a solution to our problem. That is, we shall give the blueprint of a ganglion functional model so that only the correspondences defined on the sensory configurations actually present during the offspring lifespan are computed and, then, stored. In other words, we shall give the CM so to store and allow the computation only of the correspondences defined on the $I[t]$ values actually present, for some t values, in the SV succession. So there is no need to take into account all the possible, as opposed to the actually present, $I[t]$ values. In practice, we are going to implement the rules to control the proper *learning* to concatenate sequences, see the 4, of the previously *learned* concatenations of primitive correspondences. As is well known, eg see [4,6], there are many results on how to control statistically the convergence of the MVSs, ie, on how to control the IDMEs freezing for SV successions generated by the application of rules different from the Caianiello transform. Or for the CM successions generated by rules different from the Hebbian rule. Here, we are interested in the algebraic controlled freezing of the IDMEs with the same, one at most, first index.

Without any loss of generality, we consider the two symbol alphabet $\{0,1\}$ corresponding to a proper subset of the input set, see the 2. That is, for $1 < j \le n$, the input set instance $I[1]$ characterized by $f_{k[1]}[t] = 1$ and $f_{k[j]}[t] = 0$ corresponds to the symbol 0. And, for $2 < j \le n$, the input set instance $I[2]$ characterized by $f_{k[1]}[t] = 0$, $f_{k[2]}[t] = 1$ and $f_{k[j]}[t] = 0$ corresponds to the symbol 1. For simplicity sake, let us consider an initial CM and an initial SV with the output set containing the two elements $f_{h[N-1]}[t]$ and $f_{h[N]}[t]$, the *primitive components*, identified with a delay d, see the 1, the former by the input element $f_{k[1]}[t]$ and the latter by the input element $f_{k[2]}[t]$, for suitable d. In other words, each primitive component has the value one at the iteration $t+d$, if the corresponding component belonging to the input set has the value one at the iteration t and the remaining components of the input set have the value zero, at the very same iteration t.

Let τ represent the generic iteration, and $I[i]$, $I[j]$ and $I[r]$ three elements of the input set, with $I[i] \ne I[j]$ and $I[i] \ne I[r]$. We represent with $I[i;t]$ the input set element $I[i]$ at the iteration t. For m and n constants and t variable, we consider the input successions of the type $I[i;t], \tau, \ldots, \tau, I[j;t+p], \tau, \ldots, \tau, I[r;t+q]$, where a comma separates two consecutive iterations and the number of iterations, ie, the delay between $I[i;t]$ and $I[j;+p]$ is represented by p τs and the delay between $I[i;t]$ and $I[r;t+q]$ is represented by q τs. The said delays depend on the particular Boolean functions, we shall discuss in the next Section, computed by the non zero SVCs appearing in $I[i]$, in $I[j]$ and in $I[r]$. Both i) if the two input set elements $I[j;t+p]$ and $I[r;t+q]$ identify, with different delays, either $f_{h[N-1]}[t]$ or $f_{h[N]}[t]$ or both, ie, if the first generates the output succession $O[1]$ and the second the output succession $O[2]$, and ii) if the input set element $I[i]$ identifies neither $f_{h[N-1]}[t]$ nor $f_{h[N]}[t]$ nor an output succession whatever, we call *example* the finite sequence $I[i;t], \tau, \tau, \ldots, \tau, I[j;t+p], \tau, \tau, \ldots, \tau, I[r;t+q]$.

If the very same example, ie, if a succession of the input set elements $I[i; t]$, $I[j; t + p]$ and $I[r; t + q]$, with $I[i] \neq I[j]$, $I[i] \neq I[r]$, p and q constants and t variable, belongs to the input succession for a number of times, dependent on the values chosen for the Hebbian parameters, sufficient for the non zero components present in $I[i]$ to identify either $f_{h[N-1]}[t]$ or $f_{h[N]}[t]$ or both, the first with the delay p and the second with the delay q, we shall say the MVS *has definitively acquired the property, or has autonomously learned, or has autonomously adapted itself*, to compute, in response to the input set element $I[i]$, the particular output succession $O[1]O[2]$, ie, the succession obtained by concatenating the execution of the succession $O[2]$ after the execution of the succession $O[1]$. To sum it up, the MVS *has definitively acquired the property or has definitively acquired the property*, or *has autonomously adapted itself*, to concatenate two output successions whenever at least one IDME has been frozen.

4   An Illustrative Example

As some diseases testify, e. g. the Alzheimer or the Parkinson or the bovine spongiform encephalopathy, the systematic, as opposed to the occasional, and unchecked modification of the nerve cell functionality and connectivity does not lead to a properly working new nervous system, in general. That is, to modify a set of well formed formulae so to obtain, always, a different set of well formed formulae we must apply carefully chosen rules. E. g., for simplicity sake it is better to modify one formula at the time, to be sure that each new formula is defined on the range of values its independent variables assume and does not modify the proper working of the previously defined formulae and so on. Accordingly, for each IDME we must set some IICMEs so to guarantee the proper freezing of each one of the IDMEs. In other words, we must implement the algorithms needed to control the way each new correspondence is computed and stored. Among the infinitely many sets of algorithms to this end, we present one of the simpler.

We shall give an initial CM and an initial SV generating the MVS learning to execute the output successions in response to the input element $I[i]$ whenever the examples are of the type:

$I[i; t], \tau, I[j; t + 2], \tau, \tau, \tau, I[r; t + 6], \ldots$,

where i) $I[i] \neq I[j]$; ii) $I[i] \neq I[r]$; iii) $I[j]$ is either $I[1]$ or $I[2]$; iv) $I[r]$ can be any of the input set elements.

We have chosen the initial CM, the initial SV, the output set and the examples for simplicity sake: their choice does not limit the universality of the systems presented, only their generality. Actually, to have larger output sets or to eliminate the condition on $I[j]$ to be either $I[1]$ or $I[2]$, larger initial matrices and vectors are needed, eg see [4,5].

To have a MVS controlling the proper IDMEs freezing, we must consider the initial SV as composed by two different SVC subsets, apart from the input subvector, ie, apart from the first n components. The first subset contains $[[N - n - 4]/7]$ *assemblies*: an assembly is a seven SVC sub-subset. The assembly A

is composed by the seven SVCs $[A, i]$, where $0 < A \leq [N - n - 4]/7$ and $i = 1, 2, 3, 4, 5, 6, 7$. Because for simplicity sake we consider a SV with an output set containing just two elements, the second subset contains just two elements, the two *primitive* sub-subsets: a primitive is a five SVC sub-subset. The primitive P is composed by the five SVCs $[P, i]$, with $P = [[N-n-4]/7]+1, [[N-n-4]/7]+2$ and $i = 1, 2, 3, 4, 5$. The two SVCs $[[[N-n-4]/7]+1, 3]$ and $[[[N-n-4]/7]+2, 3]$, to be defined next, are the SVCs called $f_{h[N-1]}[t]$ and $f_{h[N]}[t]$ in the 3 Obviously, the latter two components are identified, with a delay d, by the input set elements $I[1]$ and $I[2]$, defined at the 3 end.

We choose the input set cardinality n so to characterize all the $[[N - n - 4]/7] + 2$ assemblies and primitives by means of a one-to-one correspondence between the n digits binary numerals and both the assemblies and the primitives. Accordingly, any n digit binary numeral is the name of either an assembly or a primitive and, vice versa to each assembly and to each primitive is associated just one n digit numeral. Accordingly, we choose $c_{[A,1],k[i]}$ and $c_{[P,1],k[i]}$, for $\forall A$, for $\forall P$ and for $2 < i \leq n$, so that each combination of the input element values identify either one assembly or one primitive and, vice versa, so that each of the SVCs $[A, 1]$, respectively $[P, 1]$, for $\forall A$ and $\forall P$, are identified by just one input element. We represent compactly all the n corresponding IICMEs as $c_{[A,1],B[I[A]]}$, respectively $c_{[P,1],B[I[P]]}$, where the CMEs with the second index identifying a SVC equal to one, zero, are greater, smaller, than the threshold, taken with the minus sign. If the SVC $r - thEffectorEnd$ assumes the value one every time the $r - theffector$ terminates its activity, the functions computed by the assembly A and the primitive P components are defined by the CMEs:

THE ASSEMBLY A:

$c_{[A,1],B[I[A]]}; \forall A' \neq A :: c_{[A,1],[A',7,H]};$

$c_{[A,2],[A,1]} > T;$

$T/2 < c_{[A,3],[A,2]} < T; \; T/2 < c_{[A,3],[A,4]} < T;$

$c_{[A,4],[A,1]} > T; \; c_{[A,4],[A,4]} > T; \; \forall P :: c_{[A,4],[P,5]} < -T;$

$c_{[A,5],[A,4]} > T;$

$c_{[A,6],[A,5]} > T; \; c_{[A,6],[A,4]} < -T;$

$c_{[A,7],[A,6]} > T;$

THE PRIMITIVE P:

$c_{[P,1],B[I[P]]}; \forall A :: [c_{[P,1],[A,3,H]}; \; c_{[P,1],[A,7,H]}];$

$c_{[P,2],[P,1]} > T;$

$c_{[P,3],[P,1]} > T; \; c_{[P,3],[P,3]} > T; \; c_{[P,3],r-thEffectorEnd} < -T;$

$c_{[P,4],[P,3]} > T;$

$c_{[P,5],[P,3]} < -T; \; c_{[P,5],[P,4]} > T.$

If the assembly IDMEs, ie, if $c_{[A,1],[A',7,H]}[t]$, for $\forall A' \neq A$, and if the primitive IDMEs, ie, if $c_{[P,1],[A,3,H]}[t]$ and $c_{[P,1],[A,7,H]}[t]$, for $\forall A$, have initial values both positive and no greater than the smaller Hebbian parameter and if the assembly and primitive SVCs compute the given functions, then, $I[1]$ and $I[2]$ are the only input set elements identifying, respectively, the output set elements $h[N-1]$ and $h[N]$. We leave to the interested reader to verify that all the remaining input set elements or succession of input set elements do not identify output set elements or succession of output set elements. However, as the number of iterations increase and the very same example is the input succession a sufficient number of times for some of the above given IDMEs to be frozen, ie, for the MVS to have adapted itself to execute a new output succession.

As an illustrative example let us consider the MVS obtained by iterating the above given initial CM and the vectors given next. Initially, ie, for $t < t^*$, let the input set element $I[A^{**}; t]$ identifies no output succession. Moreover let the MVS to have been autonomously adapted, from the iteration t^* onward, to execute the sequence $O[A^*; t'' > t']$ in response to the input set element $I[A^*; t' > t^*]$, where $I[A^*]$ identifies the first component $[A^*, 1]$ of the assembly A^*. In turn, the first component $[P^*, 1]$ of the primitive P^* is identified by $I[1]$ or $I[2]$, depending whether the sequence $O[A^*; t'']$ first symbol is 0 or 1. Accordingly, from the iteration t^* onward, the component $[A^*, 1], [P^*, 1]$, computes the function defined by the CMEs:

$$c_{[A^*,1],B[I[A^*]]}; \forall A \neq A^* :: c_{[A^*,1],[A',7,H]};$$
$$c_{[P^*,1],B[I[P^*]]}; c_{[P^*,1],[A^*,3]}; \forall A \neq A^* :: [c_{[P^*,1],[A,3,H]}; c_{[P^*,1],[A,7,H]}].$$

Now, if the example $I[A^{**}; t > t^*], \tau, I[2; t + 2], \tau, \tau, \tau, I[A^*; t + 6]$ is the input succession a sufficient number of times to freeze both $c_{[P,1],[A^{**},3,H]}[t]$ and $c_{[A^*,1],[A^{**},7,H]}[t]$, then, i) the component $[A^*, 1]$ computes the function defined by the CMEs:

$$c_{[A^*,1],B[I[A^*]]}; c_{[A^*,1],[A^{**},7]}; \forall A \neq A^* :: c_{[A^*,1],[A',7,H]}$$

ii) if P^* is identified by $I[1]$, the component $[P^*, 1]$ computes the above given function and the component $[P, 1]$ computes the function defined by the CMEs:

$$c_{[P,1],B[I[P]]}; c_{[P,1],[A^{**},3]}; \forall A \neq A^{**} :: [c_{[P,1],[A,3,H]}; c_{[P,1],[A,7,H]}]$$

otherwise, ie, if P^* is identified by $I[2]$, namely by the same input set element identifying P, then $[P^*, 1] \equiv [P, 1]$ and it computes the function defined by the CMEs:

$$c_{[P,1],B[I[P]]}; c_{[P,1],[A^*,3]}; c_{[P,1],[A^{**},3]}; \forall A \neq A^*, A^{**} :: [c_{[P,1],[A,3,H]}; c_{[P,1],[A,7,H]}].$$

Accordingly, once both $c_{[P,1],[A^{**},3,H]}[t]$ and $c_{[A^*,1],[A^{**},7,H]}[t]$ have been frozen, from the iteration t^{**} onward, the input set element $I[A^{**}]$ identifies the output succession $1O^*$. To conclude, *whereas $I[A^{**}; t < t^{**}]$ does not identify an output succession, the very same $I[A^{**}; t > t^{**}]$ identifies the output succession $1O^*$, ie, the MVS has autonomously learned to execute the output succession $1O^*$ in response to the input element $I[A^{**}]$.*

For a more complete discussion on some, out of the infinitely many possible, MVSs autonomously adaptable to concatenate sequences of a general type, ie, without the constraints given here and, moreover, composed by assembly and primitive learning their own identifiers and on the resulting MVS simulation results, see [5].

References

1. Caianiello, E. R.: Outline of a theory of thought processes and thinking machines. J. of Theor. Biol, Vol. 2 (1961) 204-235. 36
2. Hebb, D. O.: The organization of behavior. J. Wiley & Sons, New York, (1966) 335 + xix. 37

3. Hassoun, Mohamad H.: Fundamentals of artificial neural networks. MIT Press, Cambridge (Mass.) USA (1995) 511 + xxvi. 37
4. Lauria, F. E., M. Sette, S. Visco: Adaptable Boolean neural networks. Fridericiana Scientia, Liguori, Napoli, (1997) 212,ISBN 88-207-2676-9 http://www.na.infn.it/Gener/cyber/report.html. 37, 39, 40
5. Lauria, F. E., R. Prevete: An algebraic approach to the autonomously self-adaptable Boolean neural nets. Acc. Sc. Fis. e Mat., Napoli, (2001), 299 + xi. ISBN 88-207-3266-1. http://www.na.infn.it/Gener/cyber/report.html. 37, 40, 42
6. de A. Barreto, G., Araujo, A. F. R.: Storage and recall of complex temporal sequences through a contextually guided self-organizing neural network. IJCNN2000 Como, Italy (EU). Amari, S-I, Giles, C. L., Gori, M., Piuri, V. eds.: Neural Computing: New Challenges and Perspectives for the New Millennium. IEEE Computer Soc. (Los Alamitos, CA, USA) Vol. 3 (2000) 207 - 212. ISBN: 0-7695-0619-4. 39

Part III

Francesco E. Lauria Lecture

Hybrid Automatic Trading Systems: Technical Analysis & Group Method of Data Handling

Marco Corazza[1], Paolo Vanni[2], and Umberto Loschi[2]

[1] Department of Applied Mathematics - University Ca' Foscari of Venice
Dorsoduro n. 3825/E - 30125 Venice, Italy
`corazza@unive.it`
`http://pluto.dma.unive.it/~marco/`
[2] T4T s.r.l. - Tools for Trading
via Risorgimento n. 36 - 35137 Padua, Italy
`{paolovanni,umbertoloschi}@t4t.biz`
`http://www.t4t.biz`

Abstract. For building an automatic trading system one needs: a significant variable for characterizing the financial asset behaviours; a suitable algorithm for finding out the information hidden in such a variable; and a proper Trading Strategy for transforming these information in operative indications. Starting from recent results proposed in literature, we have conjectured that the Technical Analysis approach could reasonably extract the information present in prices and volumes. Like tool able to find out the relation existing between the Technical Analysis inputs and an output we properly defined, we use the Group Method of Data Handling, a soft-computing approach which gives back a polynomial approximation of the unknown relationship between the inputs and the output. The automatic Trading Strategy we implement is able both to work in real-time and to return operative signals. The system we create in such a way not only performs pattern recognition, but also generates its own patterns. The results obtained during an intraday operating simulation on the US T-Bond futures is satisfactory, particularly from the point of view of the trend direction detection, and from the net profit standpoint.

Keywords: Automatic Trading Strategy (or Trading System), technical Analisys, GMDM.

1 Introduction

To build an automatic system for intraday trading one needs:

- a significant variable for characterizing the price-volume behaviour of given financial assets;
- an interpretative algorithm able to find out the information hidden in the considered variable;

M. Marinaro and R. Tagliaferri (Eds.): WIRN VIETRI 2002, LNCS 2486, pp. 47–55, 2002.

- and a suitable Trading Strategy (TS) able to transform these information in operative indications.

Even if in literature the debate is still open, starting from the results proposed by Lee et al. [4], and Lo et al. [5], we have conjectured that the Technical Analysis (TA) interpretative key could reasonably extract the information present in prices and volumes. Like tool able to find out the relation existing between the TA inputs and an output indicator we properly defined, we use the Group Method of Data Handling (GMDH), a soft-computing approach which gives back a polynomial approximation of the unknown relationship between the input variables and the output one. The automatic TS we implement is able both to work in real-time and to return operative signals.

The remainder of this paper is organized as follows: in Section 2 we synthetically describe the trading methodology we propose; in section 3 we detail all the functional areas characterizing our automatic intraday trading system; in section 4 we report the results obtained during an intraday operating simulation on the US T-Bond futures; and in section we give some final conclusions and remarks.

2   Methodology

Our target consists in implementing a complex system, as TA-GMDH is, and an automatic TS, both able to work in real-time and return operative signals. The inputs we use are the reports of transactions: time, price, and volume. Despite the traditional trading systems based on TA rules, the system we create not only performs pattern recognition, but also generates its own patterns[1]. The architecture of our system is articulated in three functional areas:

- the TA receives the data and processes them giving back information as suitable TA indicators;
- the GMDH uses the information obtained by the TA, recognizes the market trend, and returns the strength of the phenomenon;
- the automatic TS optimizes the use of the GMDH output.

A considerable problem consists in coordinating these areas in order to obtain the most profitable results.

GMDH is a soft-computing approach able to model in a non parametric and non linear way real phenomena, so it can be used when there is neither qualitative knowledge nor strong analytical one about these phenomena, and also when the related available data sets are highly noisy [3]. Because of these peculiarities, GMDH seem to be a promising tools for building automatic intraday trading systems.

Notice that our approach differs from the ones proposed in literature. In fact, we do not ask to the GMDH to generate a suggestion about the trend, but

---

[1] Because of that it is more flexible than standard ones, from pattern recognisers to pattern builders.

"only" to give an operating support to the TS by determining the Emergent Trend Intensity (ETI, see section 4), an original TA's indicator able to suggest both the existence of specific conditions and the way to operate (when and how). In particular, our TS has to extrapolate operative signals from the indications provided by the GMDH, and to include the necessary rules for a correct risk and money management. The philosophy followed by the TS is to buy the minima in an up-trend[2] and sell the maxima in a down-trend of the price pattern.

3   Application

3.1   Technical Analysis

To realize our automatic trading system, we employ the TA approach for building specific indicators. In particular, we do not modify at all their original definitions, which are well founded in literature. Any case, it is necessary to face the problem of the choice of the inputs to give to the GMDH, and to the TS.

Now, we present the main variables we select as inputs. At first, there are four variables linked to the time: $x_1 =$ date; $x_2 =$ month; $x_3 =$ hour (measured by number of bars; one bar is a period of 30 minutes); and $x_4 =$ day of the week. The first one gives only a chronological reference, the others three are used as cyclical indicators.

Then, the variables directly linked to the prices are: $x_5 = C_t$, the close price of the last contract in the period that end at time t; $x_{15} = H_t$, the higher price the contract reaches in the period from $t - 1$ to t; $x_{16} = L_t$, the lower price the contract reaches in the period from $t - 1$ to t.

Finally, the variables strictly following TA indicators are: $x_7 = EMA_{N,t}$, the Exponential Smoothing Average of $N = 21$ periods, at time t [1]. It is defined by $C_t \alpha + (\alpha - 1)EMA_{N,t-1}$, where $\alpha \leq 1$ is the smoothing constant. It is possible to determine the constant α by $\alpha = 2/(1 + N)$. So x_7 becomes $EMA_{21,t} = (C_t + 10EMA_{21,t-1})/11$; $x_{14} = R_t$, the logarithmic return of C_t, i.e. $R_t = \ln(C_t) - \ln(C_{t-1})$; $x_6 = V_t$, the volume, which is given by the number of contracts that have been recorded in the period of the bar, $V_t = \sum_{i=t-1}^{t} n_i$, where n_i is number of contracts at time i; $x_9 =$ an original index of movement persistence, which is based on the number of bars that compose the actual movement; $x_{10} = RSI_{14,t}$, the Relative Strength Index on 14 bars, which gives an estimation of the strength below tendency. Its value at time t is computed as $RSI_{14,t} = 100 - 100/(1 + \Delta^+/\Delta^-)$ [7], where Δ^+ is the $EMA_{14,t}$ of upward price changes, and Δ^- is the $EMA_{14,t}$ of the downward prices; $x_{11} = MACD_t$, the Moving Average Convergence Divergence, is a trend-following momentum indicator. Its basic formulation is: $MACD_t = EMA_{12-bars,t} - EMA_{26-bars,t}$ [1]; $x_{12} = \%K_{N,t}$ is a stochastic oscillator. We compute it over the last 14 bars as follows: $\%K_{14,t} = 100(C_t - \min\{L_t, \ldots, L_{t-13}\})/(\max\{H_t, \ldots, H_{t-13}\} - \min\{L_t, \ldots, L_{t-13}\})$; $x_{13} = ATR_{14,t}$, the Average True Range, is a measure of volatility [7]. $ATR_{N,t}$ is a moving average of the True Range indicator $TR_t =$

---

[2] Do not confuse with a purchase at a low price.

$\max\{H_t - L_t, C_{t-1} - H_t, C_{t-1} - L_t\}$. Again we consider $N = 14$, from which $ATR_{14,t} = \sum_{i=t-14}^{t} TR_i/15$.

Data. During the development phase, we used the a proper time series of prices and volumes of the US T-Bond futures, starting from the 1st June 1995 up to 25th may 2000; then, we used the real-time data. The tick-by-tick time series was provided by the Chicago Board of Trade, and we built 30-minute time series; so, every pit session is articulated in 30-minute intervals, starting from the market opening at 7:20 AM standard central time. The operating simulations period consisted of $17,293$ 30-minute periods.

Input Selection. During the testing period we performed a sensitivity analysis related to different variables and their combinations in order to improve the GMDH learning. Due to informative redundancy among variables directly connected to the prices - namely: C_t, $EMA_{21,t}$ and R_t - we noted a decline in the output quality when we jointly considered them as inputs. After some analyses we stated to use only R_t. Moreover we recorded the basic role of V_t in cleaning up[3] the GMDH output (notice that V_t does not bring about the output, but defines some qualitative characteristic).

3.2   GMDH Approach

Generally, given a variable y representing a phenomenon, and given $M \geq 2$ other variables $x_1, x_2, \ldots, x_M$ representing possible explicators for y, the GMDH technique searches for a polynomial approximation of the unknown relationship between y and $x_1, x_2, \ldots, x_M$. The basic GMDH determines its "optimal" polynomial form and the "optimal" values of the parameters specifying such a form by means of an iterative procedure whose target consists in minimizing a predefined cost function. The related iterative procedure can be itemized as follows:

step 1: initialize the iteration counter t to 0, and consider the starting input-output data set $D(t) = \{(x_{1,l}(t), x_{2,l}(t), \ldots, x_{M,l}(t); y_l), \ l = 1, \ldots, L\}$,[4] where L indicates the number of input-output pattern (notice that $x_i(0) = x_i$ and $M(0) = M$), and set an upper bound for the modelling error, $\overline{E}(t) > 0$;
step 2: randomly split $D(t)$ in two not-overlapping sub-sets: a training one, $D_T(t) \subset D(t)$, and a checking one, $D_C(t) = D(t) \backslash D_T(t)$;

---

[3] The volume improves the output of the bars in trend, which are not maxima or minima.
[4] The data set $D(t)$ is determined by properly using a fuzzy-like filtering methodology. Going into simple details, starting from the conjecture following which to similar inputs should be correspond similar outputs, the filtering methodology we use selects from all the past input-output patterns only the ones whose input side is similar (in a suitable fuzzy way) to the input side of the current pattern, i.e. the one whose output side is unknown.

step 3: for each pair of different explicators $x_i(t)$ and $x_j(t)$, with $i \neq j$, consider the following (approximate) relationship $y \cong a_{i,j}(t) + b_{i,j}(t)x_i(t) + c_{i,j}(t)x_j(t) + d_{i,j}(t)x_i^2(t) + e_{i,j}(t)x_j^2(t) + f_{i,j}(t)x_i(t)x_j(t)$, where $a_{i,j}(t)$, $b_{i,j}(t)$, $c_{i,j}(t)$, $d_{i,j}(t)$, $e_{i,j}(t)$, and $f_{i,j}(t)$ are real parameters;

step 4: for each of the previous $M(t)[M(t) - 1]/2$ relationships fit an ordinary least square (OLS) regression by using the sub-data set $D_T(t)$;

step 5: for each of the fitted OLS regressions determine the modelling error $E_{i,j}(t) = \{\sum_{l=1}^{L_C}[\hat{y}_{i,j,l}(t) - y_l]^2\}/L_C$, where $\hat{y}_{i,j,l}(t) = \hat{a}_{i,j}(t) + \hat{b}_{i,j}(t)x_i(t) + \hat{c}_{i,j}(t)x_j(t) + \hat{d}_{i,j}(t)x_i^2(t) + \hat{e}_{i,j}(t)x_j^2(t) + \hat{f}_{i,j}(t)x_i(t)x_j(t)$,[5] by using the L_C input-output patterns of the sub-data set $D_C(t)$; for each $E_{i,j}(t) \leq \overline{E}(t)$ initialize $\hat{x}_k(t + 1)$ to $\hat{y}_{i,j}$, where k is a suitable non negative counter lower or equal to $M(t)[M(t) - 1]/2$, and set up $\overline{E}(t + 1)$ to $\min\{E_{i,j}(t)\}$;

step 6: if $\max\{k\} \geq 2$ then update t to $t + 1$, update $M(t)$ to $\max\{k\}$, update $D(t)$ to $\{(x_{1,l}(t) = \hat{x}_{1,l}(t), x_{2,l}(t) = \hat{x}_{2,l}(t), \ldots, x_{M(t),l}(t) = \hat{x}_{M(t),l}(t); y_l)$, $l = 1, \ldots, L\}$ and go to **step 2**; else if $\max\{k\} = 1$ then $\hat{x}_k(t)$ is the best GMDH estimation for y; else if $\max\{k\} = 0$ the best GMDH estimation for y is that $\hat{y}_{i,j}(t)$ to which is associated the lowest $E_{i,j}(t)$.

A drawback characterizing this soft-computing technique is the fact that it provides "only" a point estimation of y. In order to fill this lack, we originally improve the basic GMDH technique by implementing a simple bootstrap-based approach. In fact, at each utilization of the presented procedure, instead of splitting $D(t)$ only once into a training sub-set and in a checking one, we randomly split it several times for the purpose of obtaining a population of such not-overlapping sub-sets, respectively $D_{T,n}(t)$ and $D_{C,n}(t)$, with $n = 1, \ldots, N$. So, starting from this population of training and checking sub-sets, we can get a population of "optimal" GMDH estimations of y, $\hat{y}_n$, by which to determine its empirical frequency distribution [2].

3.3 Trading Strategy

Trading financial markets requires a tool able to transform a simple forecast in a complete set of orders. The development of an automatic TS able to exploit the GMDH output results in an easier task then building a strategy based on usual TA indicators. This is primary because of the characteristics and flexibility of the soft-computational approach which we choose, and then because of the output variable *ETI* which directly supplies an instruction pattern to the automatic TS.

In designing such a TS, our primary goal was to assess: at first the possibility to use GMDH results to generate operative signals, and then its profitability. Due to our purposes, TS architecture has:

– to properly simulate the operational environment (taking into account the involved costs, and being able to generate the required instructions to real time trading and real risk management);

---

[5] The symbol "^" means the estimator of the corresponding parameter.

– and do not interfere the with GMDH results by trying to translate them in operative signals.

The only operational filters we employed to implement this TS were two suitable moving averages characterized by different lengths. By means of the respectively moving averages position[6], we define the actual trend. This allowed us, from a trend follower point of view, to make a selection of long/short operating signals avoiding to be always in the market as GMDH approach suggest. At first, the starting indicator's definition of a strong change in the trend direction led us to consider stop and reverse strategies[7], which demonstrated their operating inefficiency because of: the GMDH signals issued the strategy signal in advance with respect to the market; the steady use of the investor's own resources (we are not ever flat); the risk derived from systematically facing the overnight market; and the usual low levels of the estimated trend durations which do not ensure the necessary price swing to profitably work out the trade.

Since for these reasons, almost all professional traders show some perplexities in using strategies which limit their possibility to be flat; so we needed to take into account these requirements otherwise our product would miss the necessary characteristics to be considered a practical real time trading tool.

The following steps present a simple buy signal in an uptrend move (the downside is treated just using the opposite set of rules):

– if an emerging trend is detected, then the trading procedure begins;
– the first condition states that the trend direction has to be upward, and that its duration has to be greater than a fixed positive treshold λ; the second one is that the $MACD_t$ has to be positive[8];
– if both are true you can go long.

Notice that the estimations of the emerging trend detector, the trend direction detector, and the trend duration are all given by ETI (see section 4).

To test the effectiveness of ETI and GMDH we preferred use no particular exit strategy, so we close out our position every day when the market closes. This is not the best way to exploit all the GMDH's predictive power but, for the time being, we prefer a neutral signal that does not affect the GMDH's performance and allow us to assess, in a qualitative way, its profitability (all tests and real-time were carried out by Trade Station 2000i provided by Omega Research).

4 Results

4.1 GMDH Results

As first output, GMDH returns a population of ETI's forecasts. As second output, GMDH suitably extracts the ETI's value which will be employed by the

---

[6] We consider the $MACD_t$, the same oscillator we use with the GMDH.

[7] When we close to go long, we go short immediately.

[8] A positive $MACD_t$ means that the shorter period $EMA_{N,t}$ is above the longer one, and it identifies an uptrend.

Table 1. Evaluation of y_1 performance

Variable	Sample size	True	Wrong	% True
$y_1 = 0$	51,760	19,760	32,000	38.18%
$y_1 = 1$	21,640	15,504	6,136	71.65%
$y_1 = 0 \vee y_1 = 1$	73,400	35,264	38,136	48.05%

Table 2. Evaluation of y_2 performance

Variable	Sample size	True	Wrong	% True
$y_2 = $ Down	13,000	12,344	656	99.50%
$y_2 = $ Up	12,880	12,216	664	99.48%
$y_2 = $ Down $\vee$ $y_2 = $ Up	25,880	24,560	1,320	99.49%

TS; in this second step we faced the problem to interpret the empirical frequency distribution. The data generated by this operating way have characteristics that reflects the ETI's complexity. ETI is a vector of three elements, $\mathbf{y} = \{y_1, y_2, y_3\}$, where $y_1 \in \{0,1\}$ is a binary variable that shows if a reversal point exists or not, y_2 shows the trend direction (if $y_1 = 1$), and $y_3 \in \mathbf{N}$ shows the future duration of the movement just begun. At the current development state, GMDH results able to adequately estimate the first two ETI's elements. In general, the not negligible percentage of wrong values for $y_1 = 0$ (Table 1) can be due to two facts: GMDH signals in little advance the existence of a reversal point (but this advance does not seem to be a problem for the TS); moreover, we use a quite restrictive definition[9] for y_1, as we search only for those reversal trend which justifies financial interest (often reversals are too weak and the market faces a period of engulfing).

The results relative to the element y_2 (Table 2) are highly satisfying, and they show that GMDH can correctly characterize the trend however.

The interpretative problems concerning the empirical frequency distribution of the GMDH output are strictly correlated with y_3. Synthetic indicators as mean, variance, skewness, and kurtosis offer enough information to define an operative range for y_3; hence, we can extract an activation level for the TS, though it is a small part of the global information we could obtain. Notice that the frequency distribution morphology seems more informative than the point estimation.

In the figures which follow we show three typical different configurations of the distribution. The first one (on the left upside of Fig. 1) shows a low dispersion,

---

[9] We want that an inversion point have a minimum number of preceding and following points in trend.

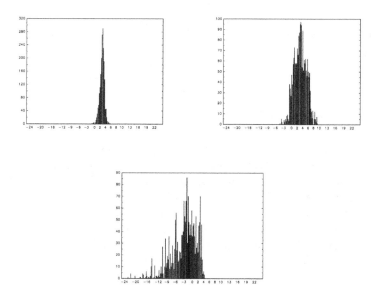

Fig. 1. On the x-axis we report the characteristics of the price movement: the number signum indicates the movement trend (negative values mean down-trend, positive values mean up-trend); the number absolute value (1 to 24) indicates the movement duration in term of bars. On the y-axis we report the absolute frequency

and a mode very close to zero; it seems to be the typical appearance of a trend point. The second one (on the right upside of Fig. 1) is platikurtic, and its mode is less close to zero; it seems characterizing the intraday weak trends (few hours). The third one (on the central downside of Fig. 1) appears heavy skewed, and more frayed as it goes away from zero; it seems to be characteristic of persistent trends.

4.2 Trading Strategy Results

In the test phase we used only one US T-Bond futures, and we charged a fixed commission of 12.5\$ per trade. We did not consider slippage[10] on entry prices; moreover, we did not consider any other bank costs. In (Table 3) we show the strategy performance.

---

[10] The slippage is the difference between the entry/exit price of the TS and the entry/exit price really made at the market.

Table 3. TS performance

Net profit	Gross profit	Maximum draw down	% Win	Average trade
12, 618$	46, 468$	5, 687$	56.49%	52.80$

5 Conclusions and Remarks

In times of "financial fidgetiness", a tool which has the formal rigour and the flexibility typical of the GMDH approach, joined with the soft-knowledge and the psychological stoutness of an automatic TS, seems to give back a big reward.

In spite of the extremely comforting results, currently we are not completely satisfied by them; in fact, during the system development we detected some potentialities of this tool which are not yet exploited.

Our new efforts will be addressed to improve the information flow quality the system receive. We shall do it: by searching for new TA's indicators able to be used as inputs for GMDH; by developing more sophisticated architectures for GMDH; and improving the GMDH-TS interface.

References

[1] Appel, G.: The Moving Average Convergence-Divergence Method. Signalert, Great Neck (1979) 49

[2] Efron, B., Tibshirani, R. J.: An Introduction to the Bootstrap. Chapman & Hall, London Weinheim New York Tokyo Melbourne Madras (1993) 51

[3] Farlow, S. J.: The GMDH Algorithm. In: Farlow, S. J. (ed.): Self-Organizing Methods in Modeling. Marcel Dekker, New York Basel (1984) 1-24 48

[4] Lee, C. M.C,Swaminathan, B.: Price Momentum and Trading Volume. Journal of Finance, LV(5) (2000) 2017-2069 48

[5] Lo, W. A., Mamaysky, H., Wang, J.: Foundations of Technical Analysis: Computational Algorithms, Statistical Inference, and Empirical Implementation. Journal of Finance, LV(4) (2000) 1705-1769 48

[6] Nison, S.: Japanese Candlesticks Charting Technique. Prentice Hall Press, New York (1991)

[7] Wilder, J. W.: New Concepts in Technical Trading. Trend Research, Greensboro (1978) 49

Interval TOPSIS for Multicriteria Decision Making

Silvio Giove

Department of Applied Mathematics, University Ca'Foscari of Venice
Dorsoduro n. 3825/E - 30125 Venice, Italy
sgiove@unive.it

Abstract. In this paper, an interval version of the classical multi-criteria TOPSIS method is proposed. In particular, the so-called Bag-Based TOPSIS proposed by Rebai will be considered, and suitably modified to treat with interval number, using the *acceptability* index suggested by Sengupta. Interval analysis can be a powerful tool to deal with complex decision problems where the values of the criteria for each alternatives can be characterized by uncertainty.

Keywords: Interval analysis, multi criteria decision problem.

1   Introduction

This paper introduces the I-TOPSIS approach (Interval TOPSIS), a new paradigm for a multi criteria decision problem, extending what proposed by Rebai [7] to the case of interval data. Interval analysis is a simple and intuitive way to introduce data uncertainty for complex decision problems, and can be used for a lot of practical applications.

2   The TOPSIS Method for MCD Problems

The TOPSIS method (Technique for Order Preference by Similarity to Ideal Solution), is one of the most used approach for multi criteria decision problems (MCD for brevity). Let us briefly introduce the basic procedure, the reader interested in deeper details can refer to any one of the specialised references, see for instance [3], [5]. To this aim, let be: $A = \{X_i\}, i = 1, .., n,$, the set of alternatives, $\{C_h\}, h = 1, .., m$, the set of criteria, while n, m are the number of alternatives and criteria respectively. Moreover, let be assigned an alternative-criterion table of interval values, $T = \{\nu_h(X)\}, \quad h = 1, .., m$. Each criterion is defined in the set $D(C_h)$, its real domain. Furthermore, let be assigned a set of criterion weights $\{w_h\}, h = 1, .., m$, measuring the importance of each criterion. First of all, the data are normalized in the following way:

$$C_h(X) = \frac{\nu_h(X)}{\sqrt{\sum_{k=1}^{n} \nu_h^2(X_i)}}, \quad \forall X \in A \tag{1}$$

M. Marinaro and R. Tagliaferri (Eds.): WIRN VIETRI 2002, LNCS 2486, pp. 56–63, 2002.

Afterwards, the algorithm computes the so-called *ideal* and *anti-ideal alternatives*, I^-, I^+:

$$I^+ = \{\max_i(C_h(X_i))\}, \quad I^- = \{\min_i(C_h(X_i))\} \tag{2}$$

Subsequently, using a suitable metric, the algorithm computes, for each alternative X_i, the two distances d_i^+, d_i^- of X_i from I^+, I^-:

$$d_i^+ = \|I^+ - X_i\| = \sum_{h=1}^{m} w_i |C_h(I^+) - C_h(X_i)| \tag{3}$$

$$d_i^- = \|I^- - X_i\| = \sum_{h=1}^{m} w_i |C_h(I^-) - C_h(X_i)| \tag{4}$$

and the following separation index $\zeta_i \in [0,1]$:

$$\zeta_i = \frac{d_i^-}{d_i^- + d_i^+} \tag{5}$$

Finally, the alternatives are ranked on the basis of the index ζ_i.

3   The Fuzzy Bag and the BB-TOPSIS Method

Rebai [7] introduced the BB-TOPSIS method (Bag Based TOPSIS) in the context of MCD problems. Here we limit to recall the main items, keeping the notation as most as possible similar to the original one. We can define a fuzzy bag $B(X)$ over a finite set $X, card(X) = m$ as the following function $B_X : X \rightarrow R^{2m}$:

$$B_X = \{C_1(X)/w_1, C_2(X)/w_2, \ldots, C_m(X)/w_m\} = \{\prod_{h=1}^{m} C_h(X)/w_h\} \tag{6}$$

where X can represents an alternative described by the values of criteria $\{C_h(X)\}$, and w_h is the weight for the h-th criterion, while the symbol $\prod$ stays for the cartesian product. We limit to quote some elementary operations. Given two bags B_X, B_Y defined over the sets X, Y, with $card(X) = card(Y)$ we can define:

$$cardinality: \quad |B_X| = \sum_{h=1}^{m} C_h(X)w_h \tag{7}$$

$$symmetric \quad difference: B_1 \Delta B_2 = \{\prod_{h=1}^{m} |C_h(X) - C_Y(X)|w_h\} \tag{8}$$

$$distance: d(B_1, B_2) = |B_X \Delta B_Y| \tag{9}$$

Other types of distance function can be defined, but the one in (9) is the only satisfying a set of useful properties[1]. A bag can than be assigned to each alternative, collecting the values for each criterion and the relative weights. Given an alternative, a dominance value for a criterion is nothing else that the sum of all the dominated counts, that is the sum of the cases where the criterion in an other alternative is inferior (or not greater, depending on the desired choice). The quoted Author called it superiority (or inferiority, or non-inferiority) score. For instance, the superiority score for the alternative X referring to the h-th criterion is given by:

$$S_h(X) = card\{Y : C_h(Y) < C_h(X), \quad Y \in A \} \tag{10}$$

being A the set of alternatives. The superiority $MCFB^>$ (Multi-attribute Canonical Fuzzy Bag), is the following bag:

$$MCFB^>(X) = \{\prod_{h=1}^{m} S_h(X)/C_h\} \tag{11}$$

The ideal and anti-ideal alternatives are defined as:

$$MCFB_>^+(X) = \vee MCFB^>(X) = \{\prod_{h=1}^{m} \vee S_h(X)/C_h\} \tag{12}$$

$$MCFB_>^-(X) = \wedge MCFB^>(X) = \{\prod_{h=1}^{m} \wedge S_h(X)/C_h\} \tag{13}$$

---

[1] Moreover, in the quoted paper, three functions were proposed when comparing the alternatives; the suitable choice depends by the attitude of the Decision Maker (pessimistic or optimistic, see [7]).

where the symbols $\wedge, \vee$ stay for the operators minimum and the maximum respectively. Next, given an alternative X, the algorithm computes the two distances between $MCFB^{>}(X)$ and $MCBFB_{>}^{+}(X)$ and between $MCFB^{>}(X)$ and $MCFB_{>}^{-}(X)$, where the distances between two bags is given by (9):

$$d_{>}^{+} = d(MCFB^{>}(X), MCFB_{>}^{+}) \tag{14}$$

$$d_{>}^{-} = d(MCFB^{>}(X), MCFB_{>}^{-}) \tag{15}$$

and the separation measure is like as (5):

$$C_{>}(X) = \frac{d_{>}^{-}}{d_{>}^{-} + d_{>}^{+}} \tag{16}$$

Finally, the alternatives are ranked according to the index $C_{>}(X), \in A$, as in the classical TOPSIS method.

4   I-TOPSIS, an Interval Version for TOPSIS

From now on, we suppose that the criteria values are positive closed intervals of R, sometimes called *interval numbers*. The following operations[2] can be defined for the two interval numbers $\bar{a} = [a^{inf}, a^{sup}], \bar{b} = [b^{inf}, b^{sup}]$

$$\bar{a} + \bar{b} = [a^{inf} + b^{inf}, a^{sup} + b^{sup}], \bar{a}\bar{b} = [a^{inf}b^{inf}, a^{sup}b^{sup}] \tag{17}$$

$$\bar{a} - \bar{b} = [a^{inf} - b^{sup}, a^{sup} - b^{inf}], \bar{a}/\bar{b} = [a^{inf}/b^{sup}, a^{sup}/b^{inf}] \tag{18}$$

Furthermore, we note that different methods were proposed in the specialized literature to compare two real intervals. Among them, we limit to quote [4], [6], [8]. In the direction of the method proposed by Sengupta [8], we propose the following *acceptability* index $\xi_{\bar{a}>\bar{b}}$, measuring how much the first interval is greater than the second one[3]:

$$\xi_{\bar{a}>\bar{b}} = \frac{m(\bar{a}) - m(\bar{b})}{w(\bar{a}) - w(\bar{b}) + 1} \tag{19}$$

---

[2] See [1] for a complete description of interval algebra.
[3] Unlike in Sengupta original formulation, we add the term 1 in the denominator of (19) to avoid loss of significance where both the spreads are null.

where:

$$m(\bar{a}) = \frac{1}{2}(a^{inf} - a^{sup}), \tag{20}$$

are the medium values and the spreads of the two intervals respectively. For the rational that justifies such a definition, please refer to the quoted literature. Here we limit to observe that the index is positive if the medium point of the first one is greater than the medium point of the second, and vice versa (it is null if both the two medium points are equal). Moreover, the index decreases with the sum of the two spreads. Anywise, some remarks could be discussed about the definition (19), but other comments and criticisms are beyond the purpose of this paper. We can now proceed in a similar way as in the BB-TOPSIS method. Let us fix the attention on the alternative X. Using interval data, the h-th criterion is expressed by a positive interval in the form $\bar{C}_h(X) = [C_h^{inf}(X), C_h^{sup}(X)]$. The BB-TOPSIS algorithm simply counts for all the alternatives dominated by X with respect to the h-th criterion. Using interval numbers, we substitute the values $S_h(X)$ in (10), with the sum of values $\xi_h(X, X_i) \equiv \xi_{C_h(X) > C_h(X_i)}$ with respect to i, that is:

$$IS_h(X) = \sum_{\substack{i=1 \\ i \notin g(X)}}^{n} \xi_h(X, X_i) \tag{21}$$

where $g(X)$ is the index function[4] of the alternative X for the set A, and I stays for Interval. Then, the bag:

$$IMCFB^>(X) = \{\prod_{h=1}^{m}(IS_h(X)/w_h)\} \tag{22}$$

can be assigned to the alternative X, with the same meaning that the definition (11). Subsequently, we compute the ideal and anti-ideal bags:

$$IMCFB_>^+ = \vee MCFB^>(X) = \{\prod_{h=1}^{m} \vee IS_h(X)/w_h)\} \tag{23}$$

$$IMCFB_>^- = \wedge MCFB^>(X) = \{\prod_{h=1}^{m} \wedge IS_h(X)/w_h)\} \tag{24}$$

---

[4] That is, if $A = \{X_1, X_2, \ldots, X_n\}$, it follows $g(X_i) = i$.

Finally, the distances (14), (15) can be replaced by the two analogous ones:

$$id_>^+ = d(IMCFB^>(X), IMCFB_>^+) \tag{25}$$

$$id_>^- = d(IMCFB^>(X), IMCFB_>^-) \tag{26}$$

and the separation index (16) by:

$$IC_>(X) = \frac{id_>^-}{id_>^- + id_>^+} \tag{27}$$

by which the alternatives can be ranked. The following theorem can be easily proved from the definition (19) and from the continuity properties of minimum and maximum operators.

Theorem: the separation index (27) is a continuous function of the values $\bar{C}_h^{inf}$, $(X_i), \bar{C}_h^{sup}(X_i), h = 1, .., m; i = 1, .., n$.

5 An Example of the Algorithm

For a better comprehension of the algorithm, let us consider the following example. Let be assigned an interval MCD problem described in the Table 1, where each element is a closed interval of R^+, and $m = n = 3$.

The Table 2 reports the index $\xi_h(X, X_i)$ for each alternative X. For instance, we have for the two first alternatives and the first criterion: $\xi_1(X_1, X_3) = \frac{m([5,7]) - m([6,10])}{w([6,10]) + w([5,7]) + 1} = \frac{6-8}{4+2+1} = \frac{-2}{7}$.

Next we computes the values $IS_h(X), X \in \{X_1, X_2, X_3\}, h = 1, 2, 3$ as reported in the the Table 3.

We can compute the ideal and anti-ideal bags, that are, from (23), (24):

$$IMCFB_>^+ = (\frac{32}{63}/0.3, \frac{1}{3}/0.5, \frac{29}{77}/0.2) \tag{28}$$

Table 1. Interval criterion values

alternative	$C_1/0.3$	$C_2/0.5$	$C_3/0.2$
X_1	[5,7]	[4,8]	[1,9]
X_2	[4,8]	[2,6]	[5,7]
X_3	[6,10]	[3,7]	[2,6]

Table 2. Values of acceptability index

alternative	C_1	C_2	C_3
X_1	$\xi_1(X_1, X_2) = 0$ $\xi_1(X_1, X_3) = -2/7$	$\xi_2(X_1, X_2) = 2/9$ $\xi_2(X_1, X_3) = 1/9$	$\xi_3(X_1, X_2) = -1/11$ $\xi_3(X_1, X_3) = 1/13$
X_2	$\xi_1(X_2, X_1) = 0$ $\xi_1(X_2, X_3) = -2/9$	$\xi_2(X_2, X_1) = -2/9$ $\xi_2(X_2, X_3) = -1/9$	$\xi_3(X_2, X_1) = 1/11$ $\xi_3(X_2, X_3) = 2/7$
X_3	$\xi_1(X_3, X_1) = 2/7$ $\xi_1(X_3, X_2) = 2/9$	$\xi_2(X_3, X_1) = -1/9$ $\xi_2(X_3, X_2) = 1/9$	$\xi_3(X_3, X_1) = -1/13$ $\xi_3(X_3, X_2) = 2/7$

Table 3. Values of $IS_h(X)$

alternative	$h = 1$	$h = 2$	$h = 3$
X_1	$-2/7$	$1/3$	$-2/143$
X_2	$-2/9$	$-1/3$	$29/77$
X_3	$32/63$	0	$-33/91$

Table 4. Ideal and anti-ideal distances

alternative	$id_>^+(X)$	$id_>^-(X)$
X_1	0.3162	0.4031
X_2	0.5524	0.1669
X_3	0.3145	0.4048

$$IMCFB_>^- = (-\frac{2}{7}/0.3, \frac{11}{3}/0.5, (-\frac{33}{91})/0.2) \tag{29}$$

Finally, from (25), (26), (27) the two distances $id_>^+(X), id_>^-(X)$ are computed together with the separation index, as represented in the Tables 11.
It follows that the final alternative ranking is: $X_3 \succ X_1 \succ X_2$.

6 Conclusion

In this paper we proposed an modified version of the so-called BB-TOPSIS method for MCD problems. Using the properties of interval algebra and a suitable index, we computed the alternatives ranking in the case where the criterion values are expressed in the form of interval numbers. In so doing, we can introduce a source of uncertainty in the data, that is typical of real decision problems.

Table 5. Separation index

X_1	X_2	X_3
0.5604	0.2320	0.5627

We remark that other approaches are possible, for instance, stochastic methods or fuzzy logic approach, see [2] for a fuzzy approach to TOPSIS. Anywise, interval number data formulation is a simple and intuitive way to represent uncertainty. Possible extensions to fuzzy data is straightforward, even if the price to pay consists into a more computational effort. As a next step, we intend to extend the method to the case of possible interactions among criteria.

References

[1] ALEFELD G., MAYER G., Interval Analysis: theory and applications, *Journal of Applied Mathematics*, 121,1996, 421-464. 59

[2] CHEN C.-T, Extensions of TOPSIS for group decision-making under fuzzy environment, *Fuzzy Sets and Systems*, 114, 2000, 167-189. 63

[3] CHEN S.-J., HWANG C.-L., HWANG F. P., *Fuzzy multiple attribute decision making*, Springer-Verlag, Berlin, 1992. 56

[4] FACCHINETTI, G., GHISELLI RICCI, R., MUZZIOLI S., Note on ranking fuzzy triangular numbers, *International Journal of Intelligent systems*, 13, 1998, 613-622. 59

[5] HWANG C. L., YOON K., *Multiple attribute decision making - methods and applications: a state of the art survey*, Springer-Verlag, New York, 1981. 56

[6] ISHIBUCHI H., TANAKA H., Multiobjective programming in optimization ofthe interval objective function,*European Journal of Operational Research* , 48, 1990, 219-225. 59

[7] REBAI A., BB-Topsis: A bag based technique for order preference by similarity to ideal solution, *Fuzzy Sets and Systems*,60, 1993, 143-162. 56, 57, 58

[8] SENGUPTA A., PAL T. K., CHAKRABORTY D, Interpretation of inequality contraints involving interval coefficients and a solution to interval linear programming, *Fuzzy Sets and Systems*, 119, 2001,129-138. 59

A Distributed Algorithm for Max Independent Set Problem Based on Hopfield Networks

Giuliano Grossi[1] and Roberto Posenato[2]

[1] Dipartimento di Scienze dell'Informazione, Università degli Studi di Milano
Via Comelico 39, 20135 Milano, Italy
grossi@dsi.unimi.it
[2] Dipartimento di Informatica, Università degli Studi di Verona
CV2, strada le Grazie 15, 37134 Verona, Italy
roberto.posenato@sci.univr.it

Abstract. A distributed algorithm to find a maximal independent set of an undirected graph is proposed. It is borrowed by a centralized one and it is based on a sequence of Hopfield neural networks. We refer to the synchronous model of distributed computation in which the topology is described by the graph. We give an upper bound on the number of messages sent during the entire process of computation.

To test the algorithm we experimentally compare it with a probabilistic heuristic derived by Ant Colony Optimization technique and with the standard greedy algorithm.

Keywords: Max Independent Set, Hopfield networks, synchronous distributed algorithms.

1 Introduction

Computing the size of the largest independent set in a graph G, i.e., the maximum subset of vertices of G such that no two vertices are joined by an edge (Max Independent Set problem), is one of the first problems shown to be NP-hard [7]. Considering the result of Feige et al. [2] for the Maximum Clique problem (the same problem as Max Independent Set on the complementary graph), even approximating Max Independent Set within a constant factor is NP-hard. In particular, if NP $\neq$ ZPP[1], no polynomial time algorithm can approximate Max Independent Set within a factor $n^{1-\varepsilon}$ for any $\varepsilon > 0$, where n is the number of vertices of the graph [5].

This problem is relevant for many theoretical research areas and practical applications. As an example, we mention the clustering problem for peer-to-peer mobile wireless networks that can be easily reduced in the problem of finding a maximum independent set of nodes in the network graph [4].

---

[1] The class of problems RP $\cap$ coRP, denoted by ZPP, is the class which admits polynomial-time randomized algorithms with zero probability of error (Las Vegas algorithms) [9].

M. Marinaro and R. Tagliaferri (Eds.): WIRN VIETRI 2002, LNCS 2486, pp. 64–74, 2002.
© Springer-Verlag Berlin Heidelberg 2002

In this paper we propose both centralized and distributed version of a neural algorithm for the Max Independent Set problem. It consists of a finite sequence the discrete-time Hopfield networks [6] which attractors converge to an admissible solution locally optimal. In the distributed variant we adopt the synchronous model of computation and the topology of the network of processors is described by the graph. It finds the same solutions of the centralized one by means of a significant number of messages, for which we give an upper bound.

To test the solution quality of our algorithm, we experimentally compare it with a very good probabilistic heuristic derived by the so called Ant Colony Optimization technique and standard greedy algorithm, widely used in the distributed case. The solution quality found by the algorithm on various instances, i.e., randomly generated and belonging to DIMACS benchmark, shows it has on average the same performances of the other two algorithms.

Another interesting feature of this technique is that it is enough general and can be applied to other combinatorial optimization problems with local constraints as Min vertex Cover.

2   Preliminaries

Let $G = \langle V, E \rangle$ be an arbitrary undirected graph, where $V = \{1, \ldots, n\}$ is the set of vertices and $E \subseteq V \oplus V$ (not ordered pairs) is the set of edges $e = \{i, j\}$. A set $S \subseteq V$ of vertices is a *independent set* of G where no two vertices in S are joined by an edge in E. An independent set is *maximal* if it is not a subset of another independent sets, while among the maximal independent set the *maximum* are those of greatest size.

The Max Independent Set problem is a maximization problem which consists in finding a maximum independent set of a give graph G. Formally

Max Independent Set
INSTANCE: Graph $G = \langle V, E \rangle$.
SOLUTION: An independent set G, i.e., a subset $S \subseteq V$ such that no two vertices in S are joined by an edge in E.
MEASURE: Cardinality of the independent set, i.e., $|S|$.

The *adjacency matrix* of G is the boolean matrix $A = (a_{ij})$, where $a_{ij} = 1$ if $\{i, j\} \in E$ and $a_{ij} = 0$ otherwise; the degree d_i of the vertex i is the number of edges incident with i.

Since in the next section we will present an approximation algorithm for Max Independent Set based on the discrete Hopfield model, we briefly recall here some notations about the neural model used.

A Hopfield network [6] $\mathcal{R}$ of n neurons with states in $\{0, 1\}$ is described by the pair $\mathcal{R} = \langle W, \boldsymbol{\lambda} \rangle$, where $W = (w_{ij})_{n \times n}$ is a symmetric matrix with $w_{ii} = 0$ $(i = 1, \ldots, n)$, and $\boldsymbol{\lambda} = (\lambda_i)_{1 \times n}$ is a vector. The matrix W is called *weights matrix* and the vector $\boldsymbol{\lambda}$ is called *thresholds vector*. In this paper we will consider weights matrix and thresholds vector with integer components.

For this model we consider the discrete-time dynamics with *sequential* updating. Let $U_i(t)$ be the state of the neuron i at time t, the dynamics is formally described as follows:

$$U_i(t+1) = \mathrm{HS}\left(\sum_{1 \leq j < i} w_{ij}U_j(t+1) + \sum_{i < j \leq n} w_{ij}U_j(t) - \lambda_i\right) \quad i = 1, \ldots, n, \quad (1)$$

where $\mathrm{HS}(x) = 1$ if $x \geq 0$, 0 otherwise.

Equations (1), given the initial condition $\mathbf{U}(0) = \mathbf{U}_0$, describe a unique trajectory $\{\mathbf{U}(t)\}_{t \geq 0}$.

To every network $\mathcal{R} = \langle W, \boldsymbol{\lambda} \rangle$ can be associated the following Lyapunov function called *energy*:

$$\mathcal{E}_{\mathcal{R}}(U_1, \ldots, U_n) = -\frac{1}{2}\sum_{i \neq j} w_{ij}U_iU_j + \sum_i \lambda_iU_i.$$

Known results concerning Hopfield networks can be summarized in the following:

Theorem 1. *The trajectory $\{\mathbf{U}(t)\}_{t \geq 0}$ generated by the Hopfield network $\mathcal{R} = \langle W, \boldsymbol{\lambda} \rangle$ with initial condition $\mathbf{U}_0$ admits an attractor $\tilde{\mathbf{y}}$, and the length $l_{\mathcal{R}, \mathbf{U}_0}$ of the transient is bounded by*

$$l_{\mathcal{R}, \mathbf{U}_0} \leq \frac{1}{2}\left(\max_{\mathbf{U}}\{\mathcal{E}_{\mathcal{R}}(\mathbf{U})\} - \min_{\mathbf{U}}\{\mathcal{E}_{\mathcal{R}}(\mathbf{U})\}\right).$$

We will say that $\tilde{\mathbf{y}}$ is the attractor *of $\mathcal{R}$ initialized by $\mathbf{U}_0$.*

3   A Neural Algorithm for **Max Independent Set** Problem

In order to approximately solve the Max Independent Set problem with the Hopfield networks we transform it in a problem of constrained quadratic optimization. As regards to this, let $S \subseteq \{1, \ldots, n\}$ and let $(x_1, \ldots, x_n)$ be a characteristic vector of S. Then $\sum_{i<j} a_{ij}x_ix_j$ counts the number of edges in E with end-points in S. It is easy to show that S is an independent set if and only if $\sum_{i<j} a_{ij}x_ix_j = 0$.

Based on this remarks, the Max Independent Set problem can be expressed as:

$$\text{maximize} \quad \Psi_G(\mathbf{x}) = \alpha\sum_{i=1}^{n} x_i$$

$$\text{subject to} \quad \Omega_G(\mathbf{x}) = \sum_{\{i,j\} \in E} 1 - x_ix_j = |E| - \sum_{i<j} a_{ij}x_ix_j \quad (\text{P})$$

$$= |E|, \qquad \mathbf{x} \in \{0, 1\}^n$$

where $\alpha \geq 1$ is an integer constant which role is discussed in Section 5 and $(a_{ij})_{n \times n}$ is the graph adjacency matrix.

We now present an algorithm, called INDEPENDENT-SET-HOPFIELD-NETS (ISHN), that finds approximate solutions for (P). This algorithm is based on a sequence of discrete Hopfield networks in which the neurons correspond to the vertices of G.

The sequence $\{\mathcal{R}_k\}_{k \geq 0}$ of Hopfield networks is inductively defined by

1. $\mathcal{R}_0$ is the network with energy function $\Phi_0(\mathbf{y}) = -(\Psi_G(\mathbf{y}) + \Omega_G(\mathbf{y}))$, and $\tilde{\mathbf{y}}^{(0)}$ is the attractor of $\mathcal{R}_0$ initialized with $(1, \ldots, 1)$;

2. let $\tilde{\mathbf{y}}^{(k)}$ be the attractor of the network $\mathcal{R}_k$ initialized with $\tilde{\mathbf{y}}^{(k-1)}$ $(k > 0)$; $\mathcal{R}_k$ is the network with energy function

$$\Phi_k(\mathbf{y}) = \Phi_{k-1}(\mathbf{y}) + \sum_{\tilde{y}_i^{(k)} = \tilde{y}_j^{(k)} = 1} a_{ij} y_i y_j. \tag{2}$$

For all k, the set $\left\{ \{i, j\} \mid \{i, j\} \in E \text{ and } \tilde{y}_i^{(k)} = \tilde{y}_j^{(k)} = 1 \right\}$ is the set of violated constraints by the attractor $\tilde{\mathbf{y}}^{(k)}$.

The algorithm consists of two alternating phases: one is the evolution of the current network, the other is the weights updating when the current network has reached an attractor. The approximation ISHN algorithm is sketched below:

ISHN Algorithm
___

Input: a graph $G = \langle V, E \rangle$, an integer α;

$\mathcal{R}_0$:= Hopfield net with energy $\Phi_0(\mathbf{y}) = -(\Psi_G(\mathbf{y}) + \Omega_G(\mathbf{y}))$;

$\tilde{\mathbf{y}}^{(0)}$:= attractor of $\mathcal{R}_0$ initialized with $(1, \ldots, 1)$;

F_0 := $\left\{ \{i, j\} \mid \{i, j\} \in E \text{ and } \tilde{y}_i^{(0)} = \tilde{y}_i^{(0)} = 1 \right\}$;

k := 0;

while [$F_k \neq \emptyset$] **do**

   k := $k + 1$;

   $\mathcal{R}_k$:= net with energy $\Phi_k(\mathbf{y}) = \Phi_{k-1}(\mathbf{y}) + \displaystyle\sum_{\{i,j\} \in F} y_i y_j$;

   $\tilde{\mathbf{y}}^{(k)}$:= attractor of $\mathcal{R}_k$ initialized with $\tilde{\mathbf{y}}^{(k-1)}$;

   F_k := $\left\{ \{i, j\} \mid \{i, j\} \in E \text{ and } \tilde{y}_i^{(k)} = \tilde{y}_j^{(k)} = 1 \right\}$;

   S := $\left\{ i \mid \tilde{y}_i^{(k)} = 1 \right\}$;

Output: a maximal independent set S of G.
___

As far as the analysis of ISHN is concerned, the following result proves that the algorithm converges, i.e., the Hopfield networks sequence is finite:

Theorem 2. *For every input graph* $G = \langle V, E \rangle$, *the algorithm* ISHN *outputs a maximal independent set of* G *after* $\alpha \cdot |E|$ *iterations of the* **while** *cycle at most.*

4   The Distributed ISHN Algorithm

The ISHN algorithm presented in the previous section is centralized and consists of two alternating phases: evolution of a given neural network and updating of the weights to build a new network. Let us observe that:

1. the neurons updating, in the evolution phase, depends only on the states of adjacent neurons;
2. the weights updating is done locally by each neuron.

Here we propose a directly implementation of the ISHN algorithm on a network of processors $p_1, \ldots, p_n$, with a topology described by the graph for which we wish to find a maximal independent set of the vertices (Max Independent Set problem). Each processor is an independent processing unit equipped with local memory; it executes a local algorithm with internal operations, sends and receives messages respectively to and from its neighborhoods (i.e., the adjacent processors). We assume, for sake of simplicity, that all processors refer to a global time t, the local computations are instantaneous (negligible time), while the communication time is at most Δ. The processor p_k, which simulates the neuron k, keeps in memory the state of neuron, the states of its neighborhoods and the weights of the adjacent connections.

In the first phase (simulation of the network evolution), the processor p_k at times $\langle z \rangle_k \cdot \Delta$ (with $z = 1, 2, \ldots$) updates the state of neuron k and, if the state of neuron changes, it sends the message *Continue* to its neighborhoods and stores z in a local variable M_k. Observe that the single step of equation (1) is executed in n steps of simulation.

In order to determine if a stable state of the neural network has been reached, at times $t = 2^s \Delta n$ (with $s = 1, 2, \ldots$) the processor p_k computes $f = 2^s n - M_k$. If $f < n$, a local flag F_k, initialized to 0, is set to 1, then the message *Continue1* is sent to its neighborhoods. When the processor p_j receives the message *Continue1* it sets the flag F_j to 1 and, in his turn, it sends the message *Continue1* to its neighborhoods. Following this schema, at times $(2^s + 1)\Delta n$, we have that either $F_k = 1$ for all $k = 1, \ldots, n$ (the neural network is in a stable state) or $F_k = 0$ for all $k = 1, \ldots, n$ (the neural network is not in a stable state). In the first case, at times $(2^s + 1)\Delta n + 1$, each processor sets its flag F_k to 0 and the neural network simulation restarts. In the second case each processor evaluates the presence of constraint violations and, if that is the case, it upgrades the weights following the rule (2), then sends the local violation message *Continue2* to its neighborhoods. If at times $t = (2^s + 2)\Delta n$ no processor receives the message

Continue2, the processors which are in the state 1 identifies a minimal cover and the algorithm stops.

If $T_{\max}$ is the maximum length of a transient, R the number of networks in the sequence, $d_{\max}$ the maximum degree of the graph and S the number of the state changes in all the neurons, the algorithm previously described requires at most $d_{\max} \cdot S + R \cdot |E| \cdot \log T_{\max}$ messages.

5   Experiments and Results

In this section the behavior of ISHN is experimentally analyzed and compared with that of others heuristics for Maximum Independent Set Problem. We concentrate our analysis on goodness of solutions because it is invariant respect to the algorithm implementation.

First of all, we discuss the dependence of the performances of ISNH on parameter α. Small values of α (w.r.t. n) give fast execution time, but poor performances in terms of solution quality. On the contrary, according to the theoretic results, large values of α cause large execution time without significantly increase the performances. This behavior has been observed in the following experiment: for various values of n and p ($100 \leq n \leq 600$, $p = 0.1, 0.5, 0.9$), 30 p-random graphs have been generated and fixed; for all α ($1 \leq \alpha \leq n$) the average size of the independent set found by ISHN has been computed. Experimental results give evidence that:

1. if $\alpha < \frac{n}{10}$ the quality of the solutions is poor;
2. if $\alpha > \frac{n}{10}$ the quality of the solutions do not significantly increase.

Therefore, for the following experiments, we have fixed α parameter to be $1/10$ of the graph size.

To experimentally compare ISHN with other heuristics, we have decide to limit the comparison to the AS-MISP (Ant System for Maximum Independent Set Problem) algorithm [8] and Greedy heuristic[2]. AS-MISP is a probabilistic (parallel) algorithm that still represents one of the most interesting heuristics for Max Independent Set as concern the goodness of the solutions. In [8] there is a wide comparison between AS-MISP and other heuristics such as the genetic algorithm of Khuri et al. [1] and GRASP program of Resende et al. [3]. On the other end, Greedy heuristic is the most known and used algorithm in distributed environments. To compare evenly the effectiveness of algorithms, we have considered three groups of instances as done in [8].

The first group of instances was generated according to two different methods as used by Khuri et al. [1]. One method consists in to generate graphs having n nodes, a density d ($d \in \{0.1, 0.2, 0.3, 0.4, 0.5\}$) and a known maximum independent set m. These instances are denoted by Mn-d-m. The other methods

---

[2] The Greedy heuristic sorts the vertices of the graph respect to their degree, repeatedly picks a nodes in order and places it in the solution if it is not adjacent to any vertex already present.

builds a *scalable* graph, which can be constructed for an even number of nodes n ($n > 6$). It is possible to show that, if n is a multiple of 4, two equivalent global maxima of value $|V^*| = n/2$ are obtained by partitioning the set of vertices into those of even (respectively odd) node numbers, otherwise the unique global maximum is given by $V^* = \{1, 3, \ldots, n/2, n/2 + 1, \ldots, n\}$, with $|V^*| = n/2 + 1$. We denote this type of graphs by *scal-n*.

The second group of instances is given by the so-called *p-random* graphs. A *p*-random graphs of size n is a graph $\langle V, E \rangle$ where $V = \{1, \ldots, n\}$ and E is obtained selecting $\{i, j\}$ as edge with probability p ($1 \leq i < j \leq n$ and $0 \leq p \leq 1$).

Finally, the third group of instances was derived from the Second DIMACS implementation challenge benchmarks. Actually, these benchmarks are instances for the Max-Clique problem, but by a reduction process it is possible to obtain instances for Max Independent Set for which the size of the optimum is the same as the max-clique of the reverse graph.

The results for the three groups of instances are shown in the following tables. The AS-MISP results are reported as in [8]. The IHSN and Greedy results have been calculated by two implementation programs written in C language and executed on a workstation with Pentium III 450 MHz processor and Linux 2.2.19 operating system.

Table 2 displays the results obtained for the instances corresponding to the first group. For each type of instance, we have generate a trial of 100 random instances. Column BF represents the best size of independent set found in the trial while column avg(BF) represents the mean value of BF on the trial. The results indicate that, besides *M100-0.1-45*, IHSN performs very well and better than both AS-MIPS and Greedy for all instances. For instances of *M100-0.1-45* type, we have experimental proved that IHSN does not always find an optimal solution for different values of α parameter.

Table 2 displays the results obtained for the instances corresponding to the second group. For each type of instance, we have considered a trial of 10 random instances. The AS-MISP results are reported even if they are been calculated on trials different from ours. The results indicate that, besides the instance generated with $p = 0.2$, IHSN performs as well as AS-MIPS and outperforms Greedy heuristics. As for instances of *M100-0.1-45* type, we have verified that for sparse graphs (instances with $p = 0.2$), independently of α parameter, IHSN usually finds solutions that are not good as AS-MISP ones. Note that even AS-MISP doesn't usually find optimal solutions for this type of instances: in [8] authors assert that *the graphs generated with probability $p = 0.2$ were the hardest, independent of the size of the graph.*

Table 3 displays the results obtained for the instances corresponding to the third group. We have reported known optimal values of the independent set in the column Optimum. The ISHN performance is better than AS-MISP one for 60% of instances and a little lower (1% at most) for others. Only with *san200_0.9_2.cmpl* instance, ISHN calculates a very strange solution (39), very far from the optimal one (60). We are investigating on such behavior.

Table 1. Results of ISHN compared with results of AS-MIPS and Greedy on different graphs of first group. $\alpha = n/10$

Instance	ISHN			AS-MIPS			Greedy		
	BF	avg(BF)	#hits	BF	avg(BF)	#hits	BF	avg(BF)	#hits
M100-0.10-45	48	45.34	98	46	46.0	100	48	42.97	25
M100-0.20-45	46	45.01	100	45	45.0	100	45	44.51	85
M100-0.30-45	45	45.00	100	45	45.0	100	45	44.95	99
M100-0.40-45	45	45.00	100	45	45.0	100	45	45.00	100
M100-0.50-45	45	45.00	100	45	45.0	100	45	45.00	100
M200-0.10-90	90	90.00	100	90	90.0	100	90	88.71	64
M200-0.20-90	90	90.00	100	90	90.0	100	90	90.00	100
M200-0.30-90	90	90.00	100	90	90.0	100	90	90.00	100
M200-0.40-90	90	90.00	100	90	90.0	100	90	90.00	100
M200-0.50-90	90	90.00	100	90	90.0	100	90	90.00	100
M300-0.10-135	135	135.00	100	135	135.0	100	135	134.81	96
M300-0.20-135	135	135.00	100	135	135.0	100	135	135.00	100
M300-0.30-135	135	135.00	100	135	135.0	100	135	135.00	100
M300-0.40-135	135	135.00	100	135	135.0	100	135	135.00	100
M300-0.50-135	135	135.00	100	135	135.0	100	135	135.00	100
scal-100	50	50.00	100	50	50.0	100	50	50.00	100
scal-200	100	100.00	100	100	98.1	74	100	100.00	100
scal-300	150	150.00	100	150	143.7	27	150	150.00	100
scal-102	52	52.00	100	52	50.0	49	52	52.00	100
scal-202	102	102.00	100	102	99.1	13	102	102.00	100
scal-302	152	152.00	100	152	147.5	15	152	152.00	100

Table 2. Results of ISHN compared with results of AS-MIPS and Greedy on different graphs of second group. $\alpha = n/10$

Instance	ISHN		AS-MISP	Greedy	
	BF	avg(BF)	BF	BF	avg(BF)
M200-0.2	25	22.70	26	20	17.6
M200-0.5	12	10.30	11	10	8.4
M200-0.6	9	8.70	9	8	7.1
M200-0.83	5	5.00	5	5	4.0
M200-0.9	5	4.04	5	3	3.0
M400-0.2	28	27.20	30	23	21.8
M400-0.5	13	12.20	12	11	9.1
M400-0.6	11	10.00	10	8	7.2
M400-0.83	6	6.00	6	4	4.0
M400-0.9	5	5.00	5	4	4.0
M600-0.2	31	30.00	33	25	23.4
M600-0.5	13	13.00	13	11	10.2
M600-0.6	11	10.20	11	9	8.2
M600-0.83	7	6.40	6	5	4.6
M600-0.9	6	5.10	6	4	3.8

Table 3: Results of ISHN compared with results from AS-MIPS on graphs of third group. $\alpha = n/10$

Instance	Size	Optimum	ISHN result	AS-MISP result	Greedy result
MANN_a27.cmpl	378	126	125	123	125
MANN_a45.cmpl	1035	345	340	335	342
brock200_1.cmpl	200	21	19	21	16
brock200_2.cmpl	200	12	11	12	7
brock200_3.cmpl	200	15	14	14	10
brock200_4.cmpl	200	17	15	16	13
brock400_1.cmpl	400	27	24	25	19
brock400_2.cmpl	400	29	24	25	20
brock400_3.cmpl	400	31	22	25	20
brock400_4.cmpl	400	33	24	26	18
brock800_1.cmpl	800	23	19	20	15
brock800_2.cmpl	800	24	20	20	14
brock800_3.cmpl	800	25	22	20	14
brock800_4.cmpl	800	26	19	20	14
c-fat200-1.cmpl	200	12	12	12	12
c-fat200-2.cmpl	200	24	23	24	24
c-fat200-5.cmpl	200	58	58	58	58
c-fat500-1.cmpl	500	14	14	14	14
c-fat500-2.cmpl	500	26	26	26	26
c-fat500-5.cmpl	500	64	64	64	64
c-fat500-10.cmpl	500	126	126	126	126
johnson16-2-4.cmpl	120	8	8	8	8
johnson32-2-4.cmpl	496	16	16	16	16
keller4.cmpl	171	11	11	11	8
keller5.cmpl	776	27	27	26	17
p_hat300-1.cmpl	300	8	8	8	7
p_hat300-2.cmpl	300	25	24	25	23
p_hat300-3.cmpl	300	36	33	36	30
p_hat500-1.cmpl	500	9	9	9	6
p_hat500-2.cmpl	500	36	36	36	29
p_hat500-3.cmpl	500	≥ 50	49	50	42
p_hat700-1.cmpl	700	11	11	11	7
p_hat700-2.cmpl	700	44	43	44	38
p_hat700-3.cmpl	700	≥ 62	60	62	55
san200_0.7_1.cmpl	200	30	30	24	16
san200_0.7_2.cmpl	200	18	18	15	12
san200_0.9_1.cmpl	200	70	70	70	45
san200_0.9_2.cmpl	200	60	39	60	37
san200_0.9_3.cmpl	200	44	44	44	31
san400_0.5_1.cmpl	400	13	13	13	7

Table 3: continued

san400_0.7_1.cmpl	400	40	40	22	21
san400_0.7_2.cmpl	400	30	30	18	15
san400_0.7_3.cmpl	400	22	22	16	12
san400_0.9_1.cmpl	400	100	100	100	42
sanr200_0.7.cmpl	200	18	17	18	14
sanr200_0.9.cmpl	200	≥42	41	42	36
sanr400_0.5.cmpl	400	13	13	13	10
sanr400_0.7.cmpl	400	≥21	21	21	16

6   Conclusions

In this paper a distributed deterministic heuristic for the Max Independent Set problem is proposed and experimentally compared with other known heuristics. The results obtained show that the solution quality is comparable with that of a very good probabilistic heuristic, i.e., Ant Colony System.

Future work must be done with the aim to generalize the distributed algorithm in order to apply it also when the topology of the graph dynamically changes, as in the peer-to-peer mobile network framework.

Acknowledgments

We wish to thank Alberto Bertoni for the useful suggestions and for carefully readings the paper.

References

[1] T. Bäck and S. Khuri. An evolutionary heuristic for the maximum independent set problem. In Z. Michalewicz, J. D. Schaffer, H. P. Schwefel, D. B. Fogel, and H. Kitano, editors, *Proc. First IEEE Conf. Evolutionary Computation, IEEE World Congress on Computational Intelligence*, volume 2, pages 531–535, Orlando FL, June 27–29, 1994. IEEE Press, Piscataway NJ. 69

[2] U. Feige, S. Goldwasser, S. Safra L. Lovàsz, and M. Szegedy. Approximating clique is almost NP-complete. In *Proceedings of the 32nd Annual IEEE Symposium on the Foundations of Computer Science*, pages 2–12, 1991. 64

[3] T. A. Feo, M. G. C. Resende, and S. H. Smith. Greedy randomized adaptive search procedure for maximum independent set. *Operations Research*, 41, 1993. 69

[4] M. Gerla and J. T-C. Tsai. Multicluster, mobile, multimedia radio network. *Wireless Networks*, 1(3):255–265, 1995. 64

[5] J. Håstad. Clique is hard to approximate within $n^{1-\epsilon}$. In *Proc. of the 37rd Annual IEEE Symposium on the Foundations of Computer Science*, pages 627–636. IEEE, 1996. 64

[6] J. J. Hopfield. Neural networks and physical systems with emergent collective computational abilities. *Proceedings of the National Academy of Sciences of the United States of America*, 79(8):2554–2558, 1982. 65

[7] R. M. Karp. *Reducibility among Combinatorial Problems*, pages 85–103. Complexity of Computer Computations. Plenum Press, New York, 1972. 64

[8] G. Leguizamón, Z. Michalewicz, and M. Schütz. An ant system for the maximum independent set problem. In *Proceedings of VII Argentine Congress of Computer Science (CACIC 2001)*, 2001. 69, 70

[9] C. H. Papadimitriou. *Computational Complexity*. Addison-Wesley, 1994. 64

Extended Random Neural Networks

G. Martinelli, F. M. Frattale Mascioli, M. Panella, and A. Rizzi

INFO-COM Dpt., University of Rome "La Sapienza"
Via Eudossiana 18 00184 Rome, Italy
{martin,mascioli,panella,rizzi}@infocom.uniroma1.it

Abstract. Random neural networks mimic at a very deep level the biological nervous system. However, it is difficult to meet during learning the biological constraints imposed on their parameters. In the paper two possible extensions are proposed in order to remove this difficulty. Moreover, the proposed learning algorithm is tailored to the specific architecture in order to reduce the computational cost. Two architectures are considered and illustrated by simulation tests.

Keywords: Bimodal neuron, Recurrent architecture.

1 Background and Proposed Extension

Spiked neural networks represent biologically plausible models of the real neural system. They take into account that signals are transmitted among real neurons under the form of random spikes having a shape characteristic of the neurons [1]. The exchanged information is coded by the frequencies of the spike trains.

A very interesting representative of the neural networks based on these experimental results was proposed in [2], [3], [4], [5], and discussed by Gelembe under the name of 'random neural network' (RNN in the following). RNN's were extensively applied by him to several real-world problems with satisfactory results, which proved their flexibility and efficiency, much greater than that manifested by different neural paradigms [6], [7], [8], [9], [10], [11], [12]. In particular, RNN's are able to efficiently carry out desirable functions as optimization, learning, associative memory, pattern recognition, etc. They were successfully used in some classical NP-hard combinatorial optimization problems such as the minimum vertex covering, the traveling salesman problem. Also they were very efficacious in solving compression and decompression of still and moving images, and in guiding learning agents in traversing a dangerous metropolitan grid safely and rapidly. This latter application of RNN's is particularly important, as recently pointed out in the technical literature, since regards the possibility of mimic humans by learning agents. Agents are assigned goals and then pursue these goals autonomously and adaptively. They learn from their own observations and from the experience of other agents and progressively improve their ability to accomplish their goals effectively and safely. Each learning agent starts with a given representation of the environment and uses it to make decisions.

M. Marinaro and R. Tagliaferri (Eds.): WIRN VIETRI 2002, LNCS 2486, pp. 75–82, 2002.

The RNN is characterized by neurons which receive and send spikes both to the other neurons and to the outside of the network. The spikes can be inhibitory or excitatory and are characterized by their mean rates of emission. The quantities involved in the activity of the i-th neuron are:

- $\omega^+(i, j)$ = mean rate of excitatory spikes sent to neuron j
- $\omega^-(i, j)$ = mean rate of inhibitory spikes sent to neuron j
- $\Lambda(i)$ = mean rate of excitatory spikes received by the outside of the network
- $\lambda(i)$ = mean rate of inhibitory spikes received by the outside of the network
- $\omega^+(j, i), \omega^-(j, i)$= mean rates of excitatory (inhibitory) spikes received from neuron j
- q_i= firing probability of the i-th neuron

Two types of neurons are introduced (positive and negative neurons). Under suitable assumptions regarding the firing process, the steady-state probability of the i-th neuron to fire, i.e. to be excited, is

$$q_i^{(1)} = \frac{\lambda^+(i)}{r(i) + \lambda^-(i)} \tag{1}$$

for a positive neuron

$$q_i^{(2)} = \frac{\lambda^-(i)}{r(i) + \lambda^+(i)} \tag{2}$$

for a negative neuron, where:

$$r(i) = \sum_{j=1}^{n}(\omega^+(i, j) + \omega^-(i, j)) \tag{3}$$

$$\lambda^+(i) = \Lambda(i) + \sum_{j=1}^{nP} q_j\omega^+(j, i) + \sum_{k=1}^{nN} q_k\omega^-(k, i) \tag{4}$$

$$\lambda^-(i) = \lambda(i) + \sum_{j=1}^{nP} q_j\omega^-(j, i) + \sum_{k=1}^{nN} q_k\omega^+(k, i) \tag{5}$$

nP, nN are the numbers of positive and negative neurons respectively.

In spite of their evident optimal performances, RNN's are not commonly encountered in the technical literature except for the numerous contributions by Gelembe himself. One reason for their scarce use could be the constraints they impose on their parameters due to their biological significance. The most stringent of these constraints regards the output of the neurons which should be in the range 0-1 since it represents a probability.

In the present paper, we propose two possible extensions of the RNN's which remove the previous difficulty. The first extension is based on the introduction of a new type of neuron: the *bimodal neuron*. It is characterized by:

$$q_i = min(q_i^{(1)}, q_i^{(2)}) < 1 \tag{6}$$

$$\lambda^+(i) = \Lambda(i) + \sum_{j=1}^{n} q_j \omega^+(j,i) \quad \lambda^-(i) = \lambda(i) + \sum_{j=1}^{n} q_j \omega^-(j,i) \qquad (7)$$

This type of neuron replaces the two types of neurons already used in RNN's, i.e. the positive and negative neurons. By means of this extension the previous constraint on the output is automatically satisfied, since it is easy to show that $q_i < 1$. The quantity q_i is considered as the output of the i-th neuron. The second extension is simply based on removing the constraint on q. The first alternative is suited to a feedforward architecture and the latter to the recurrent architecture. In the latter case the learning algorithm could be computationally intensive if an appropriate method of optimization were not used. For this reason we apply in this case a reinforcement learning algorithm. We will present examples of function approximation (2) and classification (Sect. 3) based respectively on the feedforward and on the recurrent architecture. Several learning procedures could be devised in both the cases. Two of them are proposed in the paper. Specifically, in the feedforward case we use a minimization tool available in MATLAB. In the recurrent case we develop suitable rules for modulating the behavior of the Extended RNN (ERNN in the following) by adopting the characteristic strategy of the reinforcement learning.

2 Feedforward Architecture and Related Learning Algorithm

The neural network is organized in successive layers having respectively n_1, n_2, ..., n_L neurons. The L-th layer corresponds to the output of the network. In the following we consider the case of a scalar output ($n_L = 1$). For simplicity, no spikes from and to the outside of the network are exchanged. The latter is excited by the input to the network whose components x_j j=1, 2, ..., N are preliminarily normalized to be non-negative. The i-th neuron of the k-th layer (i=1, 2, ..., n_k, k=2, 3, ..., L-1) receives spikes from the neurons of the (k-1)-th layer. It is characterized by equations:

$$\lambda^+(k,i) = \sum_{j=1}^{n_{k-1}} \omega_k^+(j,i)q(k-1,j) \quad \lambda^-(k,i) = \sum_{j=1}^{n_{k-1}} \omega_k^-(j,i)q(k-1,j)$$

$$r(k,i) = \sum_{j=1}^{n_{k-1}} [\omega_{k+1}^+(i,j) + \omega_{k+1}^-(i,j)]$$

$$q(k,i) = min\left\{ \frac{\lambda^+(k,i)}{r(k,i) + \lambda^-(k,i)}, \frac{\lambda^-(k,i)}{r(k,i) + \lambda^+(k,i)} \right\} \qquad (8)$$

In the case of the first layer, we have:

$$\lambda^+(1,i) = \sum_{j=1}^{N} \omega_1^+(j,i)x_j \quad \lambda^-(1,i) = \sum_{j=1}^{N} \omega_1^-(j,i)x_j$$

$$r(1, i) = \sum_{j=1}^{n_2} [\omega_2^+(i, j) + \omega_2^-(i, j)]$$

$$q(1, i) = min \left\{ \frac{\lambda^+(1, i)}{r(1, i) + \lambda^-(1, i)}, \frac{\lambda^-(1, i)}{r(1, i) + \lambda^+(1, i)} \right\} \tag{9}$$

In the case of the output layer the quantity r will be zero. Consequently, the output of the neural network is:

$$q(L, 1) = min \left(q, \frac{1}{q} \right) \quad q = \frac{\displaystyle\sum_{j=1}^{n_{L-1}} \omega_L^+(j, i) q(L-1, j)}{\displaystyle\sum_{j=1}^{n_{L-1}} \omega_L^-(j, i) q(L-1, j)} \tag{10}$$

The parameters of the network are:

$$\omega_k^+(j, i), \ \omega_k^-(j, i) \ k = 2, 3, \ldots, L; j = 1, 2, \ldots, n_{k-1}; \ i = 1, 2, \ldots, n_k$$
$$\omega_1^+(j, i), \ \omega_1^-(j, i) \ j = 1, 2, \ldots, N; i = 1, 2, \ldots, n_1 \tag{11}$$

They can be determined by minimizing a suitable objective function. The latter can be chosen as the MSE of the output with respect to a training set having normalized its output values in the range [0,1]. The number of layers and neurons per layer could be determined by following a constructive approach. The constraint regarding the non negativity of the parameters is easily incorporated in the minimization process by using square values. The constraint on the output of the neurons q(h, k)¡1 is automatically satisfied as a consequence of the proposed bimodal operation of the neuron. The feedforward version of ERNN, previously described, possesses the "universal function approximation" property, since this property holds for the RNN's, as proved in [13].

2.1   Simulation Test

In order to illustrate the effectiveness of the proposed ERNN, we consider its application to the approximation of the function $y = (1 + x_1^{-2} + x_2^{-1.5})^2$, with $1 \le x_1$ and $x_2 \le 5$ considered in [14] and using the same training set, constituted by 50 input-output samples. The implementation of the learning algorithm is based on the minimization of the normalized square error [14]:

$$E = \frac{\displaystyle\sum_i (y_i - q(L, 1))^2}{\displaystyle\sum_i (y_i - Y)^2} \tag{12}$$

where Y is the mean value of the output in the training set.

The minimization of 12 is carried out by applying MATLAB FMINU to the function E, taking account of equations 8, 9 and 10. The result depends on the initialization of the parameters. In the following we report the best results obtained with two different architectures and 15 different initializations. With $n_1 = 2$, $n_2 = 3$ (number of parameters: 26) and $n_1 = 3$, $n_2 = 3$ (number of parameters: 36), we obtain respectively E=3.9 10^{-2} and 6.6 10^{-3}. In [14] the optimal architecture achieves E=7.9 10^{-3} with 66 parameters.

3   Recurrent Architecture for Classification

In this application we apply the second type of extension and therefore we use the formulas 1, 3 and 7. In order to operate the network as a classifier we must decide how to introduce the input and how to extract the result of classification. A possible choice is the following one.

If the input to the classifier is constituted by N components x_i, i=1, 2, ..., N and the number of classes is C, we consider the x_i's as the outputs of a set of fictitious "input neurons", and we assign a neuron to each class. Each of these neurons is then labeled with a label denoting the associated class. Consequently, the number n of neurons is equal to (N+C+m), where m is the number of "generic neurons". However, the true complexity of the ERNN is (C+m) since the input neurons are fictitious. The neurons are ordered as follows: input, class, generic neurons. Moreover, the quantities $\Lambda(i)$ and $\lambda(i)$ are assumed to be zero. Since the x_i's are considered as outputs of neurons, they are preliminary normalized in the range [0, 1]. The output of the previous ERNN to a specific input is the label of the neuron with the largest output among the class neurons. The parameters of the network to be determined by the learning algorithm are: $\omega^+(j, i)$, $\omega^-(j, i)$, j = 1, 2, ..., n; i = N+1, N+2, ..., n with $i \neq j$.

3.1   Reinforcement Learning Algorithm

The training set is constituted by M examples [x_i(h); c(h)], where c(h) is the class label, h = 1, 2, ..., M, i = 1, 2, ..., N. The examples may be presented either cyclically or randomly with a uniform distribution. The learning algorithm is iterative. The initialization of the parameters establishes the values of the quantities r(i)'s, which remain unaltered during the learning procedure. The generic iteration consists of the following steps:

step 1 - compute the outputs q_i's, i = N+1, N+2, ..., n of the neurons by using the values of the parameters obtained in the previous iteration and the equations 1, 3 and 7;

step 2 - determine the winning neuron, i.e. the neuron with maximum output. This neuron can be either a class neuron or a generic neuron. This result affects the successive reinforcement learning, which also depends on several other factors. The overall algorithm is implemented by developing appropriate rules which take into account the said factors. In the following we report, for the sake of illustration, the rules used in connection with the simulation test described in

Sect. 3. These rules were implemented by MATLAB, using the following notations:

qp = current vector of neuron outputs

ic = class of current example

icold = ic of the previous iteration

imax = index of winning neuron

imaxold = imax of the previous iteration

R = quantity used for the reinforcement (R=.0001)

omp = matrix of the parameters $\omega^+(i,j)$: size n by n

omn = matrix of the parameters $\omega^-(j,i)$: size n by n

n1=N; nn=n

The following lines of code depict the rules used in the simulation test of sect. 3:

```
if imax==ic&imaxold==icold
    omp(:,n1+ic)=omp(:,n1+ic)+3*R*ones(nn,1);
    omn=omn+R*ones(nn);omn(:,n1+ic)=omn(:,n1+ic)-R*ones(nn,1);
elseif imax==ic&imaxold~=icold
    omp(:,n1+ic)=omp(:,n1+ic)+R*ones(nn,1);
    omn=omn+0.3*R*ones(nn);
    omn(:,n1+ic)=omn(:,n1+ic)-0.3*R*ones(nn,1);
elseif imax~=ic&imaxold~=icold&imax==imaxold
    omp(:,n1+ic)=omp(:,n1+ic)+50*R*ones(nn,1);
    omn(:,n1+imax)=omn(:,n1+imax)+10*R*ones(nn,1);
elseif imax~=ic&imaxold==imax
    omn(:,n1+imax)=omn(:,n1+imax)+3*R*ones(nn,1);
    omp(:,n1+ic)=omp(:,n1+ic)+20*R*ones(nn,1);
end
```

step 3 - normalize the parameters:

$$\omega^\pm(j,i) = \omega^\pm(j,i)\frac{r(i)}{r^*(i)} \quad i = N+1,\ N+2,\ \ldots,\ n;\ j = 1,\ 2,\ \ldots,\ n \quad (13)$$

where the symbol $\pm$ stands for + or -; the star denotes the current values of the step 2; r(i) denotes the initial value of this quantity.

Remark: the architecture of the classifier could be improved by following several alternatives, based on the use of the parameters $\Lambda(i)$ and $\lambda(i)$ and by following a constructive approach. Also the introduction of different rules is important, since the learning algorithm is particularly sensible to them.

3.2   Simulation Test

We consider the application of the ERNN classifier to the well known IRIS benchmark, as available in MATLAB, version 4.2c. In this case C=3, N=4. The number of examples available in the benchmark is 50 per class. The training set is obtained by considering the first 40 examples of each class. The remaining

10 examples per class are used for testing the performance of the classifier. The architecture of the ERNN contains 1 generic neuron besides the 3 class neurons; therefore m=1. The previous learning algorithm is applied by randomly presenting the 120 examples of the training set with a uniform distribution. The total number of iterations is 400. The classifier yields 5 errors on the training set and no errors on the test. The 5 errors are due to well known outliers affecting the benchmark used in the simulation.

4   Conclusions

Two possible extensions of RNN's are suggested in the present paper with the purpose of simplifying their learning procedures. Both the feedforward and the recurrent architectures of ERNN's are considered in detail. The learning algorithm is specialized for them in order to avoid too intensive computational effort. Namely, in the feedforward case we use MATLAB *fminu*, while in the recurrent case we apply a reinforcement algorithm. Two simulation tests illustrate the quality of the resulting networks and of the related learning algorithms. Since what is proposed only represents particular alternatives of several possible ways for determining both the architecture and the learning algorithm, there is ample room for further improvement.

References

1. Gerstner, W., van Hemmen, J. L.: Coding and information processing in neural networks. In: Domany, E., van Hemmen, J. L., Schulten, K. (eds.): Models of Neural Networks II. Springer-Verlag, Berlin Heidelberg New York (1994) 1–118 75

2. Gelembe, E.: Random neural networks with negative and positive signals and product form solution. Neural Computation, **1(4)** (1989) 502–511 75

3. Gelembe, E.: Stability of the random neural network model. Neural Computation, **2(2)** (1990) 239–247 75

4. Gelembe, E.: Learning in the recurrent random neural network. Neural Computation, **5(1)** (1993) 154–164 75

5. Gelembe, E., Stafylopatis, A., Likas, A.: Associative memory operation of the random network model. In Proceedings Int. Conf. Artificial Neural Networks. Helsinki, Finland (1991) 307–312 75

6. Gelembe, E., Koubi, V., Pekergin, F.: Dynamical random neural network approach to the traveling salesman problem. In Proceedings IEEE Symp. Sist., Man, Cybern. (1993) 630–635 75

7. Ghanwani, A.: A qualitative comparison of neural network models applied to the vertex covering problem. Elektrik, **2(1)** (1994) 11–18 75

8. Gelembe, E., Kramer, C., Sungur, M., Gelembe, P.: Traffic and video quality in adaptive neural video compression. Multimedia Syst., **4** (1996) 357–369 75

9. Cramer, C., Gelembe, E., Bakircioglu, H.: Low bit rate video compression with neural networks and temporal subsampling. Proceedings IEEE, **84(10)** (1996) 1529–1543 75

10. Gelembe, E., Feng, Y., Krishnan, K. R.: Neural network methods for volumetric magnetic resonance imaging of the human brain. Proceedings IEEE, **84(10)** (1996) 1488–1496 75
11. Gelembe, E., Ghanwani, A., Srinivasan, V.: Improved neural heuristics for multicast routing. IEEE Journal Selected Areas Commun., **15** (1997) 147–155 75
12. Gelembe, E., Seref, E., Zhiguang, Xu: Simulation with learning agents. Proceedings IEEE, **89(2)** (2001) 148–157 75
13. Gelembe, E., Zhi-Hong, Mao, Yan-Da, Li: Function approximation with spiked random networks. IEEE Trans. Neural Networks, **10(1)** (1999) 3–9 78
14. Sugeno, M., Yasukawa, T.: A fuzzy-logic-based approach to qualitative modeling. Fuzzy Systems, **1(1)** (1993) 7–31 78, 79

Generalized Independent Component Analysis as Density Estimation

Francesco Palmieri and Alessandra Budillon

Dip. di Ingegneria dell'Informazione
Seconda Università di Napoli, Aversa, Italy
{frapalmi,alebudil}@unina.it

Abstract. We propose a new generalized ICA framework in the form of a multi-layer perceptron as a density estimator. We adopt an optimization strategy based on two criteria: a minimum reconstruction error and a minimum distance from a uniform distribution. Some simulation results are also reported to validate the proposed algorithm.

Keywords: Generalized ICA, Multilayer ICA, Density estimator.

1 Introduction

Classical Independent Component Analysis (ICA) is based on a linear transformation which is adapted through a criterion that minimizes the mutual information among the outputs. Such a system has been used with success in separating instantaneous linear mixtures and various algorithm exist in the literature for adapting the free parameters of such a block. One of the most interesting formulation in our search for Independent Components is based on an information theory criterion: search for the linear transformation whose outputs density is as close as possible, in the Kullback-Leibler sense, to a factorized multi-dimensional density which is the product of a set of given "desired" marginal density functions. The typical case is based on a linear square block trained according to a set of desired outputs marginals. Many variations to this theme have also been proposed with algorithms that assume imperfect or partial knowledge of such marginal densities. The so-defined ICA paradigm suggests that the problem could be formulated as a maximum likelihood parametric density estimation. An interesting scenario, which is useful in the applications, arises when the number of sources is smaller than the number of observations (undercomplete mixture): the ICA block projects the input vector on the linear subspace on which the observations are confined, and finds the directions that best separate the various coordinates [6]. Generalized Independent Component Analysis has been defined to deal with more general distributions such a multi-cluster and non linear manifolds [5] which are poorly handled by using PCA (Principal Components Analysis) or ICA. This paradigm is also introduced to approach the difficult problem of non linear source separation for which some attempts have already appeared in the literature [4, 8]. In our two previous papers we have proposed

M. Marinaro and R. Tagliaferri (Eds.): WIRN VIETRI 2002, LNCS 2486, pp. 83–89, 2002.
© Springer-Verlag Berlin Heidelberg 2002

a Multi-Class Independent Components analysis [6] and we have derived an algorithm for training a multi-layer neural network as a generalized independent component analyzer [5]. The limitation of our previous contribution in [5] was the nature of the neural block that, to allow exact computation of the gradients, was constrained to have square layers. This limitation, removed here, conditions the type of mappings that the network can compute and therefore it may be of limited application when the generative model of our data is strongly non linear or is composed by separate clusters. This paper reports an algorithm to train a multi-layer perceptron to perform generalized independent component analysis. A successful simulation on the identification of a nonlinear manifold is reported.

2   Generalized Independent Component Analysis

Consider a random variable $\mathbf{x} \in \mathbf{X} \subseteq R^n$ and a parametric function class $\mathbf{g}$ such that

$$\mathbf{z} = \mathbf{g}(\mathbf{x}, \boldsymbol{\theta}) \ , \tag{1}$$

where $\mathbf{z} \in \mathbf{Z} \subseteq R^m$, $m \leq n$ and $\boldsymbol{\theta}$ is a set of parameters. Suppose now that a set of parameters $\boldsymbol{\theta} = \boldsymbol{\theta}_o$ can be found such that the output density function is uniform and separable, i.e. $f_{\mathbf{z}}(\mathbf{z}) = \mathbf{U}(\mathbf{z}; \boldsymbol{\beta}, \boldsymbol{\alpha} + \boldsymbol{\beta}) = \prod_{i=1}^{m} U(z_i; \beta_i, \alpha_i + \beta_i)$, with $\alpha_i > 0 \ \forall \ i = 1, \ldots, m$. The function $\mathbf{g}$ can be considered an alternative representation of the input density function $f_{\mathbf{x}}(\mathbf{x})$ if a random variable $\mathbf{xg}$ with the same density can be generated as

$$\mathbf{xg} = \widehat{\mathbf{g}}^{-1}(\mathbf{zg}; \boldsymbol{\theta}_o) \ , \tag{2}$$

from uniform independent vectors $\mathbf{zg} \propto \mathbf{U}(\mathbf{z}; \boldsymbol{\beta}, \boldsymbol{\alpha} + \boldsymbol{\beta})$, as depicted in Figure a) and b). The function $\widehat{\mathbf{g}}^{-1}(\mathbf{zg}; \boldsymbol{\theta}_o)$ is the inverse of $\mathbf{g}$ if it is invertible otherwise it will be an approximation, for example obtained using pseudoinverses. We refer to $\widehat{\mathbf{g}}^{-1}(\mathbf{zg}; \boldsymbol{\theta}_o)$ as a *generative model of* $\mathbf{x}$. Learning $\boldsymbol{\theta}_o$ is essentially a parametric density function problem.

To link this formulation to classical ICA suppose that $\mathbf{g}$ can be split into two stages as in Figure 1 c) and d),

$$\mathbf{g}(\mathbf{z}; \boldsymbol{\theta}) = \boldsymbol{\phi}(\mathbf{y}) = \boldsymbol{\phi}(\mathbf{q}(\mathbf{x}; \boldsymbol{\theta})) = (\phi_1(y_1), \ldots, \phi_m(y_m))^T \ , \tag{3}$$

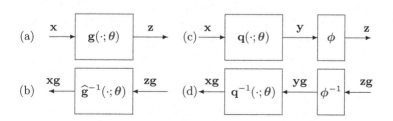

Fig. 1. a), b) General Density Estimator schemes c) and d) Generalized Independent Component Analysis forward and backward schemes

where the ϕ_i are a set of sigmoidal functions obtained from a set of m "desired" cumulative distribution functions $\{F_{Di}(y_i), i = 1, \ldots, m\}$ as $\phi_i(y_i) = \alpha_i F_{Di}(y_i) + \beta_i$. The function $\mathbf{q}(\mathbf{x}, \boldsymbol{\theta})$ is a parametric transformation possibly not square, so that its inverse is an approximation.

It is easily proven [5] that *learning the parameters* $\boldsymbol{\theta}$ *which produce output* $\mathbf{z}$ *as uniform and as independent as possible, is equivalent to force* $\mathbf{y}$ *to be distributed according to* $\prod_{i=1}^{m} f_{Di}(y_i)$ *or to maximize the differential entropy of* $\mathbf{z}$, i.e.

$$\boldsymbol{\theta}_o = \underset{\boldsymbol{\theta}}{\operatorname{argmin}} KL[f_{\mathbf{z}}; \mathbf{U}] = \underset{\boldsymbol{\theta}}{\operatorname{argmin}} KL[f_{\mathbf{y}}; \prod_{i=1}^{m} f_{Di}(y_i)] = \underset{\boldsymbol{\theta}}{\operatorname{argmax}} h(\mathbf{z}) , \qquad (4)$$

where $KL[\cdot]$ denotes the Kullback-Leiber divergence. This paradigm is what we refer to as **Generalized Independent Component Analysis**(GICA).

Linear ICA is obtained if $\mathbf{q}(\mathbf{x}; \boldsymbol{\theta}) = \mathbf{C}\mathbf{x} + \mathbf{b}$, with $\boldsymbol{\theta} = (\mathbf{C}, \mathbf{b})$, with $\mathbf{C}$ square matrix $n \times n$. The n-dimensional observed random vector $\mathbf{x}$ is the result of a n linear combinations of n independent sources and the ICA block is trained to "invert" such a system. Therefore implicitly the ICA block represents a "generative" linear model of our observations. An algorithm to find $\boldsymbol{\theta}$ is easily found observing that $h(\mathbf{y}) = h(\mathbf{x}) + log \mid C \mid$, so that the output differential entropy can be written as $h(\mathbf{z}) = h(\mathbf{x}) + log \mid C \mid + \sum_{i=1}^{n} \mathrm{E}[log f_{Di}(y_i)] + \sum_{i=1}^{n} log \alpha_i$.

3   Multi-layer ICA

We propose a multi-layer perceptron to perform generalized independent component analysis. Figure 2 shows a possible realization of the parametric function g with a multi-layer neural network. In this case $\mathbf{q}(\mathbf{x}; \boldsymbol{\theta})$ is given by an $L-$layers network where each layer is made of a linear part given by the parametric transformation $(\mathbf{C}_l, \mathbf{b}_l)$ and a non linear sigmoidal function ϕ. We emphasize that the network layers may have varying sizes since the real non linear capability of the multi-layer perceptron is obtained when the size of the various layers are different. Unfortunately a closed form expression for $h(\mathbf{z})$ cannot be derived unless the blocks are all square. Therefore we need to define a new strategy of optimization taking into account that the GICA framework requires to maximize the output entropy, while the whole transformation is kept invertible. Instead of the output entropy or equivalently the KL distance between the output density and the uniform distribution, we adopt a quadratic measure of the distance between the estimated probability density function of the network output and the probability density function of a uniform random variable (also used by Principe et al. [7]). The first cost function is

$$J_1 = \frac{1}{2} \int_{R^m} (\hat{f}(\boldsymbol{\eta}; \mathbf{z}_1, \ldots, \mathbf{z}_N) - U(\boldsymbol{\eta}))^2 d\boldsymbol{\eta} . \qquad (5)$$

To force the invertibility of the transformation we adopt as a second cost function the mean square reconstruction error

$$J_2 = \frac{1}{2} \mathrm{E}[\|\mathbf{x} - \mathbf{x}\mathbf{g}\|^2] . \qquad (6)$$

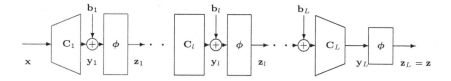

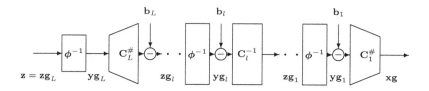

Fig. 2. Multilayer ICA Forward Network and Multilayer ICA Backward Network

This can be related to autoassociative networks that are trained to reproduce their inputs [2, 1]. We use the Parzen method to estimate the probability density function of the network last layer output

$$\hat{f}(\boldsymbol{\eta}; \mathbf{z}_1, \ldots, \mathbf{z}_N) = \frac{1}{Nh} \sum_{j=1}^{N} K\left(\frac{1}{h}(\boldsymbol{\eta} - \mathbf{z}_j)\right) , \tag{7}$$

where $\mathbf{z}_1, \ldots, \mathbf{z}_N$ are N samples of the output data, $h = (1/N)^{1/m}$, K is a gaussian kernel, i.e.

$$K\left(\frac{1}{h}(\boldsymbol{\eta} - \mathbf{z}_j)\right) = \frac{1}{(2\pi)^{m/2}} \exp\left(\frac{1}{2h^2}(\boldsymbol{\eta} - \mathbf{z}_j)^T(\boldsymbol{\eta} - \mathbf{z}_j)\right) . \tag{8}$$

These two cost functions have to be minimized with respect to the networks parameters, and their gradients must be computed:

$$\nabla_{\boldsymbol{\theta}} J_1 = \sum_{i=1}^{N} \left(\frac{\partial \mathbf{z}_i}{\partial \boldsymbol{\theta}}\right)^T \nabla_{\mathbf{z}_i} J_1 , \tag{9}$$

$$\begin{aligned}
\nabla_{\mathbf{z}_i} J_1 &= \int_{R^m} (\hat{f}(\boldsymbol{\eta}; \mathbf{z}_1, \ldots, \mathbf{z}_N) - U(\boldsymbol{\eta})) \nabla_{\mathbf{z}_i} \hat{f}(\boldsymbol{\eta}; \mathbf{z}_1, \ldots, \mathbf{z}_N) d\boldsymbol{\eta} \\
&= \sum_{j=1}^{N} \alpha_1(\mathbf{z}_j - \mathbf{z}_i) \exp\left(-\frac{\|\mathbf{z}_i - \mathbf{z}_j\|^2}{4h^2}\right) - \alpha_2 \boldsymbol{\gamma}(\mathbf{z}_1, \ldots, \mathbf{z}_N) , \tag{10}
\end{aligned}$$

where $\alpha_1 = \frac{1}{N^2 h^{m+2} 2^{m+1} \pi^{m/2}}$ and $\boldsymbol{\gamma}$ is a vector whose k^{th} components is $\gamma_k = \prod_{l=1, l \neq k}^{m} \left(1 - Q\left(\frac{1 - z_{il}}{h}\right) - Q\left(\frac{z_{il}}{h}\right)\right) \left(\exp\left(-\frac{z_{ik}^2}{2h^2}\right) - \exp\left(-\frac{(1 - z_{ik}^2)}{2h^2}\right)\right)$ and

$\alpha_2 = \frac{1}{Nh\sqrt{(2\pi)}}$. Using standard techniques from matrix differential calculus [3] we easily can derive recursive formulas for both the derivative of $\mathbf{z}_i$ with respect to $\mathbf{b}_l$ and $vec\mathbf{C}_l$, where vec is the operator the vectorize a matrix by columns:

$$\frac{\partial \mathbf{z}_i}{\partial \mathbf{b}_l} = \begin{cases} diag(\dot{\phi}(\mathbf{y}_l))\mathbf{C}_l & l = L \\ \frac{\partial \mathbf{z}_i}{\partial \mathbf{b}_{l+1}} diag(\dot{\phi}(\mathbf{y}_l))\mathbf{C}_l & l = L-1,\dots,2 \\ \frac{\partial \mathbf{z}_i}{\partial \mathbf{b}_{l+1}} diag(\dot{\phi}(\mathbf{y}_l)) & l = 1 , \end{cases} \tag{11}$$

$$\frac{\partial \mathbf{z}_i}{\partial vec\mathbf{C}_l} = \begin{cases} diag(\dot{\phi}(\mathbf{y}_l))(\mathbf{z}_{l-1} + \mathbf{b}_l)^T \otimes I & l = L \\ \frac{\partial \mathbf{z}_i}{\partial \mathbf{b}_{l+1}} diag(\dot{\phi}(\mathbf{y}_l))(\mathbf{z}_{l-1} + \mathbf{b}_l)^T \otimes I & l = L-1,\dots,2 \\ \frac{\partial \mathbf{z}_i}{\partial \mathbf{b}_{l+1}} diag(\dot{\phi}(\mathbf{y}_l))\mathbf{x}^T \otimes I & l = 1 . \end{cases} \tag{12}$$

The adapting rules are batch:

$$\begin{cases} \mathbf{b}_l = \mathbf{b}_l - \eta \sum_{i=1}^{N} (\frac{\partial \mathbf{z}_i}{\partial \mathbf{b}_l})^T \nabla_{\mathbf{z}_i} J_1 \\ vec\mathbf{C}_l = vec\mathbf{C}_L - \eta \sum_{i=1}^{N} (\frac{\partial \mathbf{z}_i}{\partial vec\mathbf{C}_l})^T \nabla_{\mathbf{z}_i} J_1 , \end{cases} \tag{13}$$

where η is the learning rate.

For the second cost function, we evaluate the gradient with respect the backward networks parameters, obtained inverting the forward network, $\boldsymbol{\theta}' = (\boldsymbol{\theta}'_1,\dots,\boldsymbol{\theta}'_L)$ with $\boldsymbol{\theta}'_l = (\mathbf{b}_l, \mathbf{C}_l^{\#})$, where $\mathbf{C}_L^{\#}$ is the pseudoinverse.

$$\nabla_{\boldsymbol{\theta}'} J_2 = \mathrm{E}\left[(\mathbf{x} - \mathbf{xg})^T \left(-\frac{\partial \mathbf{xg}}{\partial \boldsymbol{\theta}'}\right)\right] . \tag{14}$$

Also in this case using standard techniques from matrix differential calculus [3] we can derive recursive formulas for both the derivative of J_2 with respect to $\mathbf{b}_l$ and $\mathbf{C}_l^{\#}$.

$$\frac{\partial J_2}{\partial \mathbf{b}_l} = \begin{cases} \mathrm{E}[\mathbf{C}_l^{\#T} D\mathbf{b}_l] \text{ with } D\mathbf{b}_l = (\mathbf{x} - \mathbf{xg}) & l = 1 \\ \mathrm{E}[D\mathbf{b}_l] \quad \text{ with } D\mathbf{b}_l = diag(\dot{\phi}^{-1}(\mathbf{zg}_{l-1}))\mathbf{C}_{l-1}^{\#T} D\mathbf{b}_{l-1} & l = 2,\dots, L , \end{cases} \tag{15}$$

$$\frac{\partial J_2}{\partial \mathbf{C}_l^{\#}} = \begin{cases} -\mathrm{E}[D\mathbf{C}_l^{\#}] \text{ with } D\mathbf{C}_l^{\#} = D\mathbf{b}_l(\mathbf{yg}_l - \mathbf{b}_l)^T & l = 1 \\ -\mathrm{E}[D\mathbf{C}_l^{\#}] \text{ with } D\mathbf{C}_l^{\#} = D\mathbf{b}_l \mathbf{yg}_l^T & l = 2,\dots, L . \end{cases} \tag{16}$$

The adapting rules are batch:

$$\begin{cases} \mathbf{b}_l = \mathbf{b}_l - \eta' \frac{\partial J_2}{\partial \mathbf{b}_l} \\ \mathbf{C}_l^{\#} = \mathbf{C}_l^{\#} - \eta' \frac{\partial J_2}{\partial \mathbf{C}_l^{\#}} , \end{cases} \tag{17}$$

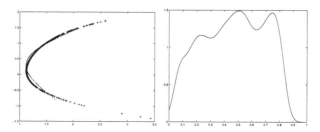

Fig. 3. Input data (.) and output of the backward network (+), estimated forward network output probability density function

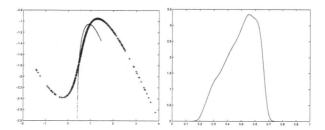

Fig. 4. Input data (.) and output of the backward network (+), estimated forward network output probability density function

where η' is the learning rate.

To sum up the algorithm consists of iteration until convergence of the following steps

a) Adaptation step for J_1
b) Network pseudoinversion
c) Adaptation step for J_2
d) Network pseudoinversion.

4   Simulation Results and Conclusions

Figures 3 and 4 show our preliminary results in training a 3-layers network with input data artificially generated by a random network, in Fig. 3 the reconstruction is almost perfect and also the output distribution is quite uniform. In Fig. 4 the reconstruction seems to be more difficult and also the output distribution is still quite concentrated.

We are encouraged by the preliminary results presented here and look forward to test our algorithm on densities with higher dimensionality and more complicated distributions. Future work will also focus on improving the algorithm convergence speed and the relative cost functions weighting.

References

[1] Karhunen J. and Joutsensalo J.: Representation and separation of signals using nonlinear PCA type learning, Neural Networks, vol. 7:113 - 127, (1994). 86

[2] Kramer M. A.: Nonlinear principal component analysis using autoassociative neural networks, AIChE J., vol. 37, n.2:233 - 243, (1991). 86

[3] Magnus J. R. and Neudecker H.: Matrix Differential Calculus with Applications in Statistics and Econometrics, John Wiley & Sons Ltd, (1988). 87

[4] Marques G. C. and Almeida L. B.: Separation of nonlinear mixtures using pattern repulsion, Proc. of Int. Worksh. on ICA and BSS, Aussois, France, (1999). 83

[5] Palmieri F., Mattera D., and Budillon A.: Multilayer Independent Component Analysis, Proc. of Int. Worksh. on ICA and BSS, Aussois, Francia, (1999). 83, 84, 85

[6] Palmieri F. and Budillon A.: Multi-Class Independent Component Analysis (MUCICA) for Rank-deficient Distributions. Advances in Independent Component Analysis, Ed. M. Girolami, Springer Verlag , (2000). 83, 84

[7] Principe J. C., Xu D., Fisher J.: Information Theoretic Learning. Unsupervised Adaptive Filtering, vol 1, Simon Haykin Editor, Wiley, (2000). 85

[8] Taleb A. and Jutten C.: Source separation in post nonlinear mixtures, IEEE Transactions on Signal Processing, vol. 47, n. 10:2807 - 2820, (1999). 83

Spline Recurrent Neural Networks
for Quad-Tree Video Coding

Lorenzo Topi, Raffaele Parisi, and Aurelio Uncini

INFOCOM dept. - University of Rome "La Sapienza"
Via Eudossiana 18, 00184 Rome, Italy
aurel@ieee.org
http://infocom.uniroma1.it/aurel

Abstract. In this paper a novel connectionist approach for video compression is presented. The basic idea is to extend to the temporal dimension the architecture used for the compression of still images. A multilayer perceptron (MLP) with infinite impulse response (IIR) synapses, embedded in a new quad-tree framework for video segmentation, is employed to take into account the video temporal dynamics. In order to reduce the computational burden and to improve the generalization performance, a flexible spline-based activation function, suitable for signal processing applications, has been used. Preliminary experimental results show that the proposed approach represents a viable alternative with respect to existing standards for high-quality video compression.

Keywords: video compression, flexible activation function, spline neural networks, recurrent neural networks.

1 Introduction

Video compression is today one of the most important topics in image processing, due to the large number of possible applications in many fields, from medicine to artificial intelligence [1].

A large class of image and video compression techniques are based on the principal component analysis (PCA) [2]. PCA is a popular tool in many applications, such as code and data compression, high resolution frequency analysis, adaptive beamforming, etc [3]. Sometimes a different terminology has been used and PCA has been called Karuhunen-Loève transform (KLT) or Hotelling transform [2]. In particular, KLT projects the input data from their original N-dimensional space onto the M-dimensional output space (with $M < N$), so performing a dimensionality reduction which retains most of the information intrinsic in the input data vector.

Under the assumption of Gaussian sources, KLT represents an optimal transform for any rate and bit allocation [2]. Moreover, KLT is asymptotically equivalent to the discrete cosine transform (DCT), which is a building block of many standard compression techniques like JPEG, MPEG, H.26x [4]. In the last years

M. Marinaro and R. Tagliaferri (Eds.): WIRN VIETRI 2002, LNCS 2486, pp. 90–98, 2002.
© Springer-Verlag Berlin Heidelberg 2002

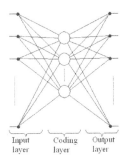

Input   Coding   Output
layer   layer   layer

Fig. 1. Two layer perceptron, as used by Cottrel [6] ($M < N$)

multilayer neural network (NN) architectures have been often used for compression of still images [5]-[9]. The most popular topology is a three-layers neural network (hereafter called neural clepsydra architecture, NCA), which is shown in Fig. 1.

Independently proposed by various authors (e.g. [6], [7]), NCA represents an autoassociative transform coding. Image compression is viewed as an encoding problem where the NN is forced to perform an identity mapping through a reduced-size layer.

NCA works similarly to KLT and represents, in some way, its generalization. The input image is divided into non-overlapping data blocks having size of N pixels. After normalization, each data block is fed to the network. The first and hidden layers perform the data coding and compression. The output layer acts as the decoder, reconstructing the normalized input data block. The NN is trained on some sample images, so that it develops an internal representation corresponding to the relevant features of a class of images.

In order to improve the compression performance, a self size-adaptive architecture was proposed in [8]. Input images are divided in sub-blocks of different dimensions (e.g. 4×4, 8×8, 16×16) according to their statistics. In [9] a three-layer NN decoder was proposed, yielding very good generalization performance. In addition, in order to reduce the computational burden, an adaptive spline neural network (ASNN) was used [10]. With this approach a 0.25 bit/pixel compression rate with good image quality was reached.

In this paper the use of NCAs for video compression is proposed and discussed. Each image in the input video sequence is segmented in data-blocks of adaptive size (similarly to the approach proposed in [8]). The size of each sub-block remains constant if the input video signal statistics is stationary.

The outline of the paper is as follows. After a short overview of standard NN techniques for the compression of still images, a new method for video compression is introduced. Finally some experimental results are described to demonstrate the effectiveness of the proposed approach.

2   Neural Networks for Image Compression

NN are mainly used for the compression of still images and often they allow to get better performance with respect to more conventional methods like JPEG.

The "*clepsydra*" network for compression was first introduced in [6], where a structure with three layers, trained by the back propagation algorithm, was employed (Fig. 1). The first and last layers had $N = W^2$ neurons (usually $W = 8$), while the hidden (or coding) layer had $M < N$ neurons.

Several other architectures were developed since then. Among the others, Parodi and Passaggio [8] studied a particular procedure based on self-adaptive masks. It is a hybrid technique, where during a pre-processing phase the optimal input mask for each block is defined, based on a typical quad-tree (QT) scheme, and a neural technique is applied for image compression. More specifically, in order to improve the image quality and the level of compression, the image is decomposed in subblocks of different size (differently from JPEG coding): the dimension of the blocks is set by comparing the variance of the pixels to a specified threshold (*th*). Each block is then coded by a specific NN, for the specific value of the activity *th*). The number M of the hidden neurons must satisfy the contrasting needs of compression level and video quality. Image reconstruction (or decompression) is performed by using the outputs of the hidden neurons, the mean value of the sub-block pixels and the number of bits of quantization, if used. The bit-rate is given by:

$$
BR = \frac{(N_{b4} \cdot N_{u4} + N_{b8} \cdot N_{u8} + N_{b16} \cdot N_{u16}) \cdot N_{bit}}{N_{pix}} +
$$
$$
+ \frac{(N_{b4} + N_{b8} + N_{b16}) \cdot (N_{net} + N_{AV}) + N_{acc}}{N_{pix}}
\tag{1}
$$

Where:
N_{bi} = number of sub-blocks processed by neural network with i^2 inputs;
N_{ui} = number of neurons of the coding layer relative to the neural network with i^2 inputs;
N_{bit} = number of bits required to code the output of the coding layer;
N_{pix} = dimension, in pixels, of the image ($P \times Q$);
N_{net} = number of bit used to identify which neural network has been used;
N_{AV} = number of bits used to code the mean value of the frame;
N_{acc} = number of bits used to code additional information about quantization.

Fig. 2 shows the scheme of a neural compressor based on three NNs. The image has been segmented, according to the QT method, in sub-blocks of 4×4, 8×8 and 16×16 pixels.

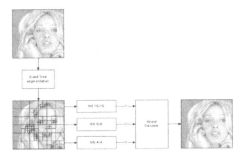

Fig. 2. Adaptive size mask structure for image compression

Video compression is currently a task of great interest, due to the spread of applications like video streaming on the web and broadcast transmissions. Techniques developed for the compression of still images can inspire an effective NN-based method for the compression of video sequences, as described in the following.

3 Adaptive Spline Recurrent Networks for Video Compression

3.1 Time Related Quad-Tree Decomposition

Video sequences are pre-processed by selecting succeeding frames that are characterized by a lower level of activity. For such frames it is possible to use the same QT structure, thus saving on the bit-rate. Methods described in the previous paragraph can be used for this task.

In Fig. 3 the creation of the so called Group of Frames (GOF) is described. Each GOF is created in this way:

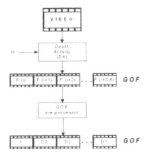

Fig. 3. Creation of the Group of Frames

- the first frame represents an image of reference (keyframe) inside the GOF;
- the depth activity (DA), that is the number of frames that will belong to the specific GOF, is calculated by comparing the value of the variance among the keyframe and the following images with a fitting threshold th;
- the frames following the keyframe (I frame) are replaced with their difference with the keyframe and are called D frames (Fig. 4). In formula:

$$d_i^k = \frac{256 + f_i^I - f_i^k}{128} \tag{2}$$

where:

$\quad d_i^k \quad = i$th pixel result of the difference
$\quad f_i^I \quad = i$th pixel of the keyframe
$\quad f_i^k \quad = i$th pixel of the kth frame from the keyframe

Frames within each GOF can be coded according to the used NN architecture. The I frame and the last one in the GOF ($D1$) are encoded with the specified QT structure (Fig. 5). The bit-rate is:

$$BR_I = \frac{(N_{b4} \cdot N_{u4} + N_{b8} \cdot N_{u8} + N_{b16} \cdot N_{u16}) \cdot N_{bit}}{N_{pix}} +$$
$$+ \frac{(N_{b4} + N_{b8} + N_{b16}) \cdot (N_{net} + N_{AV}) + N_{acc} + N_{DA}}{N_{pix}} \tag{3}$$

$$BR_{D1} = \frac{(N_{b4} \cdot N_{u4} + N_{b8} \cdot N_{u8} + N_{b16} \cdot N_{u16}) \cdot N_{bit}}{N_{pix}} +$$
$$+ \frac{(N_{b4} + N_{b8} + N_{b16}) \cdot (N_{net} + N_{AV}) + N_{acc}}{N_{pix}} \tag{4}$$

The term $N_D A$, in BR_I is required by the decoder to know the number of frames within the GOF.

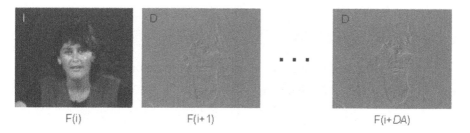

Fig. 4. Pictures within the GOF

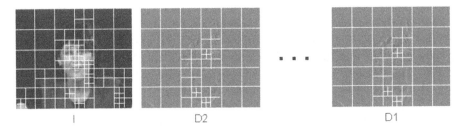

I	D2	D1

Fig. 5. QT schemes applied to the pictures within the GOF

The intermediate frames $D2$ are encoded by exploiting the QT structure used by the frame $D1$ (Fig. 5). The value of the bit-rate for these frames is:

$$BR_{D2} = \frac{(N_{b4} \cdot N_{u4} + N_{b8} \cdot N_{u8} + N_{b16} \cdot N_{u16}) \cdot N_{Bit} + N_{AV}}{N_{Pix}} \tag{5}$$

The bit-rate of the reconstructed video is an average over all the frames in the movie.

Frame differences D are used for coding because they contain fewer details compared to the original frames, so that the relative QT scheme will be made of greater sub-blocks (Fig. 5), leading to a higher compression rate.

Fig. 6 describes the procedures of the video co-decoding; the blocks Video pre-processor and Video post-processor implement the creation and reconstruction functions of the GOFs.

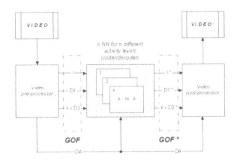

Fig. 6. Coding scheme using the proposed method

3.2 Adaptive Spline Recurrent Networks

The temporal information implicit in video sequences suggests the use of recurrent neural networks [12][13]. Temporal dynamics represents, in fact, a key tool to take into account the problem of motion compensation. Among the recurrent architectures described in literature, in [12] locally recurrent multilayer perceptron (MLPs) trained by a gradient-based procedure (recursive backpropagation) were described. In particular, infinite impulse response synapses (IIR-MLP) were considered (Fig. 7). In this work, the IIR-MLP synapse is based on the adaptive spline activation function. This new architecture called adaptive spline recurrent network (ASRN), is able to yield a great video quality with respect to the static approach. One of the most important tasks in video compression is motion detection and compensation. Due to the internal IIR synapses, that can be viewed as an internal status with memory, ASRN scheme can provide an elegant way to solve the problem of motion compensation.

4   Preliminary Experimental Results

Some preliminary tests were realized on four grey-scale videos, with 100 frames in QCIF format (176×144 pixels). The frame-rate was 30 fps (frames-per-second). A set of 3 NNs were used to encode blocks of 4×4, 8×8, 16×16 pixels. Six hidden neurons were used. Outputs were quantized with 4 bits.

Table 1. Experimental results

	$th = 8$		$th = 15$		$th = 30$	
	PSNR (*dB*)	Br (*kbps*)	PSNR (*dB*)	Br (*kbps*)	PSNR (*dB*)	Br (*kbps*)
Missa	34,62	205,63	34,02	166,05	33,02	152,85
Susi	31,11	469,53	30,91	422,31	30,38	361,52
Cup	35,27	209,85	34,55	162,07	34,04	144,51
Apple	36,27	212,5	35,76	181,84	35,3	150,36

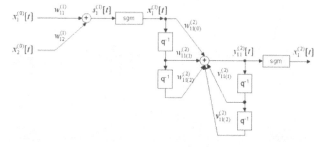

Fig. 7. : A simple example of IIR-MLP network

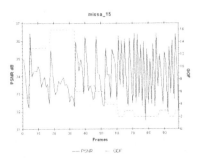

Fig. 8. Values of the PSNR and Number of frames in the GOF in Missa with TH=15

As performance indexes the pixel signal-to-noise ratio (PSNR) and the bit-rate (Br) while changing the threshold (*th*) that gives the depth activity DA were considered. Results are summarized in Table 1. The values of the two reference parameters are mean values.

It is clear that when *th* increases the level of the compression improves (the bit-rate decreases) while the quality of the restored video gets worse (the PSNR decreases). This is because the higher is the threshold, the greater is the number of frames with the same QT structure, and the worse will be the reconstruction. Analysis of the PSNR value compared to the number of frames within the GOFs, as in Fig. 8 for the *Missa* video, shows that the quality of the images decreases while the "depth" of the GOFs increases.

The quality of reconstructed videos also depends on the subject. In the presence of rapidly varying scenes GOFs will have a smaller depth activity and therefore the corresponding frames will be encoded in a better way.

Fig. 9 shows a comparison of two different video sequences. The *Missa* video represents a speaking woman and is quite static, so that the number of small GOFs is not high. *Foreman* is a quite varying video: many GOFs are made of only one frame.

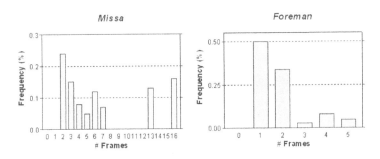

Fig. 9. Comparison among two video (with th = 15)

5 Conclusions

In the last few years many neural architectures for still images compression have been studied, yielding very promising results and suggesting the extension to video compression. In this paper a new recurrent architecture (based on flexible activation function NNs embedded in a recurrent framework) and a new quad-tree video segmentation procedure were proposed. Preliminary results obtained in standard videos demonstrated the effectiveness of the proposed approach. The topic is currently under development; further results will be described in the final paper.

References

[1] S. Y. Kung, J. N. Hwang, "Neural Networks for Intelligent Multimedia Processing", Proceedings of IEEE, Vol. 86, No. 6, pp. 1244-1272, June 1998. 90

[2] V. K. Goyal, "Theoretical Foundations of Transform Coding", IEEE Signal Processing Magazine, Vol. 18, No. 5, pp.9-21, Sept. 2001. 90

[3] S. Haykin, "Neural Networks (A comprehensive Foundation)", 2nd Edition, Prentice-Hall, 1999. 90

[4] J. Woods, T. Naveen, "A Filter Based Bit Allocation Scheme", IEEE Trans. on Image Processing, Vol. 1, pp.436-440, July 1992. 90

[5] R. D. Dony, S. Haykin, " Neural Networks to Image Compression", Proceedings of IEEE, Vol. 83, No. 2, pp. 228-303, February 1992. 91

[6] Cottrel G. W., Munro P., Zipser D., "Image Compression by back propagation: an example of extensional programming", in SHARKEY, N. E. (Ed.): "Advances in cognitive science", Ablex, Norwood, Nj., 1988. 91, 92

[7] G. L. Sicuranza, G. Ramponi, S. Marsi, "Artificial Neural Networks for Image Compression ", Electronics Letters, Vol. 6, pp. 477-479, 1990. 91

[8] Parodi G., Passaggio F., "Size-Adaptive Neural Network For Image Compression", Int. Conf. on Image Processing, ICIP '94, Austin, TX, USA, 1994. 91, 92

[9] Piazza F., Smerilli S., Uncini A., Griffo M., Zunino R., "Fast Spline Neural Networks for Image Compression", WIRN -96, Proc. Of the 8th Italian Workshop on Neural Nets, Vietri sul Mare, Salerno, Italy, 23-25 May 1996. 91

[10] Stefano Guarnieri, Francesco Piazza and Aurelio Uncini, "Multilayer Feedforward Networks with AdaptiveSpline Activation Function", IEEE Trans. On Neural Network, Vol. 10, No. 3, pp.672-683, May 1999. 91

[11] Lorenzo Vecci, Francesco Piazza and Aurelio Uncini, "Learning and Approximation Capabilities of Adaptive Spline Activation Function Neural Networks", Neural Networks, Vol.11, No.2, pp 259-270, March 1998.

[12] Paolo Campolucci, Aurelio Uncini, Francesco Piazza and Bhaskar D. Rao, "On-Line Learning Algorithms for Locally Recurrent Neural Networks", IEEE Trans. on Neural Network, Vol. 10, No. 2, pp.253-271 March 1999. 95, 96

[13] R.Parisi, E. D.Di Claudio, G.Orlandi and B. D.Rao, "Fast adaptive digital equalization by recurrent neural networks", IEEE Trans. on Signal Processing, Special number on Neural Network applications, Vol. 45, No. 11, November 1997. 95

MLP Neural Network Implementation
on a SIMD Architecture

Salvatore Vitabile[1], Antonio Gentile[2], G. B. Dammone[2], and Filippo Sorbello[2]

[1] CEntro di studio sulle Reti di Elaboratori
Italian National Research Council, Palermo, Italy
vitabile@cere.pa.cnr.it
[2] Dipartimento di ingegneria INFOrmatica
University of Palermo, Italy
gentile@unipa.it
sorbellodammone@csai.unipa.it

Abstract. An Automatic Road Sign Recognition System $\{A(RS)^2\}$ is aimed at detection and recognition of one or more road signs from real-world color images. The authors have proposed an $A(RS)^2$ able to detect and extract sign regions from real world scenes on the basis of their color and shape features. Classification is then performed on extracted candidate regions using Multi-Layer Perceptron neural networks. Although system performances are good in terms of both sign detection and classification rates, the entire process requires a large computational time, so real-time applications are not allowed. In this paper we present the implementation of the neural layer on the Georgia Institute of Technology SIMD Pixel Processor. Experimental trials supporting the feasibility of real-time processing on this platform are also reported.

Keywords: Automatic Road Sign Recognition System, SIMD Pixel Processor.

1 Introduction

The main objective of an Automatic Road Signs Recognition System $\{A(RS)^2\}$ is to recognize one or more road signs from complex digital images coming from a CCD video camera, mounted on a vehicle moving along roads and/or highways. This is a difficult task, considering the complexity of outdoor scenes and the variation of lighting and shadowing conditions. Lighting conditions is a very difficult problem to constrain and regulate. The strength of the light depends on the time of the day and season, and also on the weather conditions. Lighting conditions has an unpredictable impact on the signs color. Furthermore, the direction of the sign's face is not ideal and signs can be affected by shadows from surrounding objects.

A growing number of solutions has been proposed for road signs recognition [6], [7], [8]. Almost all of these approaches usually employ fixed threshold on the RGB or HSI color space. An $A(RS)^2$ for road signs detection and recognition

M. Marinaro and R. Tagliaferri (Eds.): WIRN VIETRI 2002, LNCS 2486, pp. 99–106, 2002.

has been proposed in [2], [3]. The system is based on a color affinity dynamic criterion for an adaptive region growing procedure used to extract useful regions and reduce the hue instability effects inside the HSV color space. Following, a shape analysis technique of previously segmented areas is performed using a similarity function in order to extract candidate sign regions. Lastly, the extracted candidate sign regions are classified using a Multi-Layer Perceptron (MLP) neural networks.

Although system performances are good from the stand point of both sign detection and classification rates, the entire process requires a large computational time, incompatible with real-time execution. In this paper we present an implementation of the neural layer on the Georgia Institute of Technology SIMD Pixel Processor (SIMPil). This implementation exploits SIMPil's large computational throughput to deliver real-time, power efficient execution of the proposed application.

2   The SIMD Pixel Processor

The SIMD Pixel Processor (SIMPil) system exploits the benefits from integrating optoelectronic devices into a high performance digital processing system [4], [5]. In SIMPil, an array of image sensors is integrated on top of and electrically interfaced to digital SIMD processing elements (PEs). This monolithic integration is the key feature of the SIMPil system, providing for an extremely compact, high frame rate, focal-plane processor. The SIMPil architecture consists of a mesh of SIMD processors. A block diagram for a 16-bit implementation is illustrated in Figure 1. The instruction set architecture allows a single PE to address a 4x4 array of image sensors. Each processor incorporates an analog to digital converter to convert light intensities, incident on the sensors, into digital values. The SAMPLE instruction simultaneously samples all sensor values and makes them available for further processing. The SIMD execution model allows the entire image projected on many PEs to be acquired in a single cycle. Each processing element has a basic RISC core, which contains the following functional units: (a) 16 bit ALU with adder/subtractor and shifter; (b) multiply-accumulator unit with a 32 bit accumulator register; (c) 16 three-ported general purpose registers; (d) up to 256 words of local memory; (e) communication unit; (f) masking unit to control PE activity.

3 $A\,(RS)^2$ System Description

The $A\,(RS)^2$ system is composed by the following main blocks:

- image acquisition: since signs are usually on roads and/or highways sides, a CCD camera with fixed orientation and zoom on a moving vehicle is used for images acquisition.
- color analysis: the *a priori* knowledge about color signs is exploited in order to implement an efficient segmentation process. The entire process can be

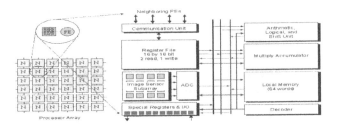

Fig. 1. Block diagram of the SIMPil SIMD system

subdivided in the following steps: (i) standard HSV color filters application according to the *h, s, v* "true" coordinates of the signs; (ii) sub-image generation and related seeds pixel determination; (iii) pixel aggregation with a dynamic threshold depending on seeds saturation value.

– shape analysis: the *a priori* knowledge about shape signs is exploited in order to select the candidate sign regions. Shape classification is done using a similarity coefficient between a segmented region and a set of image samples representing each road sign shape.

– neural classification of candidate sign regions: classification has been performed with feed-forward Two-Layers Perceptron (MLP) neural network classifiers [1]. Each extracted candidate road sign region is processed to generate relevant neural network inputs; region chromatic information is then used for the classification process.

Details on system features and implementation can be found in [2], [3]. The system has been tested using different road sign classes. Outdoor road scenes have been collected in the Palermo area (Italy), using a CCD camera. Images were acquired with different external environment conditions and were processed to extract and recognize one or more signs inside them.

MLP training was performed using 240 new real extracted signs. The training set has been enhanced artificially by addition of slightly rotated signs in both left and right direction to raise the neural network generalization capability.

The system was tested using 620 outdoor images and 24 pictogram sign classes. Classification of contents of pictogram signs is performed by three different unrelated MLP neural network classifiers. MLP topology has been fixed by the input data number, by the output classes and by making a RGB values compression (3:1) between the input layer and the hidden layer. Hence, the adopted MLP topology was 432-144-O, where O=11 for the warning signs, O=8 for the prohibitory signs and O=5 for the mandatory direction signs. Considering the sign classes distribution, the achieved segmentation and classification rates are reported in Table 1.

Figure 2 and Figure 3 show two difficult to recognize images. In the first case, the start image is characterized by a predominant blue component. Hence, a lot of regions have been detected by the blue and red color based segmentation modules. However, undesired regions have been excluded by the shape correlator

Table 1. The achieved segmentation and classification rates

Sign Classes	Signs Number	Segm. Rate %	Class. Rate %
Red Circular	318	94.6	84
Red Triangular	246	86.3	88
Blue Circular	67	95.7	100

module. The two segmented regions have been then correctly classified by the appropriate neural networks. In the second case, less than satisfactory segmentation is achieved due to the misalignment between sign orientation and camera position and orientation. However, the generalization capability of the neural classificator guarantees the correct result, thus supporting the overall robustness of the approach used.

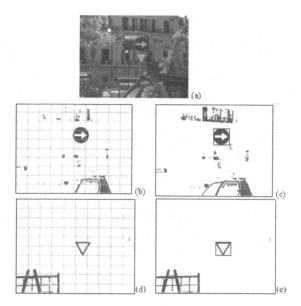

Fig. 2. A sample of the entire signs detection and recognition process: a) start image, b) blue pass-band HSV filter application, c) dynamic pixel aggregation algorithm with the related sign extraction, d) red pass-band HSV filter application, e) dynamic pixel aggregation algorithm with the related sign extraction. The signs will be correctly classified by the apposite neural module

4   MLP Implementation

We have implemented the designed neural network for the warning signs classification on the SIMPil architecture. Since in this study the warning signs classes
considered are 11, the topology of the implemented architecture is 432x144x11.
The MLP is mapped on SIMPil employing a single processing element for each
neuron. This mapping exploits the direct coupling between each SIMPil processor and a portion of the image acquired on the focal plane. The interconnection
weights are also arranged and fed to the system through the focal plane.
Presinaptic values for each hidden layer neuron are accumulated in the 32-bit
multiply-accumulate unit of the corresponding PE. This process continues until
all image values have traversed the entire processor array. The periodical feature
of the hidden activation function of the used MLP neural network [1] is mapped
to the 32 bit arithmetic precision available. Furthermore, the linear function
used in the output neurons allows a simple but effective mechanism to select
the winner neuron in the output layer. The hidden layer activation function is
computed in fixed-point, and the corresponding output values are then trans-
ferred to the PEs of the next layer. An illustration of the mapping of a single
perceptron layer on SIMPil is given in Figure 4.

In this implementation, a 13x12 SIMPil system is used to map the neural
network designed for road-sign recognition. Three neurons are mapped to each
processing element, which processes the three color component of a single image
pixel. The input image is 12x12 pixel, with a Pixel to Processing Element (PPE)
ratio currently set to 1. The connection weights are pre-computed through the
off-line training phase and stored in each PE local memory (433 words for each

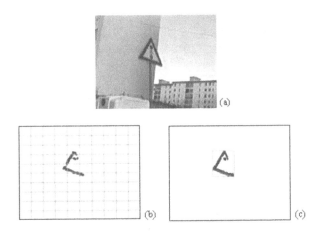

Fig. 3. A sample of the entire signs detection and recognition process: a) start
image, b) red pass-band HSV filter application, c) dynamic pixel aggregation
algorithm with the related sign extraction. The sign will be correctly classified
by the apposite neural module

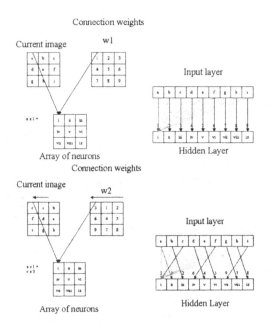

Fig. 4. The mapping of a single perceptron layer on SIMPil. A portion of the input image and the related connection weight are used for the neuron scalar product

input layer PE and 145 for each output layer PE). We use 8-bit precision for both neural network inputs and connection weights.

The sinusoidal activation function is also implemented in the PE local memory through a look-up table. The Winner Takes All unit selects the neuron with the greatest output activation level. The work flow of the SIMPil implementation is: (a) parallel weights loading phase; (b) hidden layer elaboration and pre-synaptic activation value storage; (c) post-synaptic activation computing; (d) output layer elaboration; (e) Winner Takes All elaboration.

The classification rate achieved using the described implementation is equal to 100 %: the hardware implementation has the same performances of the soft-

Table 2. System Performances

–	Weights Loading	Signs Classification
Cycle	4542	6190
System Usage	71.90 %	41.77 %
Execution Time	9.08 μs	12.38 μs
Throughput	56.11 Gops/s	32.59 Gops/s

ware implementation. In Table 2 are reported system performances for the weights loading phase and for the signs classification phase. The obtained performance assures real-time neural processing and recognition of road signs.

5   Conclusions

We have implemented the entire neural recognition system on the SIMD Pixel Processor (SIMPil) architecture developed by the PICA Research Group at the Georgia Institute of Technology. This implementation exploits SIMPil's large computational throughput to deliver real-time, power efficient execution of the proposed application with a 100 % classification rate. The obtained performance assures real-time neural processing and recognition of road signs giving ample room for real-time implementation of the entire $A\,(RS)^2$.

Acknowledgments

The authors would like to thank past and present members of the Portable Image Computation Architecture (PICA) Group at Georgia Tech and its director, Prof. D. Scott Wills, for development of the SIMPil architecture, simulator and application suite.

References

1. F. Sorbello, G. Gioiello, and S. Vitabile. *Handwritten Character Recognition using a MLP*, chapter 5, pages 91–119. L. C. Jain and B. Lazzerini - CRC Press, 1999.
2. S. Vitabile, G. Pilato, G. Pollaccia, F. Sorbello. Road Signs Recognition Using a Dynamic Pixel Aggregation Technique in the HSV Color Space. In *Proc. of 11° International Conference on Image Analysis and Processing*, Palermo - Italy, pp. 572-577, (2001), IEEE Computer Society Press.
3. S. Vitabile, A. Gentile, F. Sorbello. A Neural Network based Automatic Road Signs Recognizer. *Proc. of 2002 IEEE World Congress on Computational Intelligence - International Joint Conference on Neural Networks (IJCNN)*, Honolulu - USA, pp. 2315-2320, IEEE Computer Society Press.
4. A. Gentile, J. Cruz-Rivera, D. Wills et al. Real-time image processing on a focal plane simd array, in parallel and distributed processing. *Lecture Notes in Computer Science*, (1586):400–405, 1999. Eds. J. Rolim et al. - Springer Verlag.
5. A. Gentile, H. H. Cat, F. Kossentini, F. Sorbello ,D. S. Wills. Real-Time Vector Quantization-based Image Compression on the SIMPil Low Memory SIMD Architecture. *Proc. of the 1997 IEEE Intl. Performance, Computing, and Communications Conference (IPCCC-97)*, pp. 10-16, 1997.
6. H. Akatsuka and S. Imai. Road signposts recognition system. In *Proc. SAE vehicle highway infrastructure: safety compatibility*, pages 189–196, 1987.
7. N. Kehtarnavaz, N. Griswold, and D. Kang. Stop-sign recognition based on color shape processing. In *Machine Vision and Applications*, volume 6, pages 206–208, 1993.

8. L. Priese, J. Klieber, R. Lakmann, V. Rehrmann, and R. Schian. New results on traffic sign recognition. In *IEEE Proc. Intelligent Vehicles'94 Symposium*, pages 249–253, 1994. 99

9. L. Priese and V. Rehrmann. On hierarchical color segmentation and applications. In *Proc. CVPR*, pages 633–634, 1993.

10. G. Piccioli, E. D. Michelli, and M. Campani. A robust method for road sign detection and recognition. In *Proc. European Conference on Computer Vision*, pages 495–500, 1994.

11. G. Piccioli, E. D. Michelli, P. Parodi, and M. Campani. Robust road sign detection and recognition from image sequences. In *Proc. Intelligent Vehicles'94*, pages 278–283, 1994.

12. G. Nicchiotti, E. Ottaviani, P. Castello, and G. Piccioli. Automatic road sign detection and classification from color image sequences. In S. Impedovo, editor, *Proc. 7th Int. Conf. On Image Analysis and Processing*, pages 623–626, 1994.

Part V

Image and Signal Processing

A New Approach to Detection of Muscle Activation by Independent Component Analysis and Wavelet Transform

Bruno Azzerboni[1], Giovanni Finocchio[1], Maurizio Ipsale[1],
Fabio La Foresta[1], and Francesco Carlo Morabito[2]

[1] DFMTFA, Universitá degli Studi Di Messina
salita Sperone, 31 C.P. 57, 98166 Messina, Italy
{azzerboni,finocchio,ipsale,laforesta}@singegneria.unime.it
[2] DIMET, Universitá *Mediterranea*
via Graziella Loc. Feo di Vito, 89100 Reggio Calabria, Italy
morabito@ing.unirc.it

Abstract. Recent works have demonstrated that the Independent Components (ICs) of simultaneously-recorded surface Electromyography (sEMG) recordings are more reliable in monitoring repetitive movements and better correspond with ongoing brain-wave activity than raw sEMG recordings. In this paper we propose to detect single muscle activation, when the arms reach a target, by means of ICs time-scale decomposition. Our analysis starts with acquisition of sEMG (surface EMG) signals; source separation is performed by a neural net-work that implements on Independent Component Analysis algorithm. In this way we obtain a signal set each representing single muscle activity. The wave-let transform, lastly, is utilised to detect muscle activation intervals.

Keywords: Surface EMG,ICA.

1 Introduction

Monitoring the electrical activity of the muscle with Electromyography (EMG) can be used for exploring neuroscience questions about motor control and control of rehabili-tation devices. Clinically, needle EMG is used extensively for assessment of diseases of the peripheral nerves and muscle. However, since groups of muscles tend to be controlled by neural systems, multiple simultaneous recordings from several muscles are desirable. Surface EMG recordings provide a practical means to record from sev-eral muscles simultaneously but tend to be unreliable, i.e. recordings from a subject performing the same movement repetitively tend to have considerable trial-to-trial variability. SEMG recordings are also affected by "cross-talk" whereby several mus-cles may contribute to the recording of a given electrode, making the source of the signal difficult to be identified. Recently, Independent Component Analysis (ICA) has been proposed as a method to analyze sEMG recordings, which addresses many of these concerns. SEMG ICs have been shown to be more reliable that raw sEMG re-cordings [1] and

M. Marinaro and R. Tagliaferri (Eds.): WIRN VIETRI 2002, LNCS 2486, pp. 109–116, 2002.
© Springer-Verlag Berlin Heidelberg 2002

correspond better with ongoing brain-wave activity (measured with the EEG) than the individual sEMG recordings [2].

2   Independent Component Analysis

Independent Component Analisys (ICA) is a new statistical technique that aims at trasforming an input vector into a signal space in which the signals are statistically in-dependent. The drawback of ICA, namely the need of high order statistics in order to determine ICA expansion, is counterbalanced by its performances, which are more meaningful compared with other methods like PCA - Principal Component Analysis (see figure 1)

Let $x_k = [x_k(1), \ldots, x_k(M)]^T$ T be a set of k M-dimensional data vector corresponding to the electrode signals. We can write the ICA signal model in the vector form:

$$x_k = As_k \tag{1}$$

Here s_k is the source vector consisting of the independent signal components, $s_k(i)$, $i = 1, \ldots, N$, $A = [a(1), \ldots, a(N)]$ is a constant $M \times N$ mixing matrix whose columns $a(i)$ are the basis vectors of ICA. The aim of source separation is to determine s_k, knowing only x_k. Tipically, the basis vectors $a(i)$ are normalized to unit length and they are not mutually orthogonal. The complete procedure is implemented by using a feed forward scheme. The Neural Network (NN) inputs are the M components of vector x. There are N nodes in the hidden layer. The first layer of weights carries out a $M \times N$ whitening and compression of the input vector. The sources are then separated by means of an orthonormal

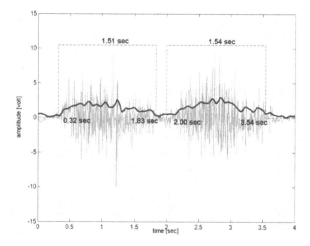

Fig. 1. The effect of projecting measurement data on the PCs and on the ICs. We can notify that PCA detect only orthogonal directions, ICA is able to capture the directions of maximum variance

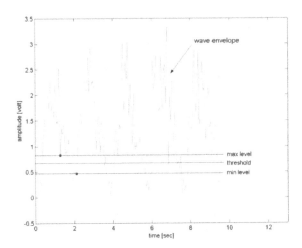

Fig. 2. Topology of feed forward Neural Network that approaches ICA

matrix (WTW=IN) that the NN should learn. The ICA network, first proposed by Karhunen (1997), is showed in figure 2. Nonlinearity (i.e., hyperbolic tangent function) is used in learning the separating matrix. The learning algorithm can be summarized as follows: whitening the original data by $v = D^{-1/2}E^T x$, where E is the matrix of the eigenvectors of the original data x and D is the diagonal matrix of eigenvalues that produces a starting point for an iterative process that finds vector W. The learning rule is:

$$W(k + 1) = E\{vg(W(k)^T v) - g(W(k)^T v)W(k)\} \qquad (2)$$

where $vg(\circ)$ is the hyperbolic tangent. After finding W, the IC's are found using the linear transformation WTv and the mixing matrix A by $A = ED^{1/2}W$. By this procedure, the ICA network allows us to determine the separating matrix.

3 Surface EMG Processing

The knowledge of individual muscles activity is important to detect muscle activation intervals. We propose to use multivariate signal processing techniques like Independent Component Analysis (ICA), in order to estimate the information content in the sEMG signals. SEMG was recorded from a single subject performing a reaching task. The subject faced a computer screen, with their right hand in a supinated position in front of them. The subject was then asked to point to the left side of the screen and return, and then point the right side of the screen, and so on. Up to 50 complete cycles were performed. Visual cues in the form of laterally-moving and shrinking circles were used to pace the movements and provide a target at the edges of the screen. SEMG signals were recorded from 16 electrodes distributed over the chest, shoulder arm and forearm (figure 3), amplified, and sampled at 1kHz. The Independent Components of the

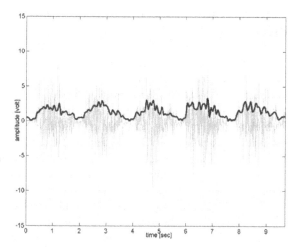

Fig. 3. SEMG signals. Mapping of electrodes is shown on top of the figure. In the bottom, each row represents the output of each electrode

sEMG have been shown to better correspond with brain activity compared to the activity from individual muscles. Further they are able to distinguish between similar motor movements, and allow for a straightforward computation of information content [1]. The first step of our procedure consists in a reduction of data dimensionality, achieved by Principal Components Analysis to capture an arbitrary percentage (e.g., > 95) of the variance of the data [1],[2]. Subsequently ICA application [2] allows the EKG artefacts to be removed and the individual muscles activity to be identified. The ICs from a 10-sec portion of recordings are shown in figure 4. Note the isolation of obvious sEMG activity (ICs [1],[3],[4],[5],[?]) from artifact (ICs [2], [6] and [?]). Although the first IC was clearly modulated by the pointing task (figure 4), it was also different from trial to trial. As such, this IC was selected for further processing. Then, wavelet analysis is used to detect the activation instant of single muscles.

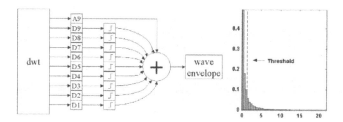

Fig. 4. Individual muscles activity detected by ICA. The rows represent the ICs of sEMG. The ICs 2,6 and 8 are artifacts, the others ICs are the individual muscles activity

4   Independent Components Processing: Time-Scale Decomposition

The most common method to detect the muscle activation is visual inspection of EMG signal (off line condition). Another approach is a "single threshold method" which compare the EMG signal to affixed threshold. Recently, "double-threshold detector" has been proposed to improve the detection [5]. We propose a new method in which the activation instant of single muscles can be determined by means of time-scale decomposition of ICs, calculated from non-invasive technique sEMG. To performe this decomposition, the discrete wavelet transform (dwt) is applied; this method is proposed to overcome the limitations of the traditional time-frequency methods. The wavelet transform acts as a "mathematical microscope" in which one can observe different parts of the signal by "adjusting the focus". This allows the detection of short-lived time components in the signal. This "adapted" method is logical since high-frequency components such as short burst need high time resolution as compared with low-frequency components, where a detailed frequency analysis is often desired. In the next subsections we will show how the dwt allows the determination of that portion of the ICs that are highly reliable (we named this wave envelope); subsequently the algorithm to detect the muscle activations will be showed.

4.1   Wave Envelope Extraction

In order to extract the wave envelope, we implemented an algorithm that optimize the choice of approximation level to fit muscle activation cycles. The first step of optimization procedure consists in a ninth level decomposition of the first IC; for example, the figure 5a shows a third level decomposition: if S was an Independent Component, we can apply a bank filter to extrapolate a low pass approximation A3 and three high pass details D1, D2, D3. This decomposition is performed by means of the Daubechies mother wavelet (see figure 5b).

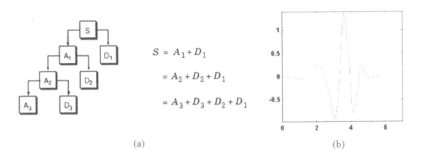

$$S = A_1 + D_1$$
$$= A_2 + D_2 + D_1$$
$$= A_3 + D_3 + D_2 + D_1$$

(a)   (b)

Fig. 5. Wavelet decomposition (a) and the mother wavelet Daubechies (b)

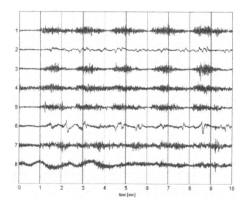

Fig. 6. Wavelet decomposition and wave envelope extraction by means of threshold algorithm

Next the algorithm adds details, with information content higher than a fixed threshold, to the ninth approximation signal, A9 (see figure 6). The figure 7 show the obtained signal; it represents the low frequency portion of the ICs that can be used to detect the information of cyclical repetition of the movement.

4.2 Muscle Activation Detection

The ICs of sEMG signals contains many bursts of high frequency. In our analysis each burst could be erroneously interpreted as the beginning or the end of muscle contraction. For these reasons we can notice the usefullness of wave envelope in which the bursts are a lot less than before. In this signal, the muscle activation intervals can be detect by means of a threshold processing. It is important to observe that an elaboration of this type couldn't be implemented directly in

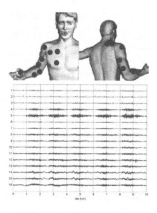

Fig. 7. The wave envelope of IC1 calculated by mean of wavelet decomposition

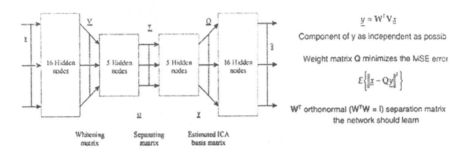

Fig. 8. Muscle activation intervals algorithm. The figure shows the three levels of threshold: max level, threshold and min level

ICs just because of its high frequency content. Let us describe our threshold algorithm. It starts with a training procedure in order to calculate the thresholds that it will utilise in a second phase. In particulary, three levels are detected: a threshold, a max level and a min level (see figure 8).

The threshold level represents the boundary between the beginning and the end of contracion. To avoid oscillations around the threshold not wished, that don't correspond to an effective activation (or deactivation), we introduced the other levels. When the muscle is active, it can't deactivate if it didn't exceed max level. Similary, when the muscle isn't active, it can't activate if it didn't come down under min level. These levels are calculated as follows. The threshold is related to mean value of wave envelope. Max level is the smallest of the maximum values of the wave envelope signal. Min level is the largest of the minimum values of the signal. These levels are recalculated every prefixed number of contractions, in order to obtain a real time performance very reliable. The figure 9 shows the obtained results by means of algorithm application to first IC after the training phase applied on five contractions. It determines that first contraction starts at 0.32 seconds and it ends at 1.83 seconds. Second contraction starts at 2.00 seconds and it ends at 3.54 seconds. Obviously, these informations are sufficient

Fig. 9. The activation intervals of IC1. First contraction starts at 0.32 seconds and it ends at 1.83 seconds. Second contraction starts at 2.00 seconds and it ends at 3.54 seconds

to calculate the duration of contraction that, in our example, is equal to 1.51 seconds in first contraction and 1.54 seconds in second contraction.

5 Conclusions

A fast and simple algorithm based on ICA and wavelet decomposition is used to process sEMG signal, in order to determine indivual muscles activity and activation intervals. The application of discrete wavelet transform (dwt) to the ICs allows the wave envelope to be calculated (see figure 7). Further, dwt allows us to isolate the wavelet approximation that characterize the arm movement. Muscle activation intervals can be identified by detecting the presence of the wavelet approximation related to the arm movement (see figure 9).

References

[1] McKeown, M. J., Torpey, D. C., Gehm W. C.: Non-Invasive Monitoring of Functionally Distinct Muscle Activations during Swallowing. Clinical Neurophysiology (2002). 109, 112

[2] McKeown, M. J.:Cortical activation related to arm movement combinations. Muscle Nerve. 9:19-25 (2000). 110, 112

[3] Jung T. P., Makeig S., McKeown M. J., Bell A. J., Lee T. W., Sejnowski T. J.: Imaging bra-indynamics using independent component analysis. Proc. IEEE. 89(7): 1107-22, (2001). 112

[4] Bell A. J., Sejnowski T. J.: An information-maximization approach to blind separation and blind deconvolution, Neural Computation, 7:1129-1159, (1995). 112

[5] Micera S.,Vannozzi G., Sabatini A. M., Dario P.: Improving Detection of Muscle Activation intervals, IEEE Engineering in Medicine and Biology, vol. 20 n.6:38-46 (2001). 112, 113

[6] Karhunen J., Oja E.: A Class of Neural Networks for Independent Component Analysis, IEEE Transactions on Neural Network, vol. 8 n. 3:486-504, (1997). 112

Learning to Balance Upright Posture: What can be Learnt Using Adaptive NN Models?

N. Alberto Borghese

Laboratory of Human Motion Analysis and Virtual Reality (MAVR)
Department of Computer Science, University of Milano
Via Comelico 39, 20135 Milano
borghese@dsi.unimi.it
www.dsi.unimi.it/~borghese/

Abstract. Human upright vertical position is unstable. A continuous activation of postural muscles is therefore required to avoid falling down. The problem is complicated by the reduced dimension of the support base (the feet) and by the articulated structure of the human skeleton. Nevertheless, upright posture is a capability, which is learnt in the first year of life. Here, the learning process is investigated by using neural networks models and the reinforcement learning paradigm. After creating a mechanically realistic digital human body, a parametric feed-back controller is defined. It outputs a set of joint torques as a function of orientation and rotational velocity of the body segments. The controller does not have any information either on the model of the human body or on the suitable set of its parameters. It learns the parameters which allow the controller to maintain the vertical position, through trial-and-error (success-fail) by using reinforcement learning. When learning is completed, the kinematics behaviour qualitatively resemble that of real experiments. The amplitude of the oscillations is larger than in the real case; this is due to the lack of any explicit penalization of the oscillations amplitude. The kinematics resembles the real one also when the body has to maintain the vertical upright position facing a tilt or displacement of the support base.

Keywords: Human posture control.

1 Introduction

Human posture is defined as the relative orientation of the body segments and their orientation in the 3D space. Upright posture is unstable and a continuous activation of postural muscles is required to avoid falling down. This is produced by a control system, which takes into account external forces (gravitational force, perturbations in the support...) as well as muscolo-skeletal mechanical properties [6]. Two are the main goals of this system: an anti-gravitational action and the stabilization in space of the body segments. The problem is complicated

M. Marinaro and R. Tagliaferri (Eds.): WIRN VIETRI 2002, LNCS 2486, pp. 117–123, 2002.

by the reduced dimension of the support base (the feet) and by the articulated structure of the human skeleton. Nevertheless, upright posture is a capability, which is learnt in the first year of life. Here, the learning process is investigated by using a neural networks model [14] and the reinforcement learning paradigm [8]. After creating a mechanically realistic digital human body, a feed-back neural controller is defined. The controller outputs a set of joints torques as a function of orientation and rotational velocity of the body segments. The controller does not have any information either on the model of the human body or on the suitable set of its parameters. It can learn the parameters only through trial-and-error (success and fail) by using reinforcement learning. Results of simulations show that the controller is able the learn the upright position. Moreover, the resulting kinematics time course closely resembles that described in the literature [4][7][10].

2   Method

From the biomechanics point of view, the human skeleton can be modeled as an articulated structure of rigid segments connected by joints [1]. It results an inverse pendulum like structure. The system is described by the length and the mechanical properties of each segment (mass, center of mass position, inertial moments). To achieve a reliable model, these quantities have been derived from the biomechanics literature [5]. The obtained model is constituted of fourteen segements: the body, the head, the two arms (constituted of the arm, forearm and hand) and the two legs (constituted of leg, inferior leg and foot). As far as joints are concerned, although the relative motion of the segments is not a pure rotation, they can be modeled as hinges, as a first approximation.

Muscle action on the segments has been modeled as torques applied to the joints ($T(t)$ in Figure 1). This represents the net contribution of the different agonist muscles. To achieve a higher realism in our model, the torque generated by muscles are implemented taking into account the mechanical properties of the muscles: limited maximum torque, finite rising and falling constant. In particular, the maximum torque generated by each muscle has been derived by the data measured during gait in [2] and the time constants reported in [9] have been adopted for modeling the muscle behavior. Moreover, a delay between the output of the controller and the torque generation has been added to simulate the processing and traveling times in the reflex circuits.

The motion of the skeleton requires to compute the acceleration of each segment at each time step, given a certain torque set. The acceleration set is then double integrated to find the actual position and velocity set ($x(t)$ and $\dot{x}(t)$). This process is carried out inside the Working Model® environment. These values are then input to the controller which produces a new control signal ($y(t)$), which represents the neural signal transmitted to the muscles. It is assumed step-like. This signal is then transformed by the neuro-muscle system model (Figure 1). The controller has been implemented in Visual Basic and interfaced with the Working Model® environment.

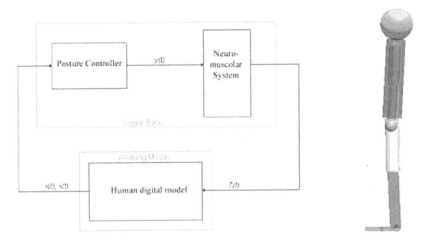

Fig. 1. On the left the schema of the learning system is schematized. The controller and the dynamical model of the muscolo-skeletal system are implemented in Visual Basic and the dynamic model of the human skeleton in Working Model. On the right the model of the body implemented. It is constituted of seven main segments: the HAT (head, arms and trunk), the upper legs, the lower legs and the feet

In the following simulations, to simplify the computational load, the arms and the head have been made solid with the body (HAT segment [11]). Moreover, sagittal symmetry has been postulated, which allows modeling learning upright posture inside the sagittal plane.

2.1   The Controller

The controller receives as input the state of the human skeleton (represented as orientation and rotational velocity of the segments) and outputs a set of neural-like signals. It is realized here with a the two-levels architecture proposed in [3] (Figure 2). Each of the two levels is represented as a parametric model, typically a neural network. The controller (first level) does not have any information either on the model of the human body or on the suitable set of its parameters. Learning to maintain an upright posture is achieved by repetitive trials which end with a failure. The system behaviour is monitored by the critic (second level). This modifies its parameters to create a reliable map on which are the "risky" states which have to be avoided. The critic outputs a signal used to tune the controller parameters.

2.2   Simulations

Simulations have been carried out using the combined system: controller plus model. The time step used in the forward integration was 4ms. Learning was

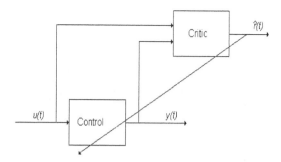

Fig. 2. The two-level architecture considered here. The first level (controller) output a set of torque, $y(t)$ as a parametric function of the position and rotational velocity of the body segments ($v(t)$). The second level, the critic transforms the failure signal $y(t)$ into a suitable modification of the parameters of the controller

considered terminated when the upright posture could be maintained for at least 20s. This is achieved on the average after 400–500 trials. The parameters in the first trial of each sequence were initialized randomly while in the subsequent trials were set equal to the parameters in the last time-step of the previous trial. The state of the system was discretized as follows: *Rotational velocity.* $(-\infty - 50\ 50\ \infty)$ deg/s; *Orientation* with respect to the vertical: $[-12-6-10+1+6+12]$ degrees, for a total of $3,402$ boxes. The body was considered out of balance for any orientation angle larger than these values.

3   Results

We have first investigated the kinematics of the model when vertical upright posture has been learnt, that is, when the parameters of the controller allow the body to maintain the upright vertical position. In Figure 3, the orientation time course of the body, upper and lower leg are plotted for the last part of a trial ($5-7$ seconds). A time correlation between the three angles has been assessed through the principle components.

This analysis has shown that only two angles are linearly independent (the covariance matrix is rank deficient). This same observation has been made experimentally in the analysis of posture and gait in humans (e.g. [6][13]). This dependency reduces the dimension of the control space and therefore the number of degrees of freedom which have to be controlled [12]. The kinematics strategies learnt in different experiments, are quite similar. They all share the characteristic that the controller tends to block the knee and to act at the ankle and hip level. This mechanism aligns the lower and upper leg, and it can be interpreted as a simplification of the control as the entire leg can be controlled as a single inverse pendulum with the body on its extremity. This same behavior has been experimentally observed [6][10]. Resorting to knee flexion in destabilizing situations is also biologically congruent. Of less realism is the amplitude of the

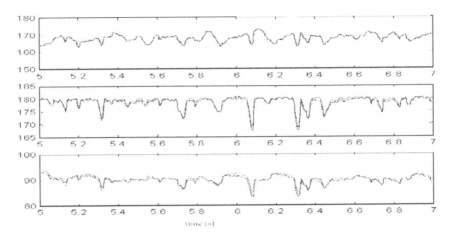

Fig. 3. The orientation time course of the upper body, upper and lower leg is plotted for a few seconds (5–7s) of a succesful trial

orientation variations. These manifest as oscillations around the vertical upright position of a certain amplitude. It is interesting to remark that, in absence of other constraints, the control system is not induced to minimize these oscillations, which are kept inside acceptable limits throughout a successful trial. An active controller would be required to minimize these oscillations, which goes beyond the possibility of the reflex controller used here. A second set of experiments has been carried out perturbing the support platform. A tilt of $+/-30$degrees or a horizontal displacement of $+/-30$cm is given to the platform. This set of experiments was made on humans by Nashner [10] and have allowed identifying two control strategies to maintain the upright posture (Figure 4). The first strategy was related to maintaining the vertical position when tilt was applied; it involves mainly a rotation of the ankle and was termed *ankle strategy*. The second strategy was related to maintaining the vertical position when displacement was applied; it involves mainly a translation of the body and therefore a hip rotation; it was termed *hip strategy*. In the simulations, only in a few trials of backwards displacement, the torques pattern described in [10] could be observed. In these experiments a different onset of torques on the different joints which produced a distal to proximal activation sequence was realized, which was similar to that observed in the real experiments (Figure 4). The kinematic strategies instead closely resemble those described in [10]. The knee is maintained close to the complete extension, and the postural stabilization is carried out through rotations around the ankle or the hip.

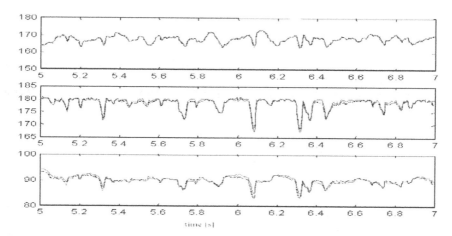

Fig. 4. On the left, the perturbation on the support is shown: tilt, forwards and backwards displacement. On the right, the time course of the torques applied to the hoints when learning has been completed are shown

4   Conclusions

The simulations described here show that to learn upright position humans do not need any structured information (constraint on the output, physical model of the body as implicitly required in [6][7][3]), but only the success-fail reinforcement signal. Moreovoer, the resulting kinematics qualitatively resembles the real one. This is true even when the support is perturbated. In this case, an ankle or hip strategy can be observed, as well as a covariation between the angles. The amplitude of the oscillations around the upright posture is larger than in real experiments and other (high order) information has to be taken into account to reduce these oscillations amplitude.

References

[1] Pedotti A. A study of motor coordination and neuromuscular activities in human locomotion. *Biol. Cybern.*, 26:53–62, 1977. 118

[2] Pedotti A., Krishnan V. V., and Stark L. Optimization of muscle-force sequencing in human locomotion. *Math. Biosc.*, 38:57–76, 1978. 118

[3] A. G. Barto, R. S. Sutton, and C. W. Anderson. Neuronlike adaptive elements that can solve difficult learning problems. *IEEE Trans. Syst. Man and Cybern.*, 13:834–846, 1983. 119, 122

[4] Ghez C. *Posture.* Elsevier, 1991. 118

[5] de Leva P. Joint center longitudinal positions computed from a selected subset of chandler's data. *J. Biomechanics*, 9:1231–1233, 1996. 118

[6] Lacquaniti F., Maioli C., Borghese N. A., and Bianchi L. Posture and movement: Coordination and control. *Archives Italiannes de Biologie*, 135:353–367, 1997. 117, 120, 122

[7] Massion J. Postural contol system. *Curr. Opin. Neurobiol.*, 4:877–887, 1994. 118, 122

[8] L. P. Kaelbling, M. L. Littman, and A. W. Moore. Reinforcement learning: A survey. *J. Artificial Intelligence Research*, 4:237–285, 1996. 118

[9] Kashima, Isurugi Y. T., and Shima M. Analysis of a muscular control system in human movements. *Biol. Cybern.*, 82:"123–131", 2000. 118

[10] Nashner L. M. Fixed patterns of rapid postural responses among leg muscle during stance. *Exp. Brain Res.*, 30:13–24, 1977. 118, 120, 121

[11] Nigg B. M. and Herzog W. John Wiley and Sons, Toronto, 1999. 119

[12] Bernstein N. Pergamon Press, Oxford, 1967. 120

[13] Borghese N. A., Bianchi L., and Lacquaniti F. Kinematic determinants of human locomotion. *J. of Physiology*, 494(3):863–879, 1996. 120

[14] R. Sutton T. Miller and P. Werbos, editors. MIT Press, 1990. 118

Detection of Facial Features

Paola Campadelli, Elena Casiraghi, and Raffaella Lanzarotti

Dipartimento di Scienze dell'Informazione
Università degli Studi di Milano, Via Comelico, 39/41 20135 Milano, Italy
{campadelli,casiraghi,lanzarotti}@dsi.unimi.it

Abstract. An algorithm for the automatic features detection in 2D color images of human faces is presented. It first identifies the eyes by means of a template matching technique, a neural network classifier, and a distance measure. It proceeds localizing lips and nose using a non-linear edge detector and color information. The method is scale-independent, works on images of either frontal, rotated or slightly tilted faces, and does not require any manual setting or operator intervention.

Keywords: Feature detection, Face recognition.

1 Introduction

Several applications like face recognition [7] [16], model-based coding of video sequences [1], 3D face reconstruction [14], facial expression analysis [17], and intelligent man-machine interfaces [1] require the localization and precise description of facial features (eyes, nose and lips).

Such is not an easy machine-vision task due to the high inter-personal variability (gender, race, ...), the intra-personal changes (pose, expression, ...), and the acquisition conditions (lighting, image resolution, ...).

Some techniques reported in literature determine feature points manually [17] [4]. Attempts to automate this phase have been done; such works can be distinguished in *color-based* and *shape-based*. The first class of methods tries to characterize the face and each feature with a certain combination of colors [6]. This is a low-cost approach, but not very robust. The shape-based approaches look for specific shapes in the image adopting either template matching (with deformable templates [19],[1], [18] or not [3]), graph matching [5], [16], snakes [13], or the Hough transform [8]. These methods work well only under restricted assumptions (regarding the head position and the illumination conditions) and they are computationally expensive.

We have proposed [9] an algorithm using both shape and color which has two hierarchical processing modules: the first identifies four sub-images, each tightly containing one of the features of interest; the latter module is specialized in localizing fiducial points on the found features with high accuracy. At that stage the most critical step was the identification of the eyes sub-images. We present here a solution based on a neural network classifier and the evaluation of the distances of pair of gray-level images.

M. Marinaro and R. Tagliaferri (Eds.): WIRN VIETRI 2002, LNCS 2486, pp. 124–131, 2002.
© Springer-Verlag Berlin Heidelberg 2002

The method we present works on images of face foregrounds. We acquire color images with homogeneous and light-colored background, and frontal and diffuse illumination. Faces can be either in frontal position or rotated around the head vertical axis of 30° at most and tilted laterally of about 10°. In any case, the completeness of the facial images is requested: no occlusions, no wearing glasses, no beard and closed mouth.

The paper is organized as follows: in section 2 image pre-processing and an initial feature localization are presented; in section 3 we describe the eyes localization using both a neural network and a distance measure; in section 4 lips and nose localization are introduced; in section 5 results on a database of 130 color images are reported and discussed.

2   Preprocessing and Initial Features Localization

The original color images have a wide variety of resolutions ranging between 480x640 to 960x1280 pixels. For computational efficiency the sub-images identification is done on down-sampled images ranging between 150x170 to 300x340 pixels.

We first cluster the gray-level image into three clusters through the clustering algorithm presented in [2]. The lightest gray-level represents the background, the intermediate the skin and the darkest represents both the features and other dark pixels of the image (for example the hair).

To localize the features of interest the largest region, S, with pixels of the intermediate gray-level (corresponding to the skin) is found. Then all the pixels surrounded by pixels of S and belonging to the darkest gray-level are identified and set to 1; all the others are set to 0. What we obtain is the *feature image* [Fig.1].

We observe that, besides the features of interest, also few regions, such as those corresponding to shadows, hair, or ears are set to 1. Further processings are therefore required to discard not interesting regions and to isolate the features of interest in separated sub-images.

We proceed localizing the eyes, then, in order to look for the lips and the nose, the attention can be concentrated upon a restricted image area.

Fig. 1. Some example of features images obtaining from the clustered images

Fig. 2. *First line*: examples of "clustered" eyes; *Second line*: Eyes Template

3   Eyes Localization

In order to determine the set of rows (*eyes band*) which contains the eyes, we apply the template matching to the *features image* [Fig.1], searching the two eyes. The difficulty is that we are not looking for an object with a fixed shape [Fig.2.*first line*]. For this reason we adopt a binary template [Fig.2.*second line*] which models the two eyes in a very rough way. It consists of two symmetric blobs placed side by side each being large enough to overlap to the region corresponding to an eye in the *features image*. A single template has been used for all the images which are of significant different size, thus showing a desirable scale-independence property.

Among the positions with the highest cross-correlation, we maintain the 10 which satisfy also the following symmetry condition: the cross correlation between half the template (one blob) and the sub-images on the left and on the right of the found position are compared and the position is rejected if the results are not similar enough, that is their ratio is lower than 0.7. Some examples of the behavior of this rule are shown in figure 3: both the blue and the red pixels have high cross-correlation, but the blue ones satisfy also the symmetry condition; the red pixels are rejected.

On all the images of our database most of the points calculated in this way are positioned in the *eyes band* (on average 8 out of 10) [Fig.3]. This allows us to select the band easily and with high reliability (100% of hits).

Fig. 3. Template matching results and identified eyes band on both frontal and rotated faces

The features are usually well separated in the *eyes band*, therefore we can isolate them in different sub-images using the vertical projection. More than two distinct peaks, due to shadows, hair and ears, are usually present in the projection; for each of them we take the corresponding gray level piece of image and use a neural network trained by standard back-propagation to recognize the eyes from the other features. We use gray-level images instead of the eye features found by the clustering algorithm since with this second representation the eyes often loose their peculiar shape.

3.1   Eyes Detection by Neural Networks

At this stage the goal is to classify all the possible sub-images extracted from the *eyes band* in two classes: eyes or non-eyes; example of them are shown in figure 4. As we can notice, their dimension are quite different (ranging from 20x20 to 50x50) and images representing the same feature have different appearences making the automatic classification problem more complex.

First, we have to reduce all the sub-images to the same dimension. We thus search the minimal input size which gives to the network enough information to perform a good classification. To this end, we have experimentally compared the performances of networks trained with different input representations. We did 3 kinds of experiments: on down-sampled images ($E1$), on images compressed by the wavelet transform [10] ($E2$), and on the coefficients of the wavelet transform ($E3$).

More precisely, for the experiment $E1$, we down-sample the original images to the size of 4x4, 8x8, 16x16 and 32x32. For the experiments $E2$ and $E3$ we adopt the Haar transform, having tried also the Daubechies and the Symmetric without observing any improvement; we consider respectively the images obtained anti-transforming from the wavelet domain and the wavelet coefficients themselves. In both cases we consider the data at different scales corresponding to images of dimensions 4x4, 8x8, 16x16 and 32x32.

We experimented different architectures for each input size, varying the number of hidden layers and the number of neurons in them. In the following we report only the best trade off between results and network complexity.

We consider network architectures with one hidden layer with different number of neurons depending on the size of the input; the output neurons are always two in order to classify an image as eye or non-eye. More precisely we consider 4 architectures: $A1$ with 16 and 5 neurons, $A2$ with 64 and 10 neurons, $A3$ with 256 and 10 neurons, and $A4$ with 1024 and 30 neurons respectively.

Fig. 4. Some example of input to the neural network: they can be both eyes and non-eyes like hair and ears

Table 1. Number of errors obtained by networks of different architectures Ai on a test set of images reduced by the three methods Ei

	$A1$	$A2$	$A3$	$A4$
$E1$	39	24	23	30
$E2$	34	25	23	29
$E3$	31	22	24	31

The images are assigned to training and test sets in two ways, $S1$ and $S2$. In $S1$ the images are randomly selected, so that eyes of the same subject are allowed to appear in both training and test set. In $S2$, no subject can appear in both training and test set; tests are performed with novel faces. In both cases the training sets are composed of 200 images, and the test set are composed of 300 images; moreover eyes and non-eyes images are present in the same proportion. We notice that, building training and test set according to the rule $S2$, the networks have more difficulties and for these reason we report only results obtained in this condition.

In table 1 we report the number of errors obtained by networks of different architectures Ai on a test set of images reduced by the three methods Ei described above.

We observe that networks $A1$ and $A4$ do not give good results; while $A2$ and $A3$ results are quite similar. We choose the architecture $A2$ which introduces a lower number of free parameters. Moreover, we notice that there is no significant difference in the performances of architectures with the same number of neurons whose input are either down-sampled images, or wavelet compressed images or the wavelet coefficients (with the exception of $A1$ which gives bad result anyway). For this reason we use (8x8) down-sampled images since down-sampling is less computationally expensive.

Integrating the classification procedure in the face image processing, and applying it to the 130 face images, we obtained that 15 images had at least a misclassification. More precisely in 12 of them only 1 error has been done, in the other 3 cases 2 errors have been done which do not compensate each other. We can only detect an error if we detect 0, 1, or 3 eyes per face-image. When the error is catched further processings are necessary (see next paragraph).

3.2   Error Correction Using Distance between Images

We suppose that, among the sub-images extracted from the *eyes band*, the two ones representing the eyes are the most similar. Thus, we have experimentally compared three methods to check the similarity. Two of them are based on distance measures between images ([11], [21]), the other is a matching technique described in [12]. The best result has been obtained with the modified Hausdorff distance [11] defined for binary images and adapted here to gray-scale ones. The distance $D_{mhg}(A, B)$ between two images A and B is described by the expression:

$$D_{mhg}(A, B) = \max \left(\frac{1}{N_a G} \sum_{a \in A} d_{p,i}(a, B), \frac{1}{N_b G} \sum_{b \in B} d_{p,i}(b, A) \right) \qquad (1)$$

where N_a and N_b are the number of pixels in image A and image B respectively, G is the number of the gray levels.

$d_{p,i}$ is the point-to-image distance function defined by the following expression:

$$d_{pi}(a, B) = \min_{b' \in W_b} (d_{p,p}(a, b)) \qquad (2)$$

where W_b is a window centered in the pixel $b \in B$ corresponding to the pixel $a \in A$ and $d_{p,p}(a, b)$ is:

$$d_{p,p}(a, b) = \sqrt{(x_a - x_b)^2 + (y_a - y_b)^2 + (z_a - z_b)^2} \qquad (3)$$

where z_i is the gray level of pixel i, and (x_i, y_i) its position.

On the 15 images on which the neural network fails, the similarity evaluated by $D_{mhg}(A, B)$ corrects all but two errors.

4   Lips and Nose Localization

Once determined the eyes' bounding boxes, we move to the lips and nose localization using both gray level and color information. On the gray-level image a non-linear edge detector is applied [20]. The detector uses local statistical information: a square window centered around a pixel P is divided into two sub-windows of equal size in four different ways [Fig.5]. For each sub-division i the following function D_i (diversity) is evaluated:

$$D_i = \alpha \Delta m - (1 - \alpha) \Delta \sigma$$

where $\Delta m = |m_a - m_b|$, $\Delta \sigma = |\Delta \sigma_a - \Delta \sigma_b|$, m_a , m_b, σ_a , σ_b are respectively the mean and the standard deviation in the regions a and b, and α is a constant $(0 \le \alpha \le 1)$.

The maximum diversity $D(P) = \max_{i=1..4}\{D_i\}$ is assigned to P. We use this method with a 7x7 window size positioned on a pixel out of 3. The lips and the nose are roughly characterized by pixels with high horizontal and vertical diversity respectively.

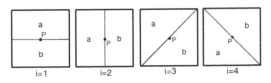

Fig. 5. Supporting windows adopeted to calculate the diversity in position P

Fig. 6. Some subdivision results on frontal, tilted, and rotated faces

To better localize the lips, we combine color information in the Cr plane with the output of the edge detector.

The nose is localized in the remaining portion of the image in the region where the horizontal diversity is different from 0.

We have thus identified four sub-images [Fig.6]. Given the sub-images, the fiducial points are detected with high accuracy on frontal faces [9]. Further improvements are required for rotated faces.

5   Results and Discussion

The method described has been experimented on 130 color images of very different scales acquired in different illumination conditions. They represent either frontal or rotated faces of Caucasian women and men. We asked to the people to have a neutral expression keeping the mouth closed and the eyes opened. We have not dealt with the case of men with beard.

The proposed method localizes the sub-images representing the features of interest with high confidence on both frontal and rotated images: on our database it fails on two images only.

A final consideration has to be done about the program running time. The algorithm has been developed in IDL, an interpreted language; its running time, on a Pentium III, 800MHz, 256Mb of RAM is, on average, of 5 seconds. More precisely, if the network manages to determine which are the two eyes subimages, the algorithm takes 4 seconds; on the contrary, if it is necessary to process the distance measures, the running time is increased of 0.7 seconds for each comparison. We observe that most of the computational time is due to the exacution of the clustering algorithm. The time can be certainly reduced developing the algorithm in a compiled language and optimizing the code.

References

[1] J. Ahlberg. A system for face localization and facial feature extraction. *Proceedings Siggraph 98*, 1999. 124

[2] M. A. Arbib and T. Uchiyama. Color image segmentation using competitive learning. *IEEE Transactions on pattern analysis and machine intelligence*, 16:1197–1206, 1994. 125

[3] R. Brunelli and T. Poggio. Face recognition: Features versus templates. *IEEE Transactions PAMI*, 15(10):1042–1062, 1993. 124

[4] P. Fua. Regularized bundle-adjustment to model heads from image sequences without calibration data. *Int. J. Computer Vision*, 2(38):153–171, 2000. 124

[5] R. Herpers and G. Sommer. An attentive processing strategy for the analysis of facial features. In Wechsler et al. [15], pages 457–468. 124

[6] R. Hsu and A. K. Jain. Face modeling for recognition. *Proceedings IEEE International Conference Image Processing*, pages 693–696, 2001. 124

[7] J. Huang, C. Liu, and H. Wechsler. Eye detection and face recognition using evolutionary computation. In Wechsler et al. [15]. 124

[8] T. Kawaguchi, D. Hidaka, and M. Rizon. Detection of eyes from human faces by hough transform and separability filter. *Proceedings ICIP, Vancouver*, 2000. 124

[9] R. Lanzarotti, N. A. Borghese, and P. Campadelli. Automatic features detection for overlapping face images on their 3d range models. *Proceedings ICIAP, Palermo*, 2001. 124, 130

[10] Stéphane Mallat. *A wavelet tour of signal processing*. Academic Press, 1999. 127

[11] M. P.Dubuisson and A. K.Jain. A modified hausdorff distance for object matching. *Proc. of 12th Int. Conf. Pattern Recognition (Jerusalem)*, 1994. 128

[12] F. Odone, E. Trucco, and A. Verri. A flexible algorithm for image matching. *Proceedings of the 11th International Conference on Image Analysis and Processing, ICIAP2001*, pages 290–295, 2001. 128

[13] M. Pardàs and M. Losada. Facial parameter extraction system based on active contours. *Proceedings ICIP, Thessaloniki*, pages 1058–1061, 2001. 124

[14] F. Pighin, J. Hecker, D. Lischinski, R. Szeliski, and D. H. Salesin. Synthesizing realistic facial expressions from photographs. *Proceedings Siggraph 98*, pages 75–84, 1998. 124

[15] H. Wechsler, P. J. Phillips, V. Bruce, F. Fogelman Soulié, and T. S. Huang, editors. *Face recognition*. London, 1998. 131

[16] L. Wiskott, J.Fellous, N. Kruger, and C. von der Malsburg. Face recognition by elastic bunch graph matching. *Intelligent biometric techniques in fingerprints and face recognition*, 1999. 124

[17] J. Cohn Y. Tian, T.Kanade. Recognizing action units for facial expression analysis. *IEEE Transactions on pattern analysis and machine intelligence*, 23(2):97–114, February 2001. 124

[18] L. Yin and A. Basu. Generating realistic facial expressions with wrinkles for model-based coding. *Computer vision and image understanding*, 84:201–240, 2001. 124

[19] A. L. Yuille, P. W. Hallinan, and D. S. Cohen. Feature extraction from faces using deformable templates. *International journal of computer vision*, 8(2):99–111, 1992. 124

[20] P. Zamperoni. Feature extraction. In H. Maitre and J. Zim-Justin, editors, *Progress in feature processing*. 1996. 129

[21] P. Zamperoni. On measures of dissimilarity between arbitrary gray-scale images. *International journal of shape modelling*, 2:189–213, 1996. 128

A Two Stage Neural Architecture for Segmentation and Superquadrics Recovery from Range Data

Antonio Chella and Roberto Pirrone

DINFO - University of Palermo and CERE-CNR
Viale delle Scienze, 90128, Palermo, Italy
{chella,pirrone}@unipa.it

Abstract. A novel, two stage, neural architecture for the segmentation of range data and their modeling with undeformed superquadrics is presented. The system is composed by two distinct neural networks: a SOM is used to perform data segmentation, and, for each segment, a multi-layer feed-forward network performs model estimation.

Keywords: SOM, Range data segmentation.

1 Introduction

The framework of the present work is the development of the vision system for an autonomous robot which is able to recognize, grasp, and manipulate the objects located in its operating environment. This step is a crucial part of the whole robot design: vision processes has to be at the same time fast, robust and accurate to guarantee the correct perception of the essential elements that are present in the operating environment. Moreover, the kind of images processed from the visual component of the robot, and the features that can be extracted from them, affect the other sensors equipment, the shape and, to some extent, the mission abilities of the robot itself.

Several approaches to segmentation and modeling of range data have been proposed in literature: all of them are based on iterative procedures to fit the model to data [9]. In general, these approaches address also segmentation of complex objects [4] [8]. In this work, a neural architecture is presented which performs segmentation of a range data set and estimates an undeformed superquadric model for each retrieved part of the scene. The architecture consists in two neural networks: a Self-Organizing Map (SOM) [3] to perform data segmentation, and a multi-layer feed-forward network trained with backpropagation which is devoted to model estimation. The SOM network is used to encode the data distribution with a low number of units which, in turn, are used for clustering. The feed-forward network for model estimation has been designed with a suitable topology and units' activation functions in order to compute the inside-outside superquadric function, starting from the range points. Connections between units, and units' activation functions are chosen to obtain

M. Marinaro and R. Tagliaferri (Eds.): WIRN VIETRI 2002, LNCS 2486, pp. 132–139, 2002.

a redundant coding of the superquadric parameters vector, starting from the weights arrangement in the trained network.

2 Description of the Architecture

The architecture presented in this work is designed to segment a range data set, and to model each part using the inside-outside function of a generic undeformed superquadric. The neural approach to this task has several advantages. First of all, both the phases of the process are fast. The SOM training algorithm preserves the topology of the data set in the arrangement of its units, so it represents a straightforward approach to perform a quick subsampling of the range points. Segments emerge as simply connected regions, and their borders are located near concavities. About the model estimation network, the error function used in backpropagation training is more simpler than the classical error functions proposed in model fitting literature, so its first and second derivatives are easier to compute.

2.1 Segmentation

The segmentation consists of a data subsampling process, clustering, and labeling phase. A SOM is trained on the whole data set, and the units in the map are arranged to follow the objects surfaces, due to the topology preserving property of this training algorithm. The units in the map tend to move towards the most convex surfaces of the data set, and are more sparse near concave regions. On the other side, neighborhood connections cause the activation of each unit to be influenced by closer ones, so the units tend to displace themselves as a sheet wrapping the data. Units' codebooks are then tuned using the well known neural gas algorithm [2]. In this way they are displaced exactly along the data surface, and a clear separation between them is obtained in those regions that correspond to occluding boundaries or concavities.

Clustering is performed using the k-means algorithm with a variable number of clusters. In this phase, a measure of the global quantization error e_{Qk} is computed for each run of the algorithm, and the right number of clusters is selected according to the rule:

$$c : e_{Qc} = \min_k(e_{Qk})$$

The quantization error is minimized by the same number of clusters as the convex blobs that are present in the data set because the neural gas trained SOM tends to group the units in these regions.

In the labeling phase each data point is assigned to the cluster that includes its best matching unit as results from the SOM training algorithm. The use of a SOM is needed not only to reduce the number of points to be clustered, but also to keep memory of the data points belonging to the sample neighborhood. In fig. 1 a segmentation example is reported for a real range data set.

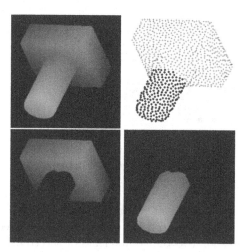

Fig. 1. From top to bottom: original data set; clustering after SOM training and neural gas vector quantization; the resulting segments

2.2   Model Estimation

Superquadrics [1] are powerful geometric primitives, widely used in computer vision to model real objects. The model of a superquadric uses two form factors to undergo simple global variations from squared shapes to rounded, and pinched ones. Moreover, global deformation operators, like tapering or bending, have been defined, leading to a family of very expressive geometrical forms.

In the case of an undeformed superquadric in a generic pose, a parameters vector made by 11 components is needed to model the shape: two form factors, three center coordinates, three axes sizes, and three pose angles (usually the Euler angles). The inside-outside equation of the primitive is defined by:

$$f(X, Y, Z) = \left[\left(\frac{X}{a_1} \right)^{\frac{2}{\varepsilon_2}} + \left(\frac{Y}{a_2} \right)^{\frac{2}{\varepsilon_2}} \right]^{\frac{\varepsilon_2}{\varepsilon_1}} + \left(\frac{Z}{a_3} \right)^{\frac{2}{\varepsilon_1}} = 1 \qquad (1)$$

where the generic point $\mathbf{X} = (X, Y, Z)$ is obtained by rotation and translation of the original data point $\mathbf{x} = (x, y, z)$, in order to refer it to the superquadric coordinate system. The direct transformation matrix to rotate and translate a point $\mathbf{X}$ expressed in the superquadric reference system to the point $\mathbf{x}$, in the world reference system, is:

$$\mathbf{x} = \mathbf{R}\mathbf{X} + \mathbf{t}$$

From the previous formula, the inverse transformation is:

$$\mathbf{X} = \mathbf{R}'\mathbf{x} + \mathbf{b} \, , \mathbf{b} = -\mathbf{R}'\mathbf{t} \qquad (2)$$

Starting from this equation the design of the network is reported in fig. 2. In this figure, the input nodes represent the original point $\mathbf{x}$, while the first layer

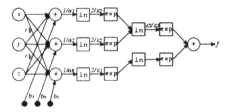

Fig. 2. Layout of the network

consists of full connected linear units which compute the $\mathbf{X}$ vector. The weights are the r'_{ij} components of the rotation matrix reported in equation (2), while the three biases correspond to the components of the translation vector in the same equation.

Successive hidden layers are made by interleaved logarithmic and exponential units. This choice derives form the need to have the form exponents as simple terms in a product, in order to treat them as weights of the units' connections. With this consideration in mind, each power in equation (1) has been expressed in the form: $a^x = \exp(x \ln(a))$. Following this approach, in the first $\ln - \exp$ couple of layers the powers of the X, Y, and Z terms in equation (1) are computed, while the second power is performed by the other couple. Finally, the output unit is again a linear one to obtain the sum of all three terms in equation (1). In fig. 2 some connections are unweighted: these weights are all fixed, and they are equal to 1. They will not be updated during the training process.

The network has been trained using backpropagation. The choice of this learning strategy is straightforward due to the multi-layer topology of the network. The classical sum-of-squares (SSE) error function has been used to train the network because it is used in curve fitting problems, but its mathematical form is much simpler with respect to the metrics proposed in superquadrics fitting literature. Weights update has been performed both with the Levenberg-Marquardt algorithm [5], and the Scaled Conjugate Gradient (SCG) [6] approach. These two methods are faster and more efficient than the classical gradient descent algorithm, and they are more suited to face the estimation of a high dimension non-linear model like superquadrics. In section 3 a detailed comparison of the two techniques will be presented.

The parameters vector is computed from the weights as follows. Considering the direct rotation matrix $\mathbf{R} = [R_{ij}]$, the approach proposed by Paul [7] can be adopted to derive the Euler angles (ϕ, θ, ψ):

$$\phi = \arctan\left(-\frac{R_{13}}{R_{23}}\right)$$
$$\theta = \arctan\left(\frac{sin(\phi) - R_{23}\cos(\phi)}{R_{33}}\right) \qquad (3)$$
$$\psi = \arctan\left(-\frac{R_{22}sin(\phi) + R_{12}\cos(\phi)}{R_{21}sin(\phi) + R_{11}\cos(\phi)}\right)$$

Fig. 3. The final reconstruction for the data set reported in fig. 1

The vector of the center coordinates is derived from the biases values:

$$\mathbf{t} = -\mathbf{Rb} \qquad (4)$$

The axes lengths can be obtained as:

$$a_k = \frac{1}{w_{2k,3k}} \ , \ k = 1, 2, 3 \qquad (5)$$

where $w_{ij,i+1k}$ is the weight of the connection between unit j of the i-th layer and unit k of the $i+1$-th layer, assuming that the input layer is labeled as layer 1. Using the previous notation, the form factors are computed from the following system of equations:

$$\begin{cases} \frac{2}{\varepsilon_2} = \frac{1}{2}(w_{31,41} + w_{32,42}) \\ \frac{2}{\varepsilon_1} = w_{33,43} \\ \frac{\varepsilon_2}{\varepsilon_1} = w_{51,61} \end{cases} \qquad (6)$$

In fig. 3 a reconstruction example is reported for the data set displayed in fig. 1.

3   Experimental Setup

Experiments have been performed on a Pentium III 1GHz equipped with 256MB RAM, and running under MS Windows ME. The Stuttgart Neural Network Simulator (SNNS) v4.2 has been used to develop and train the modl estimation network. The ln activation function, and the Levenberg-Marquardt learning function have been developed separately, using the SNNS API to compile them on the simulator kernel. The MATLAB SOM-Toolbox v.2.0 has been used to perform data segmentation.

Training samples have been selected from real range data available from the SEGMENTOR package developed by Solina and his colleagues [4]. Also Shape From Shading images have been employed, which have been obtained using the approach proposed by Tsai [10].

In current implementation, the SOM software has been let free to determine the number m of units, using the built-in heuristic formula $m = 5\sqrt{n}$, where n is the number of data points. The units have been initialized linearly along the directions of the data eigenvectors, and the map sides have been computed

Table 1. SSE values for the two learning approaches, varying the training epochs

		LeMa - Epochs					SCG - Epochs			
		1	*5*	*10*	*50*	*100*	*1*	*5*	*10*	*50*	*100*
RAN	*1*	2.784	0.319	0.100	0.009	0.008	2.829	0.309	0.995	0.008	0.007
	2	1.975	0.433	0.099	0.010	0.007	2.005	0.652	0.089	0.009	0.005
	3	2.589	0.695	0.057	0.007	0.006	2.933	0.955	0.098	0.008	0.007
	4	3.128	0.925	0.088	0.009	0.003	3.002	0.983	0.099	0.008	0.004
SFS	*1*	4.782	1.321	0.973	0.099	0.008	4.926	1.549	0.852	0.078	0.009
	2	3.821	1.003	0.782	0.058	0.007	3.027	1.297	0.925	0.049	0.008
	3	4.021	0.994	0.513	0.034	0.006	3.892	1.045	0.460	0.025	0.004

from the ratio of the two main eigenvalues. The map has a hexagonal lattice, and has been trained using the batch version of the Kohonen algorithm, with a gaussian neighborhood function. Performances are very fast, despite the fact that the algorithm is run through the MATLAB kernel. For the data reported in fig. 1 the training took about 8 secs. for rough training and 16 secs. for fine training. Each trained SOM has been tuned using 50 epochs neural gas vector quantization. Finally, the k-means algorithm has been run varying the clusters number from 2 to 5 as there were no data sets with more than 4 connected regions.

The experiments with the model estimation network were devoted mainly to determine the optimal number of learning epochs, and to select the best learning function between the SCG and the Levenberg-Marquardt (LeMa) algorithms. Reported results refer to a couple of images, one for each data type.

The network has been trained on each segment of the two images, varying the number of learning epochs, and measuring the SSE value, in order to compare performances of the two learning functions. After some trials the learning rate has been fixed to 0.5 for all the experiments. The weights have been initialized using the approach proposed by Solina [9] to perform the initial estimation of the superquadric parameters. Using the inverse procedure of the one reported in eqs (3),(4),(5),(6) it is possible to obtain the values of the weights. In table 1 are reported the SSE values obtained for each segment, varying the number of learning epochs.

Table 1 clearly shows that the two learning strategies have almost the same performance. This is a not surprising result, due to the simple mathematical

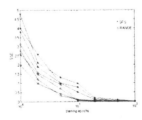

Fig. 4. Graph of the SSE vs the learning epochs, both for the range and SFS data set

form of the sum-of-squares error function. Moreover, one may argue that this result derives from an analogous finding, obtained when fitting the model to range data with classical error metrics.

Using the results reported in table 1, a precise choice on the number of learning epochs have been made. From the graph reported in fig. 4 it can be noted that the SSE value becomes negligible after 20 learning epochs, so this value has been selected to be used in the network standard operating mode.

It can be noted that the SFS image is fitted with a higher error value. This is due to the higher degree of noise in this kind of data, despite the initial smoothing, and to their original scaling along the depth dimension. Figures 5 and 6 show the recovered model for both the data sets.

The model for SFS data is not so preceptually good as the other one, but it can be noted that the same model, with a front view (the third picture in fig. 6) is very similar to the original image. This is due to the fact that SFS methods provide a relative depth estimation, and they cannot be assumed as true 3D data.

4   Conclusions

Such a system can be a useful vision tool for a manipulator robot enabling it to create an internal (symbolic) representation of the spatial structure of the objects in its operating environment. This result can be achieved, despite the possible reconstruction errors due to the eventual coarse splitting of the input image into regions of interest. In the case of fine and precise movements, the

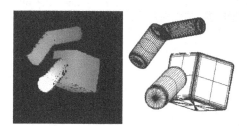

Fig. 5. Recovered model for the range data set

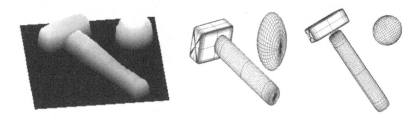

Fig. 6. Recovered model for the SFS data set

process can be iterated with higher resolution only in those regions where the cognitive module of the robot architecture will focus its attention, thus saving a large amount of computational time.

References

[1] Barr, A. H.: Superquadrics and Angle-preserving Transformations. IEEE Computer Graphics and Applications, 1:11–23, 1981. 134

[2] Fritzke, B.: Growing Cell Structures — A Self-Organizing Network for Unsupervised and Supervised Learning. Neural Networks, 7(9):1441–1460, 1994. 133

[3] Kohonen, T.: The Self–Organizing Map. Proceedings of the IEEE, 78(9):1464–1480, September 1990. 132

[4] Leonardis, A., Jaklic, A. and Solina, F.: Superquadrics for Segmenting and Modeling Range Data. IEEE Trans. on Pattern Analysis and Machine Intelligence, 19(11):1289–1295, 1997. 132, 136

[5] Marquardt, D. W.: An algorithm for least-squares estimation of non-linear parameters. Journal of the Society of Industrial and Applied Mathematics, 11(2):431–441, 1963. 135

[6] Møller, M.: A scaled conjugate gradient algorithm for fast supervised learning. Neural Networks, 6(4):525–533, 1993. 135

[7] Paul, R.: Robot Manipulators. MIT Press, Cambridge, MA, 1981. 135

[8] Pirrone, R.: Part based Segmentation and Modeling of Range Data by Moving Target. Journal of Intelligent Systems, 11(4):217–247, 2001. 132

[9] Solina, F. and Bajcsy, R.: Recovery of parametric models from range images: The case for superquadrics with global deformations. IEEE Trans. on Pattern Analysis and Machine Intelligence, 12(2):131–147, 1990. 132, 137

[10] Zhang, R., Tsai, P.-S., Cryer, J. E. and Shah, M.: Analysis of shape from shading techniques. In Proc. of international Conference on Computer Vision Pattern Recognition CVPR'94, 377–384, Seattle, Whashington, 1994. 136

Automatic Discrimination of Earthquakes and False Events in Seismological Recording for Volcanic Monitoring

E. C. Ezin[1,2], Flora Giudicepietro[3], Simona Petrosino[3],
S. Scarpetta[4], and A. Vanacore[1]

[1] International Institute for Advanced Scientific Studies
Via G. Pellegrino 19, 84019 Vietri Sul Mare, SA, Italy
Tel: +39 089 761167   Fax: +39 089 761189
[2] Institut de Mathématiques et de Sciences Physiques
BP 613 Porto-Novo, Bénin
Tel: +229 22 24 55   Fax: +229 22 24 55
[3] Osservatorio Vesuviano INGV, Napoli, Italy
[4] Dipartimento di Fisica "E.R.Caianiello", Universita di Salerno
Baronissi (SA) Italy, INFM Sez. di Salerno, Italy

Abstract. This paper reports on the classification of earthquakes and
false events (thunders, quarry blasts and man-made undersea explosions)
recorded by four seismic stations in the Vesuvius area in Naples, Italy.
For each station we set up a specialized neural classifier, able to discriminate the two classes of events recordered by that station. Feature
extraction is done using both the linear predictor coding technique and
the waveform features of the signals. The use of properly normalized
waveform features as input for the MLP network allows the network to
better generalize compared to our previous strategy applied to a similar
problem [2]. To train the MLP network we compare the performance of
the quasi-Newton algorithm and the scaled conjugate gradient method.
On one hand, we improve the strategy used in [2] and on the other hand
we show that it is not specific to the discrimination task [2] but has
a larger range of applicability.

Keywords: MLP, Seismic data.

1 Introduction

The Vesuvius Observatory at Naples, Italy founded in 1841, carries on its research and monitoring activity to improve the knowledge about the Neapolitan
volcanoes and their pre-eruptive activity with the aim of predicting an eventual
eruption. In the Vesuvius area both earthquakes and false events, like artificial
explosions and natural thunders, are recorded by the permanent seismic monitoring network, composed of ten analogic stations. Nine of them are deployed
on the volcanic edifice whereas one seismic station is located at Nola, a city at
about 15 Km from the crater axis. The seismic signals recorded by the remote

M. Marinaro and R. Tagliaferri (Eds.): WIRN VIETRI 2002, LNCS 2486, pp. 140–145, 2002.
© Springer-Verlag Berlin Heidelberg 2002

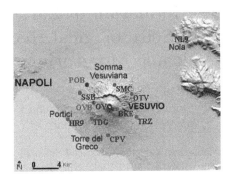

Fig. 1. Seismic monitoring network at Mt. Vesuvius

stations are frequency modulated and transmitted via radio to the Vesuvius Observatory Monitoring Center [6]. The collected analogic signals are sampled at 100 Hz, then stored on Personal Computers and made available for analyses. The Figure 1 shows the seismic monitoring network at Mt. Vesuvius.

The seismological discrimination methods are very important for the developement of the automatic processing systems, for which the reliability of the event detections is critical. Usually this functionality is carried out by procedures which associate the detected picking into the seismic events. These procedures are often based on the consistency of arrival time at the different stations with a single source. For small seismic networks, these procedures can fail and produce false events detection. Moreover local artificial and natural sources, such as thunders, man-made explosion in quarries and undersea, can generate signals similar to those produced by local earthquakes and can be detected and located as natural events. In these cases additional signal analysis can be performed to reduce the probability of false event detections. This problem can be successfully approached by using methods shown here.

2   Seismic Data

The seismic signals recorded by the remote stations are transmitted to the Vesuvius Observatory Monitoring Center. Then, the analogic signals are sampled at 100 Hz, and processed by the acquisition system. For each event, a recording of 24 seconds is taken. Since the sampling frequency is 100 Hz, each event is composed of 2400 points. For each station data have been classified in two classes by experts:

- **CPV station:** This station is located on the coast of the Gulf of Naples. It records earthquake signals and mainly man-made explosions caused by fisherman under the sea. The available dataset contains 117 earthquake events and 147 explosion events recordings.

Table 1. Training data and testing data used on each station

Station	Training data	Testing data	Total
NOLA	139	84	223
CPV	165	99	264
TRZ	129	78	207
BKE	71	43	114

- **NL9 station:** This station, located at Nola, records seismic signals like earthquakes and man-made explosions in quarries. The dataset has 114 earthquake events and 109 quarry explosion events recordings.

- **TRZ station:** This station records signal of earthquakes and mainly man-made explosions in quarries. The dataset has 106 earthquake events and 101 explosions recordings.

- **BKE station:** This station is located up on the Vesuvius, close to the crater. It records mainly earthquake events and natural false events like thunders. The dataset has 72 earthquake events and 42 thunder events recordings.

The 5/8 of the data recorded by each station, is used for the training set and the remaining for the testing set. Table 1 gives a description about the training and the testing set available for each of the four stations.

3   Feature Extraction in the Seismic Data

Feature extraction stage is critical for the success of a distrimination task. Many different techniques or algorithms have been proposed in literature for feature extraction phase (such as principal component analysis [1], linear prediction [3], etc.) for different tasks. We use the linear predictive coding (LPC) to extract spectrogram features and a discretized waveform parametrization to extract information about the amplitude versus time. In LPC technique, each event is modeled as a linear combination of its past values i.e. $s_n = \sum_{k=1}^{M} c_k s_{n-k}$ where c_k are the predictor coefficients, M represents the model order. The choice of the model order is problem dependent. We find that a good tradeoff is reached with $M = 10$. We extract 10 coefficients on each of the 15 Hanning window of 2.56 seconds of the signal overlapped with 1.28 second. Even though LPC encodes efficiently the frequency features of the signal, we would loose much of the information content of the time-domain signal if we would discharge the waveform information (i.e., the shape of the signal in terms of amplitude versus time). Waveform is usually used by experts when they classify signals empirically. Therefore, differently from the work done in [2], we take as input to the MLP network also the discretized waveform parametrization that we compute taking for each window of one second duration the value $s_{max} - s_{min}$, properly normalized (s_{max} (respectively s_{min}) is the maximum (respectively the minimum) that the signal assumes on each window). In such a way, we extract a vector of 24 components to encode

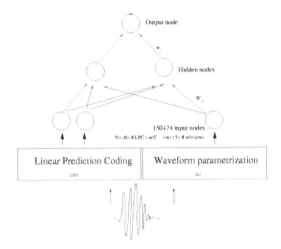

Fig. 2. Structure of the neural discriminator system

the waveform features. That leads to an input vector of 150+24 components for each signal (instead of 2400 values).

4 MLP as Classifier

A multilayer perceptron network is used to discriminate the two events. Each MLP network is trained over the dataset specific to one station, for the discrimination of the two classes specific to that station. The network architecture is shown in the Figure 2. Its configuration is the following: 174 input nodes, 1 output node, and 6 hidden nodes. The error goal is fixed to 0.001 whereas the maximum number of iterations is 80 for all the experiments carried out.

The choice of the learning algorithm is described in the following.

4.1 Learning Algorithms

Supervised learning problems have the drawbacks to require large memory and time-consuming calculations of the energy and the gradient. Many algorithms used in neural network theory involve taking a sequence of steps through weight space. With simple gradient descent, the direction of each step is given by the local negative gradient of the error function and the step size is determined by an arbitrary learning rate. A better procedure would be to exploit information from the second derivatives of the error function. This is the so called *second order* learning algorithm and it forms the basis idea for several algorithms which are considerably more powerful than the gradient descent. In this work, instead of the usual gradient descent, we use two powerful methods: the quasi-Newton algorithm and the scaled gradient descent method. We found that both gives very good performance, while the scaled conjugate gradient algorithm is faster than the quasi-newton method.

– **Quasi-Newton Algorithm:** Steepest descent suffers from a bad reputation with researchers in optimization. Considering the characteristics of supervised learning problems, the quasi-Newton method is an alternative good candidate and perform very efficiently on different problems. Let's review briefly this algorithm. Consider the vectors

$$g_n = \nabla E(w_n) \qquad p_n = w_n - w_{n-1} \qquad y_n = g_n - g_{n-1},$$

where ∇ represents the gradient operator, E is the error function, and w_n the weights of the net. The one-dimensional search direction for the n-th iteration is a modification of the gradient g_n as follows:

$$d_n = -g_n + A_n p_n + B_n y_n,$$

where the coefficients A_n and B_n are the combination of scalar products and are given by $A_n = -\left(1 + \frac{y_n \cdot y_n}{p_n \cdot y_n}\right) + \frac{p_n \cdot g_n}{p_n \cdot y_n}$ and $B_n = \frac{p_n \cdot g_n}{p_n \cdot y_n}$.
Every K steps (K being the number of weights in the network), the search is restarted in the direction of the negative gradient. More description about the algorithm can be found in [1, 7]. A potential disadvantage of the quasi-Newton method is that it requires a lot of memory for networks with few thousand weights [1].

– **Scaled Conjugate Gradient Algorithm:** The basic idea of the scaled conjugate gradient algorithm introduced by Moller [4], is to combine the *model-trust region* approach used in the Levenberg-Marquardt algorithm [1] with the conjugate gradient approach [5]. This algorithm is fast and uses small amount of storage since it only needs the calculation and storage of the second derivative of each iteration.

Table 2. MLP network performance (percentage of correct classification on the test set) using the scaled conjugate gradient descent algorithm and the quasi-Newton method for the classification of the two events over the data of four observation stations

Station	Algorithm	Computational time	Performance	Error
CPV	Conjugate GD	2.20 sec	98.98 %	1.12 %
	Quasi-Newton	69.37 sec	98.98 %	1.12 %
TRZ	Conjugate GD	2.04 sec	96.15 %	3.85 %
	Quasi-Newton	67.45 sec	96.15 %	3.85 %
NOLA	Conjugate GD	2.19 sec	100 %	0.00 %
	Quasi-Newton	67.8 sec	100 %	0.00 %
BKE	Conjugate GD	1.49 sec	100 %	0.00 %
	Quasi-Newton	67.01 sec	100 %	0.00 %

5 Performance Evaluation

We trained the MLP network using the two different algorithms previously described. As the results showed in the Table 2, the computational time required with the scaled conjugate gradient algorithm is significantly less than the one required with the quasi-Newton method. In both cases the percentage of correct classification on the test set is very high, for all the four stations. For comparison, we also compute the best results obtained on CPV data using both LPC coefficients alone as input to the network without the waveform, and we get a performance of 93 %. This means that the inputs related to the waveform features play an important role to obtain very good performance.

6 Concluding Remarks

Automatic classification of the false (natural and artificial) events and earthquakes can be done with a multilayer perceptron trained with the scaled conjugate gradient descent that is found to be a fast algorithm. This is achieved thanks to the combination of the normalized waveform parametrization and LPC algorithm that extracts the main features of the events under examination. The use of waveform information and the conjugate scaled gradient algorithm, introduced here, is useful for better performance compared to the results obtained with our previous work on a similar task. Notably, this strategy gives very good results both for artificial false events (i.e., at CPV, TRZ, NOLA) and for natural false events (i.e., at BKE). In conclusion of this work, we improve and validate on different kinds of data the strategy introduced previously. Each trained neural network will be inserted in the automatic processing in order to reduce the probability of false event detections and improve the reliability of the automatic monitoring system.

References

[1] Bishop C., *Neural Networks for Pattern Recognition*, Oxford Press, 1995. 142, 144
[2] Esposito A., Falanga M., Funaro M., Marinaro M., Scarpetta S., *Signal Classification using Neural Networks*, in Proceedings of WIRN'01, Vietri, pp. 187–1192, May 17-19, 2001. 140, 142
[3] Makhoul J., *Linear Prediction: A Tutorial Review*, in Proceedings of the IEEE, vol. 63, N°4, 1975. 142
[4] Moller M., *A Scaled Conjugate Gradient Algorithm for Fast Supervised Learning*, in Neural Networks 6(4), pp. 525-533. 144
[5] Shewchuk J. R., *An Introduction to the Conjugate Gradient Method without the Agonizing Pain* ftp://warp.cs.cmu.edu under the name quake-papers/painless-conjugate-gradient.ps. 144
[6] For more information look at the web site: http://www.ov.ingv.it. 141
[7] Numerical Recipes in C ISBN 0-521-43108-5, Cambridge University Press, 1988-1992. 144

A Comparison of Signal Compression Methods by Sparse Solution of Linear Systems

Davide Mattera[1], Francesco Palmieri[2], and Michele Di Monte[1]

[1] Dipartimento di Ingegneria Elettronica e delle Telecomunicazioni
Università degli Studi di Napoli Federico II
Via Claudio, 21, 80125, Napoli, Italy
mattera@unina.it

[2] Dipartimento di Ingegneria dell'Informazione
Seconda Universitá degli Studi di Napoli
Via Roma, 29 80131, Aversa, Italy
frapalmi@unina.it

Abstract. This paper deals with the problem of signal compression by linearly expanding the signal to be compressed along the elements of an overcomplete dictionary. The compression is obtained by selecting a few elements of the dictionary for the expansion. Therefore, signal description is realized by specifying the selected elements of the dictionary as well as their coefficients in the linear expansion. A crucial issue in this approach is the algorithm for selecting, in correspondence of each realization of the signal, the elements of the dictionary to be used for the expansion. In this paper we consider different possible algorithms for basis selection and compare their performances in a practical case of speech signal.

Keywords: Signal compression, sparse solution of linear system.

1 Introduction

Suppose we are given an information source which gives us realizations $\mathbf{s}$ of an ℓ-dimensional random vector and we want to represent these realizations in the most compressed way (with the ability of trading the amount of compression with the relative loss). Let us suppose that we have developed a "dictionary", i.e. M vectors $\boldsymbol{\Psi}_1, \ldots, \boldsymbol{\Psi}_M$ of dimension ℓ with $M >> \ell$ and we wish to represent a generic realization $\mathbf{s}$ of the source in the following way:

$$\mathbf{s} = u_1 \boldsymbol{\Psi}_1 + u_2 \boldsymbol{\Psi}_2 + \ldots + u_M \boldsymbol{\Psi}_M = \mathbf{Tu}, \tag{1}$$

with $\mathbf{T} \triangleq [\boldsymbol{\Psi}_1, \boldsymbol{\Psi}_2, \ldots, \boldsymbol{\Psi}_M]$. If the number of components of $\mathbf{u}$ different from zero is much smaller than ℓ we obtain a compression of the information contained in the vector $\mathbf{s}$, i.e., we can transmit or store simply the components of $\mathbf{u}$ different from zero rather than the ℓ components of $\mathbf{s}$. More specifically, a compression is obtained if we can represent $\mathbf{u}$ by using a number of bits smaller than the number

M. Marinaro and R. Tagliaferri (Eds.): WIRN VIETRI 2002, LNCS 2486, pp. 146–151, 2002.

needed to represent **s** with the same accuracy; note that we need to represent the coefficients as well as the information needed to specify the nonnull components. Therefore, we need to obtain a "sparse solution" (i.e., the solution **u** should have a small number of nonnull components) of

$$\mathbf{Tu} = \mathbf{s}. \tag{2}$$

In Section 2 we consider different methods for the sparse solution of a linear system and in Section 3 we compare their performances on a well-known problem of speech-signal compression in which we do not utilize any *a priori* knowledge about the considered source. In the considered method, in fact, all the *a priori* information about the source has to lie in the adopted dictionary. Consequently, the performance of any sparsification algorithm strongly depends on how much our dictionary is fit to the distribution of the considered source. Research efforts have been dedicated by the signal processing community to the problems of determining "good" dictionaries for specific sources and of learning the dictionary from a certain number of source observations [1].

2   Algorithms for Sparse Solution of a Linear System

Linear system (2) generally admits an infinity of solutions. We are interested, however, in obtaining a solution that is both accurate and sparse, i.e. an accurate solution such that a large part of its components are zero. This is motivated, as explained above, by the need for transmitting or storing the solution. Note that sparsity and accuracy constitute conflicting requirements; therefore, the minimum-square-norm solution is not sparse but one looks for a sparse vector which is sufficiently "close" to the solution in some sense. In practice, the following three settings of the problem are of interest: 1) find the most accurate solution such that the number of its nonzero components is smaller than a fixed value; 2) find the sparsest solution within a given accuracy requirement; 3) minimize a cost function that weights both the accuracy and the sparsity of the solution in some fashion. Unfortunately, an exact solution of the problem is NP-hard [2]; brute force solutions of these problems would be time-consuming. Therefore, one can simply try to find a robust sub-optimum algorithm for obtaining an approximate solution in a reasonable time. In the following, we consider some of the main techniques for obtaining a sub-optimal solution of the sparsity problem described above.

2.1   FOCUSS

The FOCal Undetermined System Solver (FOCUSS) [3] tries to solve the problem in the second setting considered above (i.e., find the sparsest solution within a given accuracy requirement); the considered optimization problem becomes

$$\begin{cases} \min_{\mathbf{u}} E(\mathbf{u}) \\[2mm] \mathbf{Tu} = \mathbf{s} \\[2mm] E(\mathbf{u}) \triangleq \sum_{i=1}^{M} |u_i|^p \end{cases} \qquad (3)$$

The adoption of the cost function (3) is motivated by the fact that the number of the nonnull components of the vector $\mathbf{u}$ can be written as $\sum_{i=1}^{M} \theta(|u_i|)$ where $\theta(x)$ is null when $x = 0$ and is equal to one when $x > 0$. Consequently, the NP-hard original problem has been replaced by a new one in that the function $\theta(x)$ is approximated as x^p. In Fig. 1 we report the shape of x^p for different values of p; note how much it is close to the ideal function $\theta(x)$ for smaller values of p. Note also that the optimization problem (3) is not convex (and, hence, suffer of the presence of many local minima) for $p < 1$.

The optimization problem is solved by determining the saddle point of the Lagrangian function

$$\begin{cases} \mathbf{G}(\mathbf{u}) + \mathbf{T}^T \lambda = \mathbf{0} \\[2mm] \mathbf{Tu} = \mathbf{s} \end{cases} \qquad (4)$$

where $\mathbf{G}(\mathbf{u})$, defined as the gradient of $E(\mathbf{u})$, is easily written as $|p|\Pi(\mathbf{u})\mathbf{u}$ with $\Pi(\mathbf{u}) \triangleq \mathrm{diag}(|\mathbf{u}|^{p-2})$. It is easy to verify that

$$\mathbf{u} = \Pi^{-1}(\mathbf{u})\mathbf{T}^T (\mathbf{T}\Pi^{-1}(\mathbf{u})\mathbf{T}^T)^{-1}\mathbf{s} \triangleq \mathbf{H}(\mathbf{u}) \qquad (5)$$

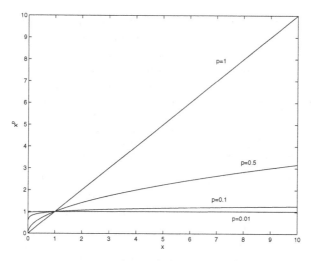

Fig. 1. The behavior of x^p for $x \in (0, 10)$

is the solution of (4). Such an equation is, then, solved by means of the recursion

$$\mathbf{u}_{k+1} = \mathbf{H}(\mathbf{u}_k). \tag{6}$$

By defining $\mathbf{W}_k = (\varPi(\mathbf{u}_k))^{-0.5}$, such a recursion can be written as

$$\mathbf{u}_{k+1} = \mathbf{W}_k\mathbf{W}_k\mathbf{T}^T(\mathbf{TW}_k\mathbf{W}_k\mathbf{T}^T)^{-1}\mathbf{s} = \mathbf{W}_k\mathbf{q}_k, \tag{7}$$

where $\mathbf{q}_k$ represents the minimum-square-norm solution of the linear system

$$(\mathbf{TW}_k)q_k = \mathbf{s}. \tag{8}$$

The minimum-square-norm solution of the system $\mathbf{Tu} = \mathbf{s}$. is utilized as starting point $\mathbf{u}_0$.

2.2 Interior Point Method (IPM)

Such an algorithm still refers to (3) and utilizes the expression

$$E(\mathbf{u}) = \mathbf{u}^T\mathbf{M}(\mathbf{u})\mathbf{u} \tag{9}$$

with

$$\mathbf{M}(\mathbf{u}) \overset{\triangle}{=} \mathrm{diag}(|\mathbf{u}|^{p-2}). \tag{10}$$

At each step, the value $\mathbf{u}_{k+1}$ is obtained by solving a quadratic problem relative to the matrix $\mathbf{M}(\mathbf{u}_k)$. At each step the quadratic problem with linear constraint is solved by means of a primal-dual infeasible interior point algorithm in a modified version due to [4].

2.3 Basis Pursuit (BP)

Such an algorithm [5] considers once again problem (3) for the special case of $p = 1$. The adoption of a value of p so far from zero is justified by the fact that, in such a case, (3) becomes a convex problem and can, therefore, be solved more easily. In fact, it can be re-written as a standard constrained linear problem with $2M$ variables by defining, in correspondence of each component of $\mathbf{u}$, two positive variables, one corresponding to the positive sign and another corresponding to the negative one.

2.4 Best Orthogonal Bases Selection (BEST)

The overall dictionary is obtained [6] as a collection of orthogonal bases. The signal expansion in each basis is easily accomplished. The best orthogonal basis (i.e., that requiring the minimum number of coefficients) is then used to represent the signal. A particular tree-structure in the set of the bases, which reduces the burden of determining the best basis, is introduced by utilizing the properties of the wavelets. The possibility of representing the signal with a few nonorthogonal elements of the overall dictionary is not exploited by this method.

2.5   Matching Pursuit and Its Variants

In this method each element to be used for the representation is introduced step-by-step in a greedy fashion. The selection is done by including among the selected elements, at each step, the one that mostly reduces the quadratic representation error. Then, in the residue, the component along the selected element is removed. This is the basic Matching Pursuit (MP) [7] algorithm. By subtracting from the current residue its component along the selected element, we re-introduce in the residue some components along the previously selected elements. The order recursive matching pursuit (ORMP) [2] solves this problem by obtaining the residue at each step on the basis of all the selected elements. In practice, this can also be accomplished by removing, at each step, the component along the selected element, not only from the residue, but also from all the other non-selected elements. This, however, increases the burden for large dictionaries. A third variant, called modified matching pursuit (MMP), at each step, simply removes from the residue the component of the selected element which is orthogonal to the previously selected elements, and represents a compromise between the two algorithms.

3   Simulation Results

In this section we test our system by compressing with the above mentioned algorithm a speech signal, sampled at 8000 samples per second and quantized with 8 bit per sample. In our experiments we consider vector dimension $\ell = 64$ and a size of the dictionary $M = 448$. Thus we require 9 bits (for each selected element) for specifying the result of the selection procedure. The number of selected elements has been set to 7. We applied the previously described algorithms to 240 different ℓ-dimensional realizations of the speech source. The utilized wavelet-packet dictionary has been constructed by means of the Coiflet basis with 8 evanishing moments. The coefficients of the linear expansion have been quantized by utilizing 4,6, and 8 bits per coefficient. As performance measure the reconstruction error E, defined as the quadratic norm of the representation error normalized to the number ℓ of its components and averaged over the above mentioned 240 independent trials, has been utilized.

In Fig. 2, in correspondence of several alternative algorithms, the reconstruction error has been reported versus the bit/rate necessary to coefficient transmission. Let us note that 7.8 kbit/s are needed for the specification of the seven selected elements. The results show significant performance advantage of the greedy algorithms based on orthogonal projections with respect to those relative to the cost function (3). The method with the best performance parameter is ORMP while the lighter orthogonal method MMP also outperforms the basis MP. The BOBS method is still better than those based on optimization problem (3), among which the best is given by IPM for which the value $p = 0.5$ has been utilized. This implies better performance of IPM with respect to BP, not reported in Fig. 2. Finally, the FOCUSS algorithm (with $p = 0.0001$), although computationally intensive, does not show performance advantages.

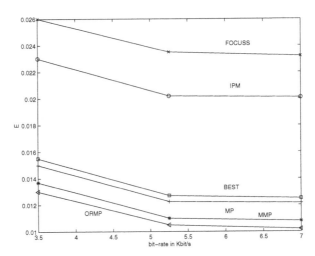

Fig. 2. The performance of different algorithms for sparse solution of a linear system

4   Conclusions

The paper deals with the problem of signal compression by utilization of algorithms for sparse solution of linear systems. We have compared some of the main algorithms proposed in the literature on a speech coding application. The simulation results show that the greedy orthogonal algorithms based on a greedy selection at each step, not only are computationally light and simple to implement but they also provide the best compression performance on this application.

References

[1] Aase, S., Husoy, J., Skretting, K., Engan, K.: Optimized signal expansions for sparse representation. *IEEE Trans. on Signal Processing* **49** (2001) 1087–1096 147

[2] Natarajan, B.: Sparse approximate solutions to linear systems. *SIAM J. Computing* **24** (1995) 227–234 147, 150

[3] Rao, B., Delgado, K.: An affine scaling methodology for best basis selection. *IEEE Trans. on Signal Processing* **47** (1999) 187–200 147

[4] Vanderbei, R. J.: LOQO user's manual – version 3.10. Technical Report SOR-97-08, Princeton University, Statistics and Operations Research (1997) Code available at http://www.princeton.edu/~rvdb/ 149

[5] Chen, S., Donoho, D., Saunders, M.: Atomic decomposition by basis pursuit. *SIAM J. Scientific Computing* **20** (1999) 33–61 149

[6] Coifman, R., Wickerhauser, M.: Entropy-based algorithms for best basis selections. *IEEE Trans. on Information Theory* **38** (1992) 713–718 149

[7] Mallat, S., Zhang, Z.: Matching pursuit in a time-frequency dictionary. *IEEE Trans. Signal Processing* **41** (1993) 3397 – 3415 150

Fuzzy Time Series for Forecasting Pollutants Concentration in the Air

Francesco Carlo Morabito and Mario Versaci

Università *Mediterranea*, Facoltá di Ingegneria
DIMET Via Graziella, Loc. Feo di Vito
89100 Reggio Calabria, Italy
`morabito,versaci`@ing.unirc.it

Abstract. The main link from Europe to Sicily and vice versa is represented by a ferry boat service from Villa San Giovanni to Messina, two towns along the homonymous strait. Consequently, the crossing and heavy vehicular traffic discharges organic and inorganic compounds in the urban atmosphere that can affect the health of citizens. In this paper, a design of a prediction system for pollutants concentration in the urban atmosphere is proposed. In this study, the exploited tool is a soft computing approach basing on Fuzzy Time Series. In particular, we exploit Two Factors Fuzzy Time Series in which the main factor is the pollutant and the secondary factor is the traffic. For our purposes, two algorithms are exploited. The obtained predictions have given good results especially regarding the prediction of pollutant concentrations one hour later, which represents the time needed to take decisions about the traffic regulation.

Keywords: Fuzzy functions, Time series forecasting

1 The Problem Under Study

To reach Sicily from Europe (and vice versa) by cars and trucks it exists a ferry boat service from Villa San Giovanni to Messina; two cities located one in front of the other along the homonymous strait. Due to the crossing vehicular traffic, these two towns are interested by a poor quality of the air. In particular, the crossing heavy traffic discharges in the air organic and inorganic compounds that affect the health citizens. The processing of environmental data represent a very difficult problem due to the correlation among (multivariate dependency with non-linear behavior) a lot of variables of different type which yield an intricate mesh of relationships. To take decisions about the traffic, it is not possible to consider devices based on black box models because the risk to take unpopular actions (like stopping vehicular traffic) is very high. It is thus essential to derive a set of rules which can support the decisions. In other words, the prediction of an episode of pollution may benefit of the knowledge on the typical meteorological, seasonal and traffic conditions of a particular area. The soft computing methodologies are naturally suitable to help in forecasting the local

M. Marinaro and R. Tagliaferri (Eds.): WIRN VIETRI 2002, LNCS 2486, pp. 152–159, 2002.

behavior of complex systems starting from the available measurements. This paper report a design of a forecasting system for pollutants concentration in the air by means of a two-factors time-variant fuzzy time series model [1]. In the past, Neural Networks and Fuzzy Inference Systems were exploited for prediction of problems about environmental problems [2, 4]. The paper is organized as follows: section 2 reports an overview on the exploited experimental database and some qualitative considerations. The novel utilized method is reported in section 3 and, finally, the best results achieved are presented and some conclusions are reported. This work is part of SMAURN Project (Monitoring System of Urban Environment through Neural Networks an European Community project on the environmental monitoring of the city of Villa San Giovanni), which purpose was to design a network of mobile terminals for monitoring some pollution parameters and predicting in real time their evolution in a urban contest. The gathered information can be used by the system manager to help local authorities in adopting action plans and administering Environmental Protection.

2   The Experimental Database: An Overview

In this work, we use an environmental database that refers to the area of the Messina Strait. The monitoring stations have been located downtown Villa San Giovanni, just along the road interested by heavy traffic to ferry boats to Sicily (Corso Italia). They were moved in different measuring points, anyway along the above mentioned road (which final part is the only access to ferries): time period devoted to collect data in each location was four weeks approximately. The time series took into account refer to the period from August 2nd to August 19th August 1998. The database is organized as follows:

- no. rows: 480
- no. columns: 14 (the first one is the time observation)
- no. pollutants: SO_2, CO, O_3, NO, NO_2, HC, PTS, PM_{10} (which statistics are reported in Table 1.)
- atmospheric parameters: wind speed, wind direction, temperature, atmospheric pressure traffic data: number of vehicles per hour in the two opposite crossing directions, from and to Sicily

The database under study presents two problems:

1. missing data (mainly due to the bad working of measurement instruments)
2. outliers (mainly due to the not proper working of the instruments or to incorrect methodology for collection and analysis).

Missing data can invalidate the statistical analysis introducing systematic components of errors in estimating parameters in the prediction model. In addition, if we estimated the parameters of the model by exploiting the observed data, we would obtain a retaliation in the estimations because many information concerning the missing data would disappear. For this study, we replace missing data by the averages of the measurements at the same time in the previous days. In the case in which an outlier occurs, it is possible to take a choice:

Table 1. Summary of statistics for the pollutants under study

	Max	Min	Average	SD	Skewness	Kurtosis
SO_2	109.4	0	7.48	9.1	4.34	36.3
CO	10.55	0	1.00	0.93	2.63	21.2
O_3	135.6	0	21	24	1.31	4.48
NO	279.2	0	15.6	25.75	4.8	36.6
NO_2	168.7	1.72	18.24	22	2.82	12.2
HC	960.2	0	308.3	159.6	0.904	4.04
PTS	396	0	59.7	33	3.53	30.32
PM_{10}	497	0	51.2	61.46	3.45	18.6
Vehicular Traffic	1190	212	673	232.2	-0.34	2.07

1. to eliminate the suspect datum making a missing datum
2. to keep the outlier and exploit more effective statistical methods. In this work, we keep the outliers because our inspection tools, fuzzy time series model, are very good when anomalous values are processed (uncertainty, inaccuracy, ...).

The presence of an outlier can constitute an indication of unusual and unexpected events. Usually, the maximum and minimum values can be considered as outliers and they must be examined by caution, because they can cause deformation in the calibration of the prediction model. On the other hand, other methodologies can be useful to evidence outliers (i.e., Shewhard's and Cusum's control cards) in which the measurements between past and present are checked.

3   The Exploited Tool: Fuzzy Time Series Models

A pollutant event may be influenced by many factors; for example, the number of vehicles circulating on a certain road section one hour before can be exploited to predict the pollutant concentrations in the air one hour later. This model make use of two factors only to predict a time series. In this contest, we exploit the fuzzy time series so called "two factors fuzzy time series" applied to the main factor (pollutant) and the second factor (traffic data). To understand how this method works, let us consider a subset of real numbers $Y(t)$ (Universe of Discourse), assuming the fuzzy sets $\mu_i(t)$, defined on Y ranging from [0 1]. $F(t)$ and $G(t)$ are two fuzzy time series of $Y(t)$. $F(t)$ is a function of time t, and $\mu_i(t)$ are linguistic values of $F(t)$, where $\mu_i(t)$ are represented by fuzzy sets. In our case, $F(t)$ is the pollutant concentration in the air (main factor) and $G(t)$ (secondary factor) is the number of vehicles (one hour before) and it aids the prediction of $F(t)$. In this contest, two algorithms, so called B and B^*-*Algorithms*, have been developed [1] in order to forecast values of a time series.

B-Algorithm

Step 1: Fuzzification of data

As for the main factor, the fuzzification of data is operated on its decreases and increases. In particular, we find the maximum decrease DL and the maximum increase DR between any two continuous data;

Step2: Definition of the universe of discourse for main factor

The universe of discourse U for main factor (pollutant) is defined as follows: $[DL - D_1, DR + D_2]$ where D_1 and D_2 are suitable positive values;

Step3:Partition of the universe of the discourse

After that, the universe of discourse is divided into several intervals which length is variable; lets call these partition by: $u_1, u_2, \ldots, u_m$

Step 4: Definition of fuzzy sets

Inside the universe of discourse U, we define fuzzy sets; by membership function, each fuzzy set, labeled by means of $A_1, A_2, \ldots, A_m$ is associated to a particular partition of the universe of discourse.

Step 5: Definition of the universe of discourse for secondary factor

We define fuzzy sets on the universe of discourse U for the factor G(t) (number of vehicles), but now the fuzzification is operated on real values. We call the corresponding labels: $B_1, B_2, \ldots, B_m$. The choose of the membership functions is forced by qualitative considerations.

Step 6: choise of the base window

To predict the data of time t, we must fix the base window, w. Once the fuzzification has been carried out, and a suitable base window w has been chosen, we introduce the criterion vector $C(t)$ and the operation matrix $O^w(t)$ at time t, respectively expressed as follows: $C(t) = f(t-1) = [C_1 C_2, \ldots, C_m]$ and: $O^w(t) = [f(t-2); f(t-3); \ldots f(t-w)]$ where $f(t-1)$ is the fuzzified variation of the main factor $F(t)$ between $t-1$ and $t-2$, m is the number of elements in the universe of discourse, C_j and O_{ij} are crisp values.

Step 7: Definition of the second factor vector

Next step is to define the second-factor vector $S(t)$, which is composed by the second factor fuzzy time series $G(t)$. It is described as: $S(t) = g(t-1) = [S_1, S_2, \ldots, S_m]$ where $S(t)$ is the second-factor vector at time t, $g(t-1)$ is the fuzzified data of $G(t)$ at time $t-1$, m is the number of partitions.

Step 8: Construction of the fuzzy relationship matrix

Last step is to introduce the fuzzy relationship matrix $R(t)$, defined as follows: $R(t) = O^w(t) \times S(t) \times C(t)$. From matrix $R(t)$, we can get the fuzzified predicted variation $f(t)$ between time t and time $t-1$ being: $F(t) =$

$[Max(R_{11}, R_{21}, \ldots, R_{(w-1)1})$
$Max(R_{12}, R_{22}, \ldots, R_{(w-1)2}) \cdots$
$Max(R_{1m}, R_{2m}, \ldots, R_{(w-1)m}]$

where $f(t)$ is the fuzzified variation of the fuzzy time series $F(t)$ between time t and time $t-1$. If all belonging degrees of the above mentioned fuzzified variations are 0, then the prediction is void. If the maximum value of $f(t)$ belongs to u_i, then the fuzzified value is the medium value of that partition. Finally, if the value of $f(t)$ falls in more than one partition, the fuzzified value is the medium values of the centers of these partitions.

B^*-Algorithm

This algorithm differs from the previous one in the defuzzification of the forecasted variations of the main factor. In this contest, we compute the a-significance level [5] ($f(t)$) a of the fuzzified predicted variation $f(t)$ as follows:

$$f(t) = [f_1 f_2 \ldots f_m], \; f(t)_\alpha = [f_{1\alpha} f_{2\alpha} \ldots f_{m\alpha}]$$

where $f(t)$ is the fuzzified predicted variation of date at time t represented by a fuzzy set in $F(t)$, m is the number of partition and $\alpha \in [0, 1]$. If $f_i > \alpha$, then $f_{i\alpha} = f_i$; otherwise $f_{i\alpha} = 0$ (i is the index of partition). If the belonging degrees of the α-significance level predicted variation have only one maximum u_i, and the midpoint of u_i, is m_i, then the predicted variation of date t is m_i. If the grades of membership of the α-significance level predicted variation have more than one maximum, then the predicted variation of date t is the average of them. The predicted data is equal to the predicted variation plus the actual data of the last day of the main-factor fuzzy time series. By using this algorithm, the prediction of a certain value of an time series is calculated by means of two main series: first one is the main factor (as was done in B algorithm), while the second one is an time series described, for example, from the corresponding value of the previous day. Once a time window has been chosen, let call it border, which represents the number of previous and subsequent samples of the sample to be predicted in the second time series, the algorithm evaluates the maximum and the minimum of the border itself; in borderline cases, if the predicted sample is lower (higher) than minimum (maximum), then the predicted value coincides with it. By Matlab Toolbox, we implemented the both algorithms.

4   Best Results

In this section of the paper the simulations for predictions of CO, SO_2, NO, NO_2 and HC will be shown; O_3, PTS and PM_{10} did not take into account because their concentrations increasing is not directly proportional to the vehicular traffic. The extracted simulations have been done with different values of w and with both the proposed algorithms and different membership functions (gaussian, triangular and trapezoidal, but other shapes can be take into account). Best results are shown in Table 2; it can be seen that results achieved by B^* best fit with best accuracy. As an example, let us consider the step-by-step characteristics of B and B^* simulations in case no.10 with overlapping triangular membership functions. Membership functions for the partitions of the main factor and for the secondary factor are the following:

Membership Value	Range	Membership Value	Range
A1=[0.2 0.4 0.6 0.8 0.9 0.3 0 0 0]	[-600 -250]	A2=[0 0.1 0.4 0.4 0.8 0 0 0 0]	[-350 -100]
A3=[0 0 0.2 0.6 0.9 0.3 0 0 0]	[-200 -50]	A4=[0 0 0.05 0.5 1 0.7 0.1 0 0]	[-100 150]
A5=[0 0 0 0.3 1 0.5 0 0 0]	[120 350]	A6=[0 0 0 0.2 0.3 0 0 0]	[300 450]
A7=[0 0 0 0.2 0.9 0.3 0 0 0]	[410 660]	A8=[0 0 0 0.3 0.9 0.8 0.4 0.1 0]	[620 820]
A9=[0 0 0 0 0.5 0.4 0 0 0]	[700 1000]		

Membership Value	Range	Membership Value	Range
B1=[0 0 0 0 0.5 0 0 0]	[0 300]	B2=[0 0 0 0 0 0 0 0]	[100 350]
B3=[0 0 0 0.88 0 0 0 0]	[200 370]	B4=[0 0 0 0 0 0.7 0.1 0 0]	[350 450]
B5=[0 0 0.51 0 0 0 0 0 0]	[300 420]	B6=[0 0 0.22 0 0 0 0 0]	[300 450]
B7=[0 0 0 0 0 0 0.05 0 0]	[410 510]	B8=[0 0 0 0 0 0 0 0]	[450 570]
B9=[0 0 0 0 0 0 0.78 0]	[520 700]		

Membership function values have been fixed taking into account that a kind of direct proportionality anyway exists between traffic parameters and hydrocarbons levels (Figure 1). The bank of rules exploits step belongings functions which values are stored in the above written single arrays. By B algorithm looking at which the quasi-adherence of the predicted results to the expected values can be observed.

5 Conclusions

In this work we exploited the two factors time-variant fuzzy time series model in order to design a device capable to predict pollutants concentration in the air. By means of two special algorithms (so-called B and B*), we have carried out the short time prediction of the pollutants concentration of a zone of the city

Table 2. Summary of Best Results

Pollutant	Algorithm	Membership Functions	RMSE		
	B	Gaussian	7.4	7.41	7.42
	case 1	Triangular	7.4	7.41	7.42
CO_2		Trapezoidal	7.4	7.41	7.42
	B^*	Gaussian	6.91	6.92	6.93
	case 2	Triangular	6.93	6.94	6.95
		Trapezoidal	7.17	7.18	7.19
	B	Gaussian	9.76	7.41	9.74
	case 3	Triangular	9.76	9.77	9.74
SO_2		Trapezoidal	9.76	9.77	9.74
	B^*	Gaussian	9.77	9.79	9.80
	case 4	Triangular	9.63	9.65	9.65
		Trapezoidal	9.76	9.78	9.79
	B	Gaussian	5.65	5.97	5.98
	case 5	Triangular	5.65	5.97	5.98
NO		Trapezoidal	5.65	5.97	5.98
	B^*	Gaussian	6.51	6.52	6.53
	case 6	Triangular	6.50	6.51	6.52
		Trapezoidal	6.85	6.89	6.90
	B	Gaussian	7.53	7.55	7.56
	case 7	Triangular	7.53	7.55	7.56
NO_2		Trapezoidal	7.53	7.55	7.56
	B^*	Gaussian	7.77	7.79	7.80
	case 8	Triangular	7.73	7.75	7.76
		Trapezoidal	8.04	8.05	8.06
	B	Gaussian	9.91	9.92	9.94
	case 9	Triangular	9.91	9.92	9.94
HC		Trapezoidal	9.91	9.92	9.94
	B^*	Gaussian	10.13	10.09	10.00
	case 10	Triangular	10.33	10.35	10.37
		Trapezoidal	10.06	10.04	10.20

of Villa San Giovanni. Fuzzy time series leads on one hand to the fuzzification of the difference between two subsequent samplings of the pollutant to be predicted and on the other hand in writing fuzzy rules to connects these differences (and then predictions) to the main reason that generates them (vehicular flow in both driving directions). The experimental case study was derived from the database available through the SMAURN project. Concerning the two exploited algorithm, the computed errors can be considered acceptable. In addition, the computational complexity allows us on-line applications. The proposed predic-

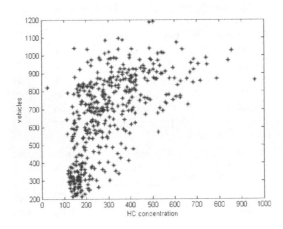

Fig. 1. Scatter plot showing the correlation between main factor and secondary factors

tions may anyway be improved by a proper knowledge of the expert and/or by optimizing the choose of the time window and the a parameter .

References

[1] Shyi, M. C, Jeng, R. H.: Temperature Prediction Using Fuzzy Time Series. IEEE Transactions on Systems, Man, And Cybernetics - Part B: Cybernetics 30 (**2**) (2000) 263-275. 153, 154
[2] F. C. Morabito, M. Versaci.: Prediction and Estimation of Atmospheric Pollutant Levels by Soft Computing Approach. In Proceedings of International Joint Conference on Neural Networks (IJCNN'01),(2001), 1415-1420. 153
[3] D. Marino, B. Ricca.: Neural Networks for Econometric and Environmental Models for Territory Management. In Proceedings of the XVII Italian Congress on Regional Sciences, Sondrio, Italy, (1999).
[4] D. Marino, F. C. Morabito.: A Fuzzy Neural Network for Urban Environment Monitoring System: the Villa San Giovanni Study Case. Neural Nets, (1999) 323. 153
[5] Y. Yuan, M. J. Shaw: Introduction of fuzzy decision trees. Fuzzy Sets Syst. 69 (**2**) (1995) 125-139. 156

Real-Time Perceptual Coding of Wideband Speech by Competitive Neural Networks

Eros Pasero and Alfonso Montuori

Politecnico di Torino, Dipartimento di Elettronica
C.so Duca degli Abruzzi, 24, 10100 Torino, Italy
pasero@polito.it, montuori@lep.polito.it
http://www.neuronica.polito.it

Abstract. We developed a real-time wideband speech codec adopting a wavelet packet based methodology. The transform domain coefficients were first quantized by means of a mid-tread uniform quantizer and then encoded with an arithmetic coding. In the first step the wavelet coefficients were quantized by using a psycho-acoustic model. The second step was carried out by adapting the probability model of the quantized coefficients frame by frame by means of a competitive neural network. The neural network was trained on the TIMIT corpus and his weights updated in real-time during the compression in order to model better the speech characteristics of the current speaker. The coding/decoding algorithm was first written in C and then optimised on the TMS320C6000 DSP platform.

Keywords: Wideband speech, Competitive Neural Network.

1 Introduction

Several applications such as teleconferencing, multimedia services and high-quality wideband telephony require advanced coding algorithms for wideband speech. In contrast to the standard telephony band of 200 to 3400 Hz, wideband speech is assigned the band 50 to 7000 Hz and is sampled at a rate of 16000 Hz for subsequent digital processing. The added low frequencies increase the voice naturalness whereas the added high frequencies make the speech sound more intelligible.

The energy spectrum in this bandwidth is not uniform. Linear prediction based algorithms, which have been used effectively in narrowband coders to achieve high quality speech at low bit rates, are inefficient for wideband speech coding because they attempt to match all frequencies equally well. Furthermore the wideband energy spectrum is time varying. A voiced/unvoiced classification, which has been often used for speech coding, is not sufficient to define the bands of the spectrum in which the energy concentrates. This uneven and time varying distribution of the signal energy provides motivation for using adaptive subband coding. We developed a real-time wideband speech coder/decoder adopting a wavelet packet transform based methodology [5].

M. Marinaro and R. Tagliaferri (Eds.): WIRN VIETRI 2002, LNCS 2486, pp. 160–167, 2002.

It has been shown that wavelets can approximate time varying non-stationary signals in a better way that the Fourier transform, representing the signal on both time and frequency domains [1] [7] [8]. Due to this property wavelet filters concentrates speech information into a few neighbouring coefficients, which is essential for a low bit rate representation. In this way we can advantageously encode them using an entropy coding system.

The transform domain coefficients were first quantized by means of a uniform quantizer on the basis of the psycho-acoustic masking phenomenon and then encoded with an arithmetic coding. In order to decode the coefficients the receiver needs to know the probability model used for the arithmetic coding. Therefore we must transmit a probability table as side information. For real-time applications, it is not advantageous to transmit a probability table for each frame. Better results can be achieved by using, for each frame, the same probability table based on the distribution of the quantized wavelet coefficients. We improved further this methodology by means of an adaptive approach, in which the probability table is updated frame by frame by selecting it in a pre-calculated codebook. The codebook was obtained by training a competitive neural network on the TIMIT corpus. The trained network is also used to select frame by frame the best table in the codebook. In order to model better the characteristics of the current signal, the codebook, i.e. the weights matrix of the network, is updated periodically during the compression too.

TMS320 DSPs have proven effective for real-time compression of audio signals [3] [4] [20] [21]. The codec algorithm was first written in C and then optimised on the TMS320C6000 DSP platform.

2   The Subband Decomposition

The design of a subband coder involves the choice of a filter bank. A filter bank is characterised by its main structure (uniform-band vs. octave-band filter bank), the type and the order of filters, their implementation and the number of bands.

Table 1. Subband decomposition for the 16 kHz sampling rate

Subbands (Hz)	Coeff.	Subbands (Hz)	Coeff.	Subbands (Hz)	Coeff.
0-125	1-2	875-1000	15-16	2500-2750	41-44
125-250	3-4	1000-1250	17-20	2750-3000	45-48
250-375	5-6	1250-1500	21-24	3000-3500	49-56
375-500	7-8	1500-1750	25-28	3500-4000	57-64
500-625	9-10	1750-2000	29-32	4000-5000	65-80
625-750	11-12	2000-2250	33-36	5000-6000	81-96
750-875	13-14	2250-2500	37-40	6000-8000	97-128

In our coder the audio signal is transformed into a time-scale representation through a non-uniform wavelet packet decomposition. The coding process first entails obtaining a frame of 128 speech samples, which are transformed into subband signals by means of a fast wavelet packet transform algorithm. The structure of the analysis tree is chosen so that the resulting 21 subbands mimic the critical bands of the human auditory system for the 0-8 kHz bandwidth, which allows to make use of the spectral masking properties of the human ear to decrease the bit-rate of the encoder while perceptually hiding the quantization error. The coefficient mapping is showed in Table 1.

The choice of the prototype filter of the transform, as well as its length, influences the separation of the subband signals and the compression performance. The filters proposed by Daubechies are the ones that best preserve frequency selectivity as the number of stages of the DWPT increases. This is due to their regularity property [1] [2]. We have obtained excellent performances with biorthogonal filters, specifically with the Filters 3 of the best biorthogonal filter banks of Villasenor [6].

3   Perceptual Noise Masking

The samples of the time-scale representation are quantized to reduce the amount of data sent to the transmission channel. The allocation of the bits to the subbands considers the perceptual noise masking characteristics of the human ear. The noise threshold, i.e. the maximum noise that can be inaudibly inserted into the signal, has been used as quantization error.

The calculus of the noise threshold involved several steps [9]. First we calculated the energy in each critical band. To estimate the effects of masking across critical bands the spreading function given in [11] [12] was used. After this step the signal to masking ratio was calculated for each subband by evaluating the tonality of the signal. In order to determine the noiselike or tonelike nature of the signal, the spectral flatness measure [10], computed by means of the wavelet packet transform, was used. Finally the maximum between the masking threshold and the threshold in quiet was taken.

The frame length was set equal to 8 ms. Since we used symmetric extension of data this length was equal to the length of the analysis window.

The transform domain coefficients were quantized by means of a mid-tread quantizer [16] and encoded with the arithmetic coding. However arithmetic coding requires the probability model to be also available to the decoder and hence the probability table must also be transmitted as side information. Transmitting the probability tables presents a challenge, since without further encoding the added information by far exceeds the coding gain achieved through arithmetic coding [13]. In order to transmit the probability tables with a low overhead, the neural network approach described in the next paragraph was used.

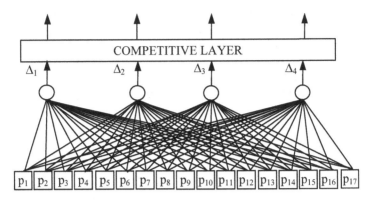

Fig. 1. The neural network topology with N=17 input symbols and M=4 output neurons

4   The Competitive Neural Network

Self-organising networks can learn to detect regularities and correlation in their input and adapt their future responses to that input accordingly. The neurons of competitive networks learn to recognise groups of similar input vectors.

The topology of the network we used is showed in Fig. 1. In our competitive network the distance between the N inputs p_i, representing the probability table of the quantized wavelet coefficient of a speech frame, and vectors formed from the columns of the input weight matrix W_{ij}, was calculated by means of the following equation [22],

$$D_j = - \left(\sum_{i=1}^{N} p_i \cdot log_2 \left(W_{ij} \right) - \sum_{i=1}^{N} p_i \cdot log_2 \left(W_{ij} \right) \right). \tag{1}$$

The quantity D_j in (1) represents the difference between the following two quantities:

1) $-\sum_{i=1}^{N} p_i \cdot log_2 \left(W_{ij} \right)$, which represents the quantized wavelet coefficient mean number of bits we would have by using an optimal arithmetic coding with the probability table $[W_{1j}, W_{2j}, \ldots, W_{Nj}]$,

2) $-\sum_{i=1}^{N} p_i \cdot log_2 \left(p_i \right)$, which represents the entropy of the probability distribution $[p_1, p_2, \ldots, p_N]$.

Finding the distances D_j and subtracting the biases b_j, we compute the Δ_j elements

$$\Delta_j = D_j - b_j. \tag{2}$$

The competitive transfer function returns neuron outputs of 0 for all neurons except for the winner, the neuron associated with the minimum element D_j. The winner's output is 1. The conditions

$$\sum_{i=1}^{N} W_{ij} = 1, \forall j \,, \tag{3}$$

$$\sum_{i=1}^{N} p_i = 1 \,. \tag{4}$$

are imposed on the weight matrix and on the inputs.

We used the Kohonen learning rule [14] to adapt the weights of the winning neuron j

$$W_{ij}(t) = W_{ij}(t-1) + \lambda \cdot (p_i(t) - W_{ij}(t-1)) \,. \tag{5}$$

This rule preserves the condition (3).

The biases b_i are updated during the training to force each neuron to classify roughly the same percentage of input vectors. In fact, one of the limitations of competitive networks is that some neuron weight vectors may start out far from any input vectors and never win the competition (dead neurons). To stop this from happening, biases are used to make a distant neuron more likely to win [15].

If M is the number of the output neurons, the probability table is encoded with only $log_2 M$ bits.

5   Real-Time Implementation

We based our tool on the TMS320C6000 platform. The TMS320C6711 DSP Starter Kit and later on the TMS320C6701 Evaluation Module were used. Both contain a floating-point DSP. The latter is equipped with a peripheral component interconnect (PCI) interface, which provides plug-and-play functionality along with the ability to support high-speed modes of data transfers.

The input voice is sampled at 16 kHz and digitalized by means of the 16-bit A/D converter, which is on the DSP board. Then the digital signal is compressed and sent in real-time to the host computer through the HPI (Host Port Interface), the parallel 16-bit interface the CPU board uses to communicate with the computer (it is possible to access the internal and external memory of the board through the HPI). The host computer packets the compressed voice with the UDP/IP protocol and sends it to the Internet.

On the host computer a server application is present too, which receives speech packets from the Internet, unpacks them and sends the compressed speech to the DSP board in real-time, where it is decompressed and converted in analog format. Two pipe structures are used to receiving and transmitting data between the coding/decoding procedure and the serial port connected to the A/D-D/A converter [19].

The arithmetic coding was implemented by using integer arithmetic to partition the cumulative frequency distribution table used at each stage. Not only this is more efficient than using floating point arithmetic, but avoids that different round-off errors can make different machines encode differently [17].

The weights matrix of the neural network is periodically updated during the compression in order to model better the speech characteristics of the current speaker. In fact the codebook of the quantized wavelet coefficient distribution, i.e. the matrix weight, is dependant on the speaker and is initially set to the result of the off line network training (see below for further details). To optimise the arithmetic coding performance the network updates this codebook by learning the characteristics of the quantized wavelet coefficient distributions of current speaker's speech. The receiver must only adapt the neural network weights too in order to correctly decode the quantized wavelet coefficients.

6   Main Results

A reconstructed signal with a segmental SNR greater than 16.5 dB was achieved at 32 kbit/s. It is possible to reduce the bit rate by using a quantization step greater than the masking noise. In this way the coding is not any more perceptually transparent, but the quantization noise is tolerable up to 8-10 kbit/s. The use of symmetric extensions of the frames causes the incorrect calculation of the masking threshold, but this drawback is compensated with a low algorithmic delay (8 ms), which is not greater than the frame duration.

The ITU-T recommendation for wideband audio compression is the G.722.1, a digital coder based on transform coding as well, using a Modulated Lapped Transform [23]. G.722.1 provides audio closer in quality to FM radio than to ordinary telephone calls at 24 kbits/s and 32 kbits/s. It operates on 20 ms frames (320 samples) of audio. Because the transform window (basis function length) is 640 samples and a 50 per cent (320 samples) overlap is used between frames, the total algorithmic delay is 40 ms. The overlapping avoids the blocking artefacts that can be listened in most DCT-based compression system, but introduces an algorithmic delay that could be unacceptable in real-time applications, such as video-conferencing, in which the telecommunication system can create echo problems.

Three neural networks were trained for the following subbands: 0-2kHz, 2kHz-4kHz and 4kHz-8kHz. Codebook of different sizes were obtained by using M=2,4,8,16 output neurons and N=9,17,33 input symbols Pi. We used as training set the TIMIT corpus sentences spoken by 64 different speakers from 8 major dialect regions of the United States. A separate set of sentences spoken by of 8 different speakers was used as test set. The best trade-off between bit rate, computation complexity and quality of the reconstructed speech was M=4 neurons and N=17 symbols. For this configuration the mean bit rate was about 2 kbit/s greater than the entropy bound of the quantized coefficients, with an overhead for the transmission of the probability tables of 250 bit/s.

The test set was also used in order to measure the suitability of the wavelet transform to concentrate speech information. We found that nearly the 90% of the Villasenor normalised wavelet coefficients are below 0.05 in module. This result was essential for a low bit rate representation of the coefficients using the arithmetic coding.

The processing delay of the coding algorithm with the TMS320C6701 CPU, which has 8 independent functional units, a 5 ns cycle time and is designed to perform up to eight 32 bit instruction per cycle [18], was less than 2 ms.

7   Conclusions and Future Work

A wavelet based real-time speech coder has been proposed and a real-time implementation on the TMS320C6000 platform has been tested. Since the coder does not rely on any source model of the signal, it can be used for all audio signals if a new training of the neural network is made.

The low algorithmic delay (8 ms) makes the coder suitable for real-time applications in which the telecommunication system can create echo problems.

The use of a neural network approach for the arithmetic coding of the quantized coefficients led to a coding performance close to the optimum (entropy-bound) coding scheme with a very low overhead for the transmission of side information. Future work includes the incorporation of a temporal masking model, the analysis of the coder performance with music signals sampled at 44.1 kHz and the use of a real-time network protocol able to minimise the audible artefacts which are caused by packet losses and jitter in the IP network.

References

[1] Daubechies, I.: Orthonormal bases of compactly supported wavelets. Comm. Pure Appl. Math., Vol. 4 (1988) 909–996 161, 162

[2] Daubechies, I.: Ten Lectures on Wavalets. SIAM, Philadelphia, PA (1992) 162

[3] Singh, I., Agathoklis, P., Antoniou, A.: Wavelet-based compression of speech signals on the TMS320C30 digital signal processor. IEEE Symposium on Advances in Digital Filtering and Signal Processing (1998) 178–182 161

[4] Fu, X., Zhang, Z.: TMS320C6000 DSP Multichannel Vocoder Technology Demonstration Kit Host Side Design. Texas Instruments Application Report, Literature Number SPRA558B (2000) 161

[5] Wickerhauser, M. V.: INRIA Lectures on wavelet packet algorithms. Lecture Notes in Computer Science. Problemes Non P.-L. Lions, Ed., Roquencourt, France (1991) 160

[6] Villasenor, J. D., Belzer, B., Liao, J.: Filter Evaluation and Selection in Wavelet Image Compression. Proceedings of IEEE Data Compression Conference (1994) 351–360 162

[7] Vetterli, M., Kovacevic, J.: Wavelets and subband coding. Prentice-Hall, Englewood Cliffs, NJ 1995) 161

[8] Mallat, S.: A wavelet tour of signal processing. 2nd edn. Academic Press (1998) 161

[9] Johnston, J. D., Sinha, D., Dorward, S., Quackenbush, S. R.: AT&T Perceptual Audio Coder. Collected Papers on Digital Audio Bit-Rate Reduction. N. Gilchrist and C. Grewin, Editors, AES (1996) 162

[10] Jayant, N. S., Noll, P.: Digital Coding of Waveforms: Principles and Applications to Speech and Video. Prentice-Hall, Englewood Cliffs, NJ (1984) 162

[11] Schroeder, M. R., Atal, B. S., Hall, J. L.: Optimizing digital speech coders by exploiting masking properties of the human ear. Journal of the Acoustical Society of America, Vol.66, no. 6 (1979) 1647–1652 162

[12] Carnero, B., Drygajlo, A.: Perceptual Speech Coding and Enhancement Using Frame-Synchronized Fast Wavelet Packet Transform Algorithms. IEEE Trans. on Signal Processing, Vol. 47, no. 6, (1999) 162

[13] Golchin, F., Paliwal, K. K.: Lossless coding of MPEG-1 Layer III encoded audio streams. Proceedings of IEEE International Conference on Acoustics, Speech, and Signal Processing, Vol. 2 (2000) 162

[14] Kohonen, T.: Self-Organization and Associative Memory. 2nd edn. Springer-Verlag, Berlin (1987) 164

[15] The Mathworks Inc. (ed.): Neural networks toolbook. (2000) 164

[16] Papamichalis, P. E.: Practical approaches to speech coding. Prentice-Hall, Englewood Cliffs New Jersey (1987) 162

[17] Press, W. H., Teukolsky, S. A., Vetterling, W. T., Flannery, B. P.: Numerical Recipes in C: The Art of Scientific Computing. Cambridge University Press (1988) 910–915 164

[18] Texas Instruments Inc. (ed.): TMS320C6201/6701 Evaluation Module Technical Reference. Literature Number SPRU305 (1998) 166

[19] Dart, D.: Understanding the Functional Enhancements of DSP/BIOS II and their Utilization in Real-Time DSP Applications. Texas Instruments Application Report, Literature Number SPRA648 (2000) 164

[20] Montuori, A., Quaglia, D.: A Tutorial on Subband Audio Coding Using the TMS320C6211 Starter Kit. Application Report, Texas Instruments DSP Challenge 2000 (2001) 161

[21] Quaglia, D., Montuori, A., De Martin, J. C., Pasero, E.: Interactive DSP Educational Platform for Real-Time Subband Audio Coding. Proceedings of ICASSP 2002, International Conference on Acoustics, Speech, and Signal Processing (2002) 161

[22] Pasero, E., Montuori, A.: Wavelet Based Wideband Speech Coding on the TMS320C67 for Real-Time Transmission. Proceedings of IEEE Multimedia Technology and Applications Conference (2001) 208–212 163

[23] ITU-T: G.722.1. Coding at 24 and 32 kbit/s for hands-free operation in systems with low frame loss. Series G: Transmission Systems and Media, Digital Systems and Networks (1999) 165

Sound Synthesis by Flexible Activation Function Recurrent Neural Networks

Aurelio Uncini

INFOCOM dept. – University of Rome "La Sapienza"
Via Eudossiana 18, 00184 Rome, Italy
aurel@ieee.org
http://infocom.uniroma1.it/aurel

Abstract. In this paper we investigate on the use of adaptive spline neural networks, to define a new general class of physical-like sound synthesis models, based on a learning from examples strategy (in particular in this paper we study single-reed woodwind instruments). It is well known that one of the main problems in physical modeling concerns the difficulty of parameter identification and the definition of the exciter nonlinear function shape (which plays a key rule in the instrument timbre). In the proposed neural model we make use of FIR-IIR synapses followed by a Catmul-Rom spline based flexible nonlinear function whose shape can be modified by adapting its control points. This general structure can imitate an entire class of instruments by learning all the parameters (synaptic weights and spline control points) from recorded sounds. In order to obtain an efficient hardware/software implementation, the synaptic weights are constrained to be power-of-two terms while the nonlinear function can be implemented as a simple spline interpolation scheme or through a small lookup table. In order to demonstrate the effectiveness of the proposed model, experiments on a single-reed woodwind instruments have been carried out.

Keywords: sound synthesis, physical model, flexible activation function, spline neural networks, power-of-two neural networks.

1 Introduction

A new neural network-based approach is presented in order to define a new class of physical-like model sound synthesis. Neural networks represent, in fact, a central technology for many ill-posed *intelligent multimedia signal processing* problems [1].

Sound synthesis by physical or physical-like model seems to be one of the best way to produce interesting and high quality sounds [2]. The physical model paradigms are, in general, based on the subdivision of the synthesizer in a nonlinear excitation part in connection with other linear parts as delay lines and/or filters [3]-[4]. The most famous model-based technique is the so-called digital waveguide filter [3], [5]. The basic idea of this approach is to simulate the

M. Marinaro and R. Tagliaferri (Eds.): WIRN VIETRI 2002, LNCS 2486, pp. 168–177, 2002.
© Springer-Verlag Berlin Heidelberg 2002

vibration-transmitting component of an acoustic musical instrument such as membrane of a drum, a string of a stringed instrument, and a bore of a woodwind instrument. One of the main problems with model-based synthesis techniques is the determination of the synthesis model parameters. Usually, a spectrum analysis of the original signal is necessary in order to design correctly the filters. Moreover many simplifications are made in order to describe the nonlinear excitation mechanism (NLEM). The NLEM is, in fact, very important so far as it characterizes the timbre of the instrument.

In the last years, several attempts have been made for modeling the NLEM. As an example J. O. Smith proposed a sophisticated digital-filter theory to characterize the formant structure of a violin sound and used that knowledge to create a physical model of the violin body [8].

A computational expensive evolutionary approach for the estimation of the nonlinear physical model of flute has been proposed in [9].

In [10], Drioli and Rocchesso proposed an interesting learning-based approach for pseudo-physical model for sound synthesis. They proposed, in fact, the use of Radial Basis Function universal approximation scheme in order to off-line learn the static or dynamic curve of NLEM.

Casey [11] has proposed neural networks learning method to perform a search through the synthesis parameter space for a given model. The inputs were a dimensionally reduced sound model, and the outputs the parameters to a physical model of a musical instrument. In order to perform a identification of frequency modulation (FM) synthesizer parameters a Genetic Algorithms approach has been proposed by Horner [12].

The estimation of parameters for physical models, however, has a particular advantage over equivalent estimation for additive, FM, or other abstract synthesis models in that the resulting parameter set has a clearly understandable interpretation, which aids in further signal manipulation. For example the parameters estimation of windowing instruments (e.g. clarinet) yields such data as "breath speed," "reed stiffness," "mouth pressure," "tube length," and so forth. In contrast to this, FM (or additive sinusoidal modeling) synthesis parameter estimation do not correspond to data spaces so easily interpretable by musicians.

In this paper a new recurrent-network-based synthesis model for single reed instruments is proposed. Although the idea of using neural networks for sound synthesis is not new (see, for example, [10] and the reference therein) this work addresses a new particularly efficient scheme. Recently, in fact, a neural architecture, based on a flexible activation function, called adaptive spline neural network (ASNN), has been proposed [13]. The ASNNs, have universal approximation property [14] and are suitable for many nonlinear signal processing applications [15].

In this works, in particular, the structure of the network is designed on the basis of a physical model of nonlinear excitation of the single-reed woodwind instrument. In general the NLEM, as in the vibrating reed, is a nonlinear system with memory so static networks cannot adequately model this system. In order to take into account this nonlinear dynamic, Time Delay Neural Networks (TDNNs) [16] with flexible activation function are used.

In order to obtain an efficient hardware/software implementation, the synaptic weights are constrained to be a power-of-two terms while the nonlinear function can be implemented as a simple Catmul-Rom (CR) spline interpolation scheme or through very small lookup table.

Due to power-of-two weights constraints and difficult derivative computation (for some particular synthesis scheme) standard or time-delay back-propagation learning algorithm cannot be developed. In the following, the learning phase, described in Section 3, has been carried out by an efficient combinatorial optimization algorithm called Tabu Search firstly proposed by Glover and Laguna [17] and recently used for power-of-two adaptive filters [18].

In order to demonstrate the effectiveness of the proposed model, experiments on a single-reed woodwind instruments have been carried out.

2   The Neural Architecture Synthesizer

2.1   The Physical Model of Woodwind Instrument

A general model for a reed woodwind instrument is reported in Fig. 1. It is composed of a delay line, a linear element (filter) and a NLEM. The single-reed and mouthpiece arrangement act as a pressure-controlled valve, which transmits energy into the instrument for the initialization and maintenance of oscillations in the acoustic resonator.

The reed can be modeled as a damped non-linear oscillator so that the motion of a second-order mass-spring system is given by the following expression

$$m_r \left[\frac{d^2x}{dt^2} + \mu\omega_r \frac{dx}{dt} + \omega_r^2(x - x_0) \right] = g(p_\Delta(t), U(t)) \tag{1}$$

where m_r is the equivalent reed-mass, μ is the damping factor, ω_r is fundamental reed frequency, $p_\Delta(t)$ is the difference between the player's oral cavity

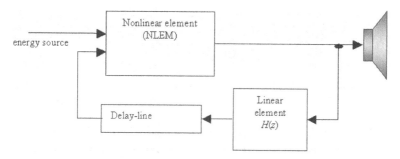

Fig. 1. General scheme of physical model synthesizer

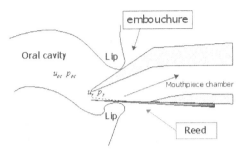

Fig. 2. Scheme of reed embouchure: reed vibrations control the air flow through the embouchure

and the pressure in the reed channel $p_\Delta = (p_{oc} - p_r)$ and U(t) is the steady volume flow through the reed and g(.) is a hard non-linear function [5]-[7]. The reed-excitation mechanism is a nonlinear system with memory and its parameters estimation can be very difficult [6]. The reed vibrations control the air flow on the embouchure (see Fig. 2). A vibrating reed is a pressure-controlled valve with two possible configurations: blown closed and blown open.

2.2   The Neural Pseudo-Physical Model Sound Synthesis

In order to define a general neural class suitable for sound synthesis, neurons with flexible activation functions based on splines interpolated curve are implemented [13]-[15]. The parameters that we optimize are the filter's weights and the control point of the CR-spline activation curve.

The flexible activation function greatly reduces the number of neurons and connections to approximate the NLEM, as it gives an increased expressive power to the neuron.

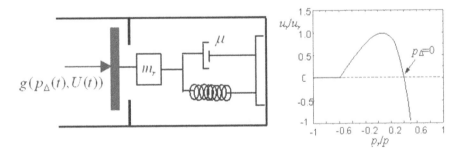

Fig. 3. The reed model as nonlinear mechanical oscillator (left). The flow pressure through the reed embouchure versus reed pressure surface (right)

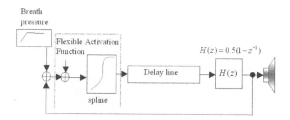

Fig. 4. Scheme of mass-less reed pseudo-physical model instrument

In a first experiment we consider a mass-less reed model shown in Fig. 4. For this model that can be used for clarinet sound, we can use a memory-less neuron: so the learning algorithm adapts only the spline control points.

For a more general sound synthesis model we make use of neural networks with FIR-IIR synapses [16]. The synthesis neural network (here called Adaptive Spline Recurrent Network (ASRN)) constructed on the basis of the previously described physical model of a single full-mass reed instrument is shown in Fig. 5. Once the parameters have been setup with the learning algorithm, the instrument works as a typical physical model instrument.

In order to obtain computationally efficient synthesizer, the ASRN make use of IIR-FIR synapse with power-of-two (or a sum of power-of-two) coefficients. This represents a great advantage in the case of hardware realization. Multipliers, in fact, can be built using few simple and fast shift registers instead of slower floating-point arithmetic, such a strategy can reduce both the VLSI silicon area and the computational time. Moreover, as specified in [13], the activation function can be efficiently implemented both in hardware and in software or after the learning, simply realized through a small lookup-table.

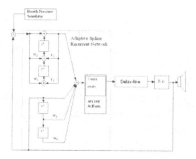

Fig. 5. Scheme of pseudo-physical model neural synthesizer. The nonlinear dynamic element of Fig. 1 is here replaced with a ASRN

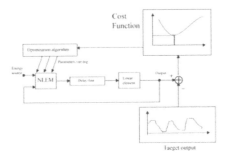

Fig. 6. Proposed Tabu Search learning scheme for the pseudo-physical model neural synthesizer

3   Learning Algorithm

Several batch or on-line algorithms to train locally recurrent neural networks have been developed (see [16] and references therein for more details). However, when the net topology is sophisticated, as in some particular synthesis scheme, it is not easy to calculate the gradient. Moreover, if others constraints are added, as in the proposed model where synaptic weights are defined over the power-of-two domain, the correct gradient computation is impossible.

Let $\mathbf{w}$ the N dimensional vector containing all the synaptic weights defined in the discrete domain ($\mathbf{w} \in D^N$), such that

$$D = \left\{ \begin{array}{l} \alpha : \alpha = \sum_{i=1}^{\lambda} c_i 2^{-g_i} \\ c_i \in \{-1, 0, 1\} \quad , g_i \in \{0, 1, \ldots, B\} \end{array} \right\} \tag{2}$$

Let M the number of control points collected in a vector $\mathbf{q}$ defined in a continuous real domain ($\mathbf{q} \in R^M$); it is possible, now, define $\mathbf{x} = \mathbf{w} \cup \mathbf{q}$, as the vector containing all network's free parameters. The learning consists on a search of a optimum x^* over the space defined by the Cartesian product ($X = R^M \times D^N$) which represents a difficult mixed continuous-discrete optimization problem over the space X.

In this work we make use of the Tabu Search (TS) algorithm [17] recently used for power-of-two adaptive filters [18]. Unlike other combinatorial optimization algorithms, like Genetic Algorithms or Simulated Annealing, where each step is performed independently from the previous moves, TS keeps trace of the visited region in the search space in order to avoid entrapment in local minima and prevent cycling. The search mechanism can be viewed as a dynamic system, which makes it possible to reduce the amount of inspected points and, consequently, the computational burden. Moreover, TS do not require a difficult problem-dependent parameters setting.

The system *learns* from its history and *reacts* trying to correct or to avoid past errors, by using the knowledge acquired in order to direct the search towards the most promising domain regions.

Let $f(x) \in X$ the function to be minimized, TS is a searching algorithm which visits the feasible region X to look for the points where the objective function reaches its minimum. It exploits a prohibiting mechanism to avoid the most recent moves to be repeated in order to escape from local minimum and prevent cycling.

Given an initial solution $x \in X$, a so called *neighborhood set* $N(x) \subset X$, is generated through a deterministic or random *move*. Then, the objective function is evaluated for each element of the *neighborhood set*, and a new solution is chosen as the minimal element of $N(x)$. The definition of neighborhood can, also, be modified to avoid cycle by introducing the concept of *tabu solution* and *tabu list* $T \subset X$. The tabu list T, consists of a set of prohibited moves most recently visited that will not have to be revisited, so a new neighborhood is defined by the set $N(x) - T$.

Finally, this simple iterative scheme can be enhanced by introducing several heuristic criteria, such as *intensification* (i.e. to explore deeply a region that look promising), *diversification* (i.e. to leave a region that does not looks promising) [17].

4   Experimental Results

We have tested this model with clarinet and saxophone sounds. The learning phase consisted of 1000 TS cycles for the clarinet, having taken into account a cost function over a window of 1024 samples.

The cost function J_{cost} minimized by the previous described learning algorithm is defined as:

$$J_{\cos t} = \alpha J_1 + \beta J_2 \tag{3}$$

where J_1 and J_2 are defined as:

$$J_1 = \sum_{\omega \in \Omega} \left(\left| D(e^{j\omega}) \right| - \left| X(e^{j\omega}) \right| \right)^2 \tag{4}$$

$$J_2 = \frac{1}{N} \sum_{t=0}^{N} w[t] \left(d[t] - x[t] \right)^2 \tag{5}$$

where $d[t]$, $x[t]$ and $D(e^{jw})$, $X(e^{jw})$, represent the desired and actual sound signals in time and frequency domain respectively and $w[t]$ is a suitable weighting function.

In other words, J_{cost} is a combination of two functionals: the first represents a distance in frequency domain while the second represents a distance in the time-domain distance combination between the real instrument sound and the generated one.

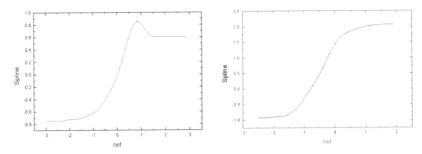

Fig. 7. Spline flexible activation function shapes obtained by learning from clarinet sound for the memory-less model of Fig. 4 (left) and IIR-MLP Fig. 5 (rigth)

We have tested the model with several FIR-IIR delay line lengths. For the clarinet we have obtained good results even without FIR synapses, just with an adaptive CR-spline neuron, while for the saxophone model it resulted better to use IIR synapses but real time was compromised. Using the model of Fig. 4 we obtained good results for clarinet, while acceptable results for saxophone-like sound have been reached using the model of Figure 5. In Figure 7 the nonlinear activation function obtained by learning from clarinet sound for the models shown in Figs. 4–5.

Our important goal is not that we reproduce the identical target sound that is impossible without complicating the model, but that our instrument can learn the parameters able to reproduce different sound types, so that the same model can be used to reproduce a class of different musical instruments.

Once fixed all the parameters for a single instrument by minimizing the cost function (learning stage) the instrument can be played (forward stage) as a normal physical-model instrument and the parameter can be controlled in order to produce sound modifications. Real time implementations of the models discussed in this paper were carried out using a platform independent, floating-point, C++ environment created by Cook and Scavone [7] and called *Synthesis ToolKit* (STK). A significant number of signal processing unit generator objects are supplied with the STK as well as with routine for MIDI control in real-time playing.

5   Conclusions

In this paper the use of ASRN as a physical-like model for sound synthesis of reed instruments has been proposed. The ASRN, represents a general computational model and we think that it is possible to make it reproduce a very large class of instruments such as: plucked, bowed and woodwind. Our base model has been made as simple as possible in order to be played in real time.

The use of IIR-FIR synapse with power-of-two (or a sum of power-of-two) coefficients represents a great advantage in the case of hardware realization.

Multipliers, in fact can be built using simple and fast shift registers instead of slower floating-point arithmetic, such a strategy can reduce both the VLSI silicon area and the computational time.

References

[1] S. Y. Kung, J. N. Hwang, "Neural Networks for Intelligent Multimedia Processing", Proceedings of IEEE, Vol. 86, No. 6, pp. 1244-1272, June 1998. 168

[2] B. L. Vercoe, W. G. Gardner, E. D. Scheirer, "Structured Audio: Creation, Transmission, and Rendering of Parametric Sound Representations", Proceedings of IEEE, Vol. 86, No. 5, pp. 922-940, May 1998. 168

[3] J. O. Smith, "Physical Modeling Using Digital Wave-guides", Computer Music Journal, vol 16, n. 4, pp 74-91, 1992. 168

[4] G. Borin, G De Poli, and A. Sarti, "Sound Synthesis by Dynamic Systems Interaction", in Readings in Computer-Generated Music, pp.139-160, IEEE Comp. Soc. Press, D. Baggi ed., 1992. 168

[5] Gary Paul Scavone, "An acoustical analysis of single-reed woodwind instruments with an emphasis on design and performance issues and digital waveguide modeling techniques", Ph.D. thesis, Music Dept., Stanford University, March 1997. 168, 171

[6] N. H. Fletcher, T. D. Rossing, "The Physics of Musical Instruments", Springer-Verlang, New-York, 1981. 171

[7] Gary P. Scavone, Perry Cook, "Real Time Computer Modeling of woodwind instruments", International Symposium on Musical Acoustics, Leavenworth, WA 1998. 171, 175

[8] J. O. Smith, "Technique for Digital Filter Design and System Identification with Application to the Violin", PhD Thesis, CCRM, Standford University, Report n. STAN-M-14, 1983. 169

[9] J. Vuori and V. Vlimki, "Parameter Estimation of Non-linear Physical Models by Simulated Evolution: Application to the Flute Model", Proc. Int. Comp. Music Conf., pp. 402-404, Tokyo 1993. 169

[10] Carlo Drioli, Davide Rocchesso, "Learning Pseudo-Physical Models for Sound Synthesis and Trasformation", IEEE International Conference on Systems, Man, and Cybernetics, vol. 2, pp 1085-1090, 1998. 169

[11] M. A. Casey, "Understanding musical sound with forward models and physical models", Connection Sci., vol. 6, pp. 355-371, 1994. 169

[12] A. Horner, B. Beauchamp, and L. Haken, "FM matching synthesis with genetic algorithms", Comput. Music J., vol. 17, no. 4, pp. 17-29, Winter 1993. 169

[13] Stefano Guarnieri, Francesco Piazza and Aurelio Uncini, "Multilayer Feedforward Networks with AdaptiveSpline Activation Function", IEEE Trans. On Neural Network, Vol. 10, No. 3, pp.672-683, May 1999. 169, 171, 172

[14] Lorenzo Vecci, Francesco Piazza and Aurelio Uncini, "Learning and Approximation Capabilities of Adaptive Spline Activation Function Neural Networks", Neural Networks, Vol.11, No.2, pp 259-270, March 1998. 169

[15] Aurelio Uncini, Lorenzo Vecci, Paolo Campolucci and Francesco Piazza, "Complex-valued Neural Networks with Adaptive Spline Activation Function for Digital Radio Links Nonlinear Equalization", IEEE Trans. on Signal Processing, Vol. 47, No. 2, February 1999. 169, 171

[16] Paolo Campolucci, Aurelio Uncini, Francesco Piazza and Bhaskar D. Rao, "On-Line Learning Algorithms for Locally Recurrent Neural Networks", IEEE Trans. on Neural Network, Vol. 10, No. 2, pp.253-271 March 1999. 170, 173

[17] F. Glover, M. Laguna, "Tabu search", Kluver Academic Publisher, 1997. 170, 173, 174

[18] Stefano Traferro and Aurelio Uncini, "Power-of-Two Adaptive Filters Using Tabu Search", IEEE Transactions on Circuits and Systems-II: Analog and Digital Signal Processing, Vol. 47, No. 6, June 2000. 170, 173

Part VI

Special Session on "Learning in Neural Networks: Limitations and Future Trends" Chaired by Marco Gori

Mathematical Modelling of Generalization

Martin Anthony

Department of Mathematics, London School of Economics
Houghton Street, London WC2A 2AE, UK
m.anthony@lse.ac.uk
www.maths.lse.ac.uk/Personal/martin

Abstract. This paper surveys certain developments in the use of probabilistic techniques for the modelling of generalization. Some of the main methods and key results are discussed. Many details are omitted, the aim being to give a high-level overview of the types of approaches taken and methods used.

Keywords: Probabilistic modelling of learning

1 Probabilistic Modelling of Learning

Suppose that X is a set of *examples* and that $Y \subseteq [0,1]$ is a set of possible *outputs*. Elements (x, y) of $Z = X \times Y$ will be called *labelled examples*. In the model, we shall assume that a *learning algorithm* $\mathcal{A}$ takes a randomly generated *training sample* of labelled examples and produces a function $h : X \to [0,1]$, chosen from some *hypothesis class* H of functions. We assume that there is some fixed, but unknown, probability measure[1] μ on Z, and that each training example is generated independently according to μ. A learning algorithm is a function $A : \bigcup_{n=1}^{\infty} Z^n \to H$, where H is a *hypothesis class* of functions from Z to $[0,1]$. We have in mind some *loss function* $\ell : [0,1] \times Y \to [0,1]$. Examples of loss functions are $\ell(r, s) = |r - s|$, $\ell(r, s) = (r - s)^2$, and the discrete loss, given by $\ell(r, s) = 0$ if $r = s$ and $\ell(r, s) = 1$ if $r \neq s$. What we hope for is that $\mathcal{A}(z)$ has a relatively small *loss*, where, for $h \in H$, the loss of h is the expectation $L(h) = e, ell(h(x), y)$ (where the expectation is with respect to μ). Since the best loss one could hope to be near is $L^* = \inf_{h \in H} L(h)$, we want $\mathcal{A}(z)$ to have loss close to L^*, with high probability, provided the sample size n is large enough. (Here, and in the rest of the paper, we use the symbol p to denote probability. In the definition that follows, the probability is with respect to μ^n.) This definition has its origins in [35, 33, 32, 19]. (See also the books [3, 4, 21, 36].)

We say that $\mathcal{A}$ is a *successful* learning algorithm for H if for all $\epsilon, \delta \in (0, 1)$, there is some $n_0(\epsilon, \delta)$ (depending on ϵ and δ only) such that, if $n > n_0(\epsilon, \delta)$, then with probability at least $1 - \delta$, $L(\mathcal{A}(z)) \leq L^* + \epsilon$. Note that if $\mathcal{A}$ is successful,

---

[1] Certain measurability conditions are implicitly assumed in what follows, but these conditions are reasonable and not particularly stringent. Details may be found in [31] for instance.

M. Marinaro and R. Tagliaferri (Eds.): WIRN VIETRI 2002, LNCS 2486, pp. 181–189, 2002.

then there is some function $\epsilon_0(n, \delta)$ of n and δ, with the property that for all δ, $\lim_{n\to\infty} \epsilon_0(n, \delta) = 0$, and such that for any probability measure μ on Z, with probability at least $1 - \delta$ we have $L(\mathcal{A}(\boldsymbol{z})) \leq L^* + \epsilon_0(n, \delta)$. The minimal $\epsilon_0(n, \delta)$ is called the *estimation error* of the algorithm.

When H is a set of binary functions, meaning each function in H maps into $\{0, 1\}$, if $Y = \{0, 1\}$, and if we use the discrete loss function, then we shall say that we have a *binary* learning problem.

We might want to use real functions for classification. Here, we would have $Y = \{0, 1\}$, but $H : X \to [0, 1]$. In this case, one appropriate loss function would be given, for $r \in [0, 1]$ and $s \in \{0, 1\}$, by $\ell(r, s) = 0$ if $r - 1/2$ and $s - 1/2$ have the same sign, and $\ell(r, s) = 1$ otherwise. We call this the *threshold loss*. Thus, with respect to the threshold loss, $\ell(h(x), y) \in \{0, 1\}$ is 0 precisely when the thresholded function $T_h : x \mapsto \text{sign}(h(x) - 1/2)$ has value y. There is some advantage in considering the *margin* of classification by these real-valued hypotheses (a fact that has been emphasised for some time in pattern recognition and learning [34], and which is very important in Support Vector Machines [13].) Explicitly, suppose that $\gamma > 0$, and for $r \in [0, 1]$, define $\text{mar}(r, 1) = r - 1/2$ and $\text{mar}(r, 0) = 1/2 - r$. The *margin* of $h \in H$ on $z = (x, y) \in Z \times \{0, 1\}$ is defined to be $\text{mar}(f(x), y)$. Now, define the loss function ℓ^γ by $\ell^\gamma(r, s) = 1$ if $\text{mar}(r, s) < \gamma$ and $\ell^\gamma(r, s) = 0$ if $\text{mar}(r, s) \geq \gamma$. The corresponding loss $L^\gamma(h)$ of a hypothesis is called the loss of h at margin γ. We say (as in [3]) that $\mathcal{A} :$ $(0, 1) \times \bigcup_{n=1}^\infty Z^n \to H$ is a *successful real-valued classification algorithm* if for all $\epsilon, \delta \in (0, 1)$ there is $n_0(\epsilon, \delta)$ such that, if $n > n_0(\epsilon, \delta)$, then with probability at least $1 - \delta$, $L(\mathcal{A}(\gamma, \boldsymbol{z})) \leq \inf_{h \in H} L^\gamma(h) + \epsilon$.

2   Techniques

Uniform Glivenko-Cantelli Classes Suppose that F is a set of (measurable) functions from Z to $[0, 1]$ and that μ is a probability measure on Z. Denote the expectation $\mathbb{E}_\mu f$ by $\mu(f)$ and, for $\boldsymbol{z} = (z_1, z_2, \ldots, z_n) \in Z^n$, let us denote by $\mu_n(f)$ the empirical measure of f on $\boldsymbol{z}$, $\mu_n(f) = n^{-1} \sum_{i=1}^n f(z_i)$. F is a *uniform Glivenko-Cantelli* class if it has the following property (also known as uniform convergence of empiricals to expectations) if for all $\epsilon > 0$, $\lim_{n\to\infty} \sup_\mu \mathbb{P}\left(\sup_{m \geq n} \sup_{f \in F} |\mu(f) - \mu_m(f)| > \epsilon\right) = 0$.

Define the *loss class* (corresponding to ℓ and H) to be $\ell_H = \{\ell_h : h \in H\}$ where, for $z = (x, y)$, $\ell_h(z) = \ell(h(x), y)$. Suppose that ℓ_H is a uniform Glivenko-Cantelli class. For $\boldsymbol{z} \in Z^n$, the *empirical loss* of $h \in H$ on $\boldsymbol{z}$ is defined to be $L_{\boldsymbol{z}}(h) = \mu_n(\ell_h) = n^{-1} \sum_{i=1}^n \ell(h(x_i), y_i)$, where $z_i = (x_i, y_i)$. Let us say that $\mathcal{A}$ is an *approximate empirical loss minimisation* algorithm if for all $\boldsymbol{z} \in Z^n$, $L_{\boldsymbol{z}}(\mathcal{A}(\boldsymbol{z})) < 1/n + \inf_{h \in H} L_{\boldsymbol{z}}(h)$. Then it is fairly easy to see [1, 3], that $\mathcal{A}$ is a successful learning algorithm.

Symmetrization A key technique is *symmetrization*. The following symmetrization result for expectations is obtainable(see [14]):

$$\mathbb{E}\left(\sup_{f \in F} |\mu(f) - \mu_n(f)|\right) \leq \frac{2}{n} \mathbb{E} \sup_{f \in F} \left|\sum_{i=1}^{n} \sigma_i f(z_i)\right|, \tag{1}$$

where, for $1 \leq i \leq n$, $\sigma_i \in \{-1, 1\}$ are *Rademacher* random variables, taking value 1 with probability $1/2$ and -1 with probability $1/2$. (Here the expectation is jointly over the distributions of the samples, and of the σ_i.) Symmetrization results for the tail probabilities $\mathbb{P}\left(\sup_{f \in F} |\mu(f) - \mu_n(f)| > \epsilon\right)$ can also be obtained; see [18, 25].

Concentration We now describe a type of *concentration result* (see [24]), a generalisation of Hoeffding's inequality. We shall call it the *bounded differences inequality*. Suppose that a function $g : Z^n \to \mathbb{R}$ has the following *bounded differences* property: for $1 \leq i \leq n$, there are constants c_i such that for any $\boldsymbol{z}, \boldsymbol{z}' \in Z^n$ which differ only in the ith coordinate (so $z_i \neq z_i'$ but $z_j = z_j'$ for all $j \neq i$), we have $|g(\boldsymbol{z}) - g(\boldsymbol{z}')| \leq c_i$. Then, if $z_1, z_2, \ldots, z_n$ are independent, we have

$$\mathbb{P}\left(|g(\boldsymbol{z}) - \mathbb{E}g(\boldsymbol{z})| \geq \alpha\right) < 2\exp\left(-2\alpha^2 / \sum_{i=1}^{n} c_i^2\right). \tag{2}$$

In particular, as observed in [14], if we take $g(\boldsymbol{z}) = \sup_{f \in F} |\mu(f) - \mu_n(f)|$, and note that g has the bounded differences property with $c_i = 1/n$, we obtain that, with probability at least $1 - \delta$,

$$\sup_{f \in F} |\mu(f) - \mu_n(f)| < \sqrt{\frac{1}{2n} \ln\left(\frac{2}{\delta}\right)} + \mathbb{E} \sup_{f \in F} |\mu(f) - \mu_n(f)|. \tag{3}$$

Using Covering Numbers Given a (pseudo-)metric space (A, d) and a subset S of A, we say that the set $T \subseteq A$ is an ϵ-*cover* for S (where $\epsilon > 0$) if, for every $s \in S$ there is $t \in T$ such that $d(s, t) < \epsilon$. For a fixed $\epsilon > 0$ we denote by $\mathcal{N}(S)\epsilon d$ the cardinality of the smallest ϵ-cover for S. (We define $\mathcal{N}(S)\epsilon d$ to be ∞ if there is no such cover.) In our setting, for $\boldsymbol{z} \in Z^n$, and $f \in F$, let $f|_{\boldsymbol{z}} = (f(z_1), f(z_2), \ldots, f(z_n))$ and let $F|_{\boldsymbol{z}} = \{f|_{\boldsymbol{z}} : f \in F\} \subseteq [0, 1]^n$. For $r \geq 1$, let $d_r(\boldsymbol{v}, \boldsymbol{w}) = \left(n^{-1} \sum_{i=1}^{n} |v_i - w_i|^r\right)^{1/r}$, and let $d_\infty(\boldsymbol{v}, \boldsymbol{w}) = \max_{1 \leq i \leq n} |v_i - w_i|$. Define the *uniform covering number* $\mathcal{N}_r F \epsilon n$ to be $\sup_{\boldsymbol{z} \in Z^n} \mathcal{N}(F|_{\boldsymbol{z}} \epsilon d_r)$. Note that if $r > s$ then $d_s(\boldsymbol{v}, \boldsymbol{w}) \leq d_r(\boldsymbol{v}, \boldsymbol{w}) \leq d_\infty(\boldsymbol{v}, \boldsymbol{w})$ and, consequently, $\mathcal{N}_s F \epsilon n \leq \mathcal{N}_r F \epsilon n \leq \mathcal{N}_\infty F \epsilon n$.

As shown in [25] (using techniques developed in [35, 27, 19] and elsewhere), if F is a set of functions from Z to $[0, 1]$, then for any $\epsilon \in (0, 1)$,

$$\mathbb{P}\left(\sup_{f \in F} |\mu(f) - \mu_n(f)| > \epsilon\right) \leq 8 \mathbb{E}_{\mu^n}\left(\mathcal{N}(F|_{\boldsymbol{z}})\epsilon/8d_1\right) e^{-n\epsilon^2/128}. \tag{4}$$

This implies that, with probability at least $1 - \delta$,

$$\sup_{f \in F} |\mu(f) - \mu_n(f)| < \sqrt{\frac{64}{n} (\ln \mathcal{N}_1 F \epsilon/8n) + \ln \left(\frac{8}{\delta}\right)}.$$

In the binary case, better bounds are possible; see [3, 14] (in particular [14, 16] by using a technique known as *chaining*).

Next, we have the following result [6, 3] which concerns real-valued classification. (See [6, 30] for similar results.) With probability at least $1 - \delta$,

$$\forall h \in H, \quad L(h) < L_z^\gamma(h) + \sqrt{\frac{8}{n} (\ln \mathcal{N}_\infty H \gamma/22n) + \ln \left(\frac{2}{\delta}\right)}. \tag{5}$$

Rademacher Complexity For $z \in Z^n$, $\mathbb{E} \sup_{f \in F} \left|2n^{-1} \sum_{i=1}^n \sigma_i f(z_i)\right|$ is denoted $R_n(F, z)$, where the expectation is over the joint distribution of the σ_i, and the *Rademacher complexity* (or Rademacher average) of F is defined to be $R_n(F) = \mathbb{E} R_n(F, z)$ (where here the expectation is over Z^n, with respect to μ^n). (See, for example [25, 9, 22, 31].) By equation (1), we see directly that $\mathbb{E} \sup_{f \in F} |\mu(f) - \mu_n(f)|$ is bounded above by $R_n(F)$. By (3), with probability at least $1 - \delta$, for $z \in Z^n$,

$$\sup_{f \in F} |\mu(f) - \mu_n(f)| < R_n(F) + \sqrt{\frac{1}{2n} \ln \left(\frac{2}{\delta}\right)}.$$

The Rademacher complexity possesses some useful structural properties; for example, the Rademacher complexities of a function class and its symmetric convex hull are the same [9]. Estimates of the Rademacher complexity for a number of function classes, including neural networks, can be found in [9].

More recently, attention has turned to *localized* Rademacher complexities, in which the supremum is taken not over the whole of F, but over a subset of those f with small variance. For details, see [25, 7, 12].

Combinatorial Measures of Function Class Complexity We have seen that the covering numbers and Rademacher complexity can be used to bound the probabilities of chief interest. These can in turn be bounded by using certain combinatorial measures of function class complexity. We shall focus here on the bounding of covering numbers, but see [25] for results relating Rademacher complexities to combinatorial parameters.

For the binary case, Vapnik and Chervonenkis [35] established that what has subsequently been known as the Vapnik-Chervonenkis dimension (or VC-dimension) is a key measure of function class complexity. (The importance for learning theory was highlighted in [10], and expositions may be found in the books [4, 3, 21, 36], and elsewhere.) In this case, for $z \in Z^n$, the set $F|_z$ is finite, of cardinality at most 2^n, and we may define the *growth function* Π_F :

$\mathbb{N} \to \mathbb{N}$ by $\Pi_F(n) = \max_{\mathbf{z} \in Z^n} |F|_{\mathbf{z}}|$. It is clear that $\mathcal{N}(F|_{\mathbf{z}} \epsilon d_r = |F|_{\mathbf{z}}|$ and $\mathcal{N}_r F \epsilon n = \Pi_F(n)$, for all r and for $\epsilon \in (0,1)$. The *VC-dimension* VCdim(F) is then defined to be (infinity, or) the largest d such that $\Pi_F(d) = 2^d$. The Sauer-Shelah lemma [28, 29] asserts that if VCdim$(F) = d < \infty$ then for all $n \geq d$, $\Pi_F(n) \leq \sum_{i=0}^{d} \binom{n}{i}$, showing that the growth function is polynomial in this case. For another description of VC-dimension, we may say that a subset S of Z is *shattered* by F if for any $T \subseteq S$ there is $f_T \in F$ with $f_T(z) = 1$ for $z \in T$ and $f_T(z) = 0$ for $z \in S \setminus T$. Then the VC-dimension is the largest cardinality of a shattered set. Note that, with the discrete loss, it is easy to see that if $F = \ell_H$ then $\Pi_F = \Pi_H$ and so VCdim$(F) = $ VCdim(H). Now, equation (4) has the following consequence for a binary class of finite VC-dimension d: with probability at least $1 - \delta$,

$$\sup_{f \in F} |\mu(f) - \mu_n(f)| < k\sqrt{\frac{1}{n}\left(d\ln\left(\frac{n}{d}\right) + \ln\left(\frac{1}{\delta}\right)\right)},$$

for a fixed constant k. (In the Boolean case, tighter bounds can be obtained (see [23]).)

Lower bounds on the sample complexity of learning algorithms can also be obtained in terms of the VC-dimension [17, 10, 3]. The VC-dimensions of many different types of neural network have been estimated; see [3, 20, 2], for example.

Suppose, more generally, that $F : Z \to [0,1]$. For $\gamma > 0$, we say that $S \subseteq Z$ is γ-*shattered* by F if there are numbers $r_z \in [0,1]$ for $z \in S$ such that for every $T \subseteq S$ there is some $f_T \in F$ with the property that $f_T(z) \geq r_z + \gamma$ if $z \in T$ and $f_T(z) < r_z - \gamma$ if $z \in S \setminus T$. We say that F has finite *fat-shattering dimension* d at scale γ, and we write fat$_\gamma F = d$, if d is the maximum cardinality of a γ-shattered set. We say simply that F has finite fat-shattering dimension if it has finite fat-shattering dimension at every scale $\gamma > 0$. Alon *et al.* [1] obtained an upper bound on the d_∞ covering numbers in terms of the fat-shattering dimension, establishing that F is a uniform Glivenko-Cantelli class if and only if it has finite fat-shattering dimension. We can apply their results to real classification learning by using (5). This leads [3] to the fact that, with probability at least $1 - \delta$,

$$\forall h \in H, \quad L(h) < L_{\mathbf{z}}^\gamma(h) + \sqrt{\frac{8}{n}\left(d\log_2\left(\frac{32en}{d}\right)\ln(128n) + \ln\left(\frac{4}{\delta}\right)\right)}, \quad (6)$$

where $d = $ fat$_{\gamma/8} H$.

For more on the fat-shattering dimension, including estimates for neural network classes, see [1, 3, 6]. See [3, 8, 25, 26] for improved bounds on covering numbers in terms of the fat-shattering dimension, particularly with respect to the metrics d_p for $p \neq \infty$.

3   Data-Dependent Learning Bounds

In this section we present some data-dependent results, in which bounds on estimation error are given that depended not only on the hypothesis class, but on the sample $\boldsymbol{z}$ itself. Data-dependent bounds have been obtained in a number of ways, in particular through deploying a general 'luckiness' framework developed in [30, 37], and, more recently, through the application of concentration inequalities, as in [11, 5].

Suppose that H is a binary function class mapping from X to $\{0, 1\}$. By proving a new concentration inequality, Boucheron, Lugosi and Massart [11], established that the *VC-entropy* $H_n(\boldsymbol{x}) = \log_2 |H|_{\boldsymbol{x}}|$ (for $\boldsymbol{x} \in X^n$) is concentrated around its expectation. With this, they were able to establish the following data-dependent result (in which the loss function is the discrete loss): with probability at least $1 - \delta$, for $\boldsymbol{z} \in Z^n = (X \times \{0, 1\})^n$,

$$\forall h \in H, \quad L(h) < L_{\boldsymbol{z}}(h) + \sqrt{\frac{6 \ln |H|_{\boldsymbol{x}}|}{n}} + 4\sqrt{\frac{\ln(2/\delta)}{n}}.$$

This should be compared with the bounds that would follow from the results presented earlier: such bounds would involve $\mathbb{E} |H|_{\boldsymbol{x}}|$ or, since μ is not known, the growth function $\Pi_H(n) = \max_{\boldsymbol{x} \in X^n} |H|_{\boldsymbol{x}}|$, and therefore would not depend explicitly on the data. It is certainly possible that $|H|_{\boldsymbol{x}}|$ is much less than $\Pi_H(n)$, and so the data-dependent bound could have significant advantage. (This result can also be expressed in terms of the *empirical VC-dimension*.)

There are also data-dependent results for real-valued classification [37, 5]. Using the concentration inequality from [11], Antos, Kégl, Linder and Lugosi [5] have obtained bounds involving the *empirical fat-shattering dimension*. For $\boldsymbol{x} \in X^n$, and $\gamma > 0$, let $\mathrm{fat}_\gamma(H|\boldsymbol{x})$ be the fat-shattering dimension of the set of functions obtained by restricting H to the set consisting of the elements of the sample $\boldsymbol{x}$. Then, in [5], it is shown that, for $\gamma > 0$, with probability at least $1 - \delta$,

$$\forall h \in H, \quad L(h) < L_{\boldsymbol{z}}^\gamma(h) + \sqrt{\frac{1}{n}\left(9d(\boldsymbol{x}) + 12.5\ln\left(\frac{8}{\delta}\right)\right)\ln\left(\frac{32en}{d(\boldsymbol{x})}\right)\ln(128n)},$$

where $d(\boldsymbol{x}) = \mathrm{fat}_{\gamma/8}(H|\boldsymbol{x})$.

This should be compared with (6). The former might look better, but the empirical fat-shattering dimension can be significantly less than the fat-shattering dimension, so in some cases the data-dependent bound is better. Moreover, the empirical fat-shattering dimension can be calculated reasonably easily in some cases. (See [5].)

We can also obtain a version of the above result in which the margin γ is not specified beforehand, and could depend on both the data and the chosen hypothesis. Using the 'method of sieves' (see [6, 3]), it can be shown that, with probability at least $1 - \delta$, the following holds, for all $h \in H$ and for all $\gamma \in (0, 1]$:

$$L(h) < L_{\boldsymbol{z}}^\gamma(h) + \sqrt{\frac{1}{n}\left(9d_1(\boldsymbol{x}) + 12.5\ln\left(\frac{16}{\delta\gamma}\right)\right)\ln\left(\frac{32en}{d_2(\boldsymbol{x})}\right)\ln(128n)},$$

where $d_1(\boldsymbol{x}) = \mathrm{fat}_{\gamma/16}(H|\boldsymbol{x})$ and $d_2(\boldsymbol{x}) = \mathrm{fat}_{\gamma/8}(H|\boldsymbol{x})$.

Turning attention now to the Rademacher complexity, Bartlett and Mendelson [9] have observed that the empirical Rademacher complexity $R_n(F, \boldsymbol{z})$ is concentrated about its expectation, which is $R_n(F)$. For, it is easy to see that $g(\mathbf{z}) = R_n(F, \mathbf{z})$ satisfies the bounded differences property with each c_i equal to $2/n$. Hence, by (3), with probability at least $1 - \delta$,

$$\forall h \in H, \quad L(h) < L_{\mathbf{z}}(h) + R_n(F, \mathbf{z}) + 3\sqrt{\frac{1}{n}\ln\left(\frac{2}{\delta}\right)}.$$

References

[1] Noga Alon, Shai Ben-David, Nicolo Cesa-Bianchi, and David Haussler: Scale-sensitive dimensions, uniform convergence, and learnability. *Journal of the ACM* **44**(5): 616–631. 182, 185

[2] Martin Anthony: Probabilistic analysis of learning in artificial neural networks: the PAC model and its variants. *Neural Computing Surveys*, **1**, 1997. 185

[3] Martin Anthony and Peter L. Bartlett: *Neural Network Learning: Theoretical Foundations*. Cambridge University Press, Cambridge UK, 1999. 181, 182, 184, 185, 186

[4] Martin Anthony and Norman L. Biggs: *Computational Learning Theory: An Introduction*. Cambridge Tracts in Theoretical Computer Science, 30, 1992. Cambridge University Press, Cambridge, UK. 181, 184

[5] András Antos, Balázs Kégl, Tamás Linder and Gábor Lugosi: Data-dependent margin-based generalization bounds for classification. Preprint, Queen's University at Kingston, Canada. magenta.mast.queensu.ca/~linder/preprints.html. 186

[6] Peter Bartlett: The sample complexity of pattern classification with neural networks: the size of the weights is more important than the size of the network. *IEEE Transactions on Information Theory* **44**(2): 525–536. 184, 185, 186

[7] Peter L. Bartlett, Olivier Bousquet and Shahar Mendelson: Localized Rademacher complexities. To appear, *Proceedings of the 15th Annual Conference on Computational Learning Theory*, ACM Press, New York, NY, 2002. 184

[8] Peter L. Bartlett and Philip M. Long: More theorems about scale-sensitive dimensions and learning. In *Proceedings of the 8th Annual Conference on Computational Learning Theory*, ACM Press, New York, NY, 1995, pp. 392–401. 185

[9] Peter Bartlett and Shahar Mendelson: Rademacher and Guassian complexities: risk bounds and structural results. In *Proceedings of the 14th Annual Conference on Computational Learning Theory*, Lecture Notes in Artificial Intelligence, Springer pp. 224-240, 2001. 184, 186

[10] Anselm Blumer, Andrzej Ehrenfeucht, David Haussler, and Manfred K. Warmuth: Learnability and the Vapnik-Chervonenkis dimension. *Journal of the ACM*, **36**(4): 929–965, 1989. 184, 185

[11] Stéphane Boucheron, Gábor Lugosi and Pascal Massart: A sharp concentration inequality with applications. *Random Structures and Algorithms*, **16**: 277–292, 2000. 186

[12] Olivier Bousquet, Vladimir Koltchinskii and Dmitriy Panchenko: Some local measures of complexity on convex hulls and generalization bounds. To appear, *Proceedings of the 15th Annual Conference on Computational Learning Theory*, ACM Press, New York, NY, 2002. 184

[13] Nello Cristianini and John Shawe-Taylor: *An Introduction to Support Vector Machines*, Cambridge University Press, Cambridge, UK, 2000. 182

[14] Luc Devroye and Gábor Lugosi: *Combinatorial Methods in Density Estimation*, Springer Series in Statistics, Springer-Verlag, New York, NY, 2001. 183, 184

[15] Richard M. Dudley: *Uniform Central Limit Theorems*, Cambridge Studies in Advanced Mathematics, 63, Cambridge University Press, Cambridge, UK, 1999.

[16] Richard M. Dudley: Central limit theorems for empirical measures. *Annals of Probability*, **6**(6): 899–929, 1978. 184

[17] Andrzej Ehrenfeucht, David Haussler, Michael Kearns, and Leslie Valiant. A general lower bound on the number of examples needed for learning. *Information and Computation*, **82**: 247–261, 1989. 185

[18] E. Giné and J. Zinn: Some limit theorems for empirical processes. *Annals of Probability* **12**(4): 929–989, 1984. 183

[19] David Haussler: Decision theoretic generalizations of the PAC model for neural net and other learning applications. *Information and Computation*, **100**(1): 78–150, 1992. 181, 183

[20] Marek Karpinski and Angus MacIntyre: Polynomial bounds for VC dimension of sigmoidal and general Pfaffian neural networks. *Journal of Computer and System Sciences*, **54**: 169–176, 1997. 185

[21] Michael J. Kearns and Umesh Vazirani: *Introduction to Computational Learning Theory*, MIT Press, Cambridge, MA, 1995. 181, 184

[22] Vladimir Koltchinskii and Dmitry Panchenko: Rademacher processes and bounding the risk of function learning. Technical report, Department of Mathematics and Statistics, University of New Mexico, 2000. 184

[23] Gábor Lugosi: *Lectures on Statistical Learning Theory*, presented at the Garchy Seminar on Mathematical Statistics and Applications, August 27-September 1, 2000. (Available from www.econ.upf.es/ lugosi.) 185

[24] Colin McDiarmid: On the method of bounded differences. In J. Siemons, editor, *Surveys in Combinatorics, 1989*, London Mathematical Society Lecture Note Series (141). Cambridge University Press, Cambridge, UK, 1989. 183

[25] Shahar Mendelson: A few notes on Statistical Learning Theory. Technical Report, Australian National University Computer Science Laboratory. 183, 184, 185

[26] S. Mendelson and R. Vershynin: Entropy, dimension and the Elton-Pajor theorem. Preprint, Australian National University. 185

[27] David Pollard: *Convergence of Stochastic Processes*. Springer-Verlag, 1984. 183

[28] N. Sauer: On the density of families of sets. *Journal of Combinatorial Theory (A)*, **13**: 145–147, 1972. 185

[29] S. Shelah: A combinatorial problem: Stability and order for models and theories in infinitary languages. *Pacific Journal of Mathematics*, **41**: 247–261, 1972. 185

[30] John Shawe-Taylor, Peter Bartlett, Bob Williamson and Martin Anthony: Structural risk minimisation over data-dependent hierarchies. *IEEE Transactions on Information Theory*, **44**(5): 1926–1940, 1998. 184, 186

[31] Aad W. van der Vaart and Jon A. Wellner: *Weak Convergence and Empirical Processes*, Springer Series in Statistics, Springer-Verlag, New York, NY, 1996. 181, 184

[32] Leslie G. Valiant: A theory of the learnable. *Communications of the ACM*, **27**(11): 1134–1142, Nov. 1984. 181

[33] Vladimir N. Vapnik: *Estimation of Dependences Based on Empirical Data*. Springer-Verlag, New York, 1982. 181

[34] Vladimir N. Vapnik: *Statistical Learning Theory*, Wiley, 1998. 182

[35] V. N. Vapnik and A. Y. Chervonenkis: On the uniform convergence of relative frequencies of events to their probabilities. *Theory of Probability and its Applications*, **16**(2): 264–280, 1971. 181, 183, 184

[36] M. Vidyasagar: *A Theory of Learning and Generalization*, Springer-Verlag, 1996. 181, 184

[37] Robert Williamson, John Shawe-Taylor, Bernhard Scholkopf, and Alex Smola: *Sample Based Generalization Bounds*, NeuroCOLT Technical Report, NC-TR-99-055, 1999. 186

Structural Complexity and Neural Networks[*]

Alberto Bertoni[1] and Beatrice Palano[2]

[1] Dipartimento di Scienze dell'Informazione
Università degli Studi di Milano
via Comelico 39, 20135 Milano, Italy
bertoni@dsi.unimi.it
[2] Dipartimento di Informatica
Università degli Studi di Torino
c.so Svizzera 185, 10149 Torino, Italy
beatrice@di.unito.it

Abstract. We survey some relationships between computational complexity and neural network theory. Here, only networks of binary threshold neurons are considered.

We begin by presenting some contributions of neural networks in structural complexity theory. In parallel complexity, the class TC_k^0 of problems solvable by feed-forward networks with k levels and a polynomial number of neurons is considered. Separation results are recalled and the relation between $TC^0 = \bigcup TC_k^0$ and NC^1 is analyzed. In particular, under the conjecture $TC \neq NC^1$, we characterize the class of regular languages accepted by feed-forward networks with a constant number of levels and a polynomial number of neurons.

We also discuss the use of complexity theory to study computational aspects of learning and combinatorial optimization in the context of neural networks. We consider the PAC model of learning, emphasizing some negative results based on complexity theoretic assumptions. Finally, we discussed some results in the realm of neural networks related to a probabilistic characterization of NP.

Keywords: Structural complexity, Neural networks, Finite state automata, Learning, Combinatorial optimization.

1 Introduction

Artificial neural networks are computational models consisting of many simple richly interconnected elementary processors. These models, originally inspired to the structure of the central nervous system, can exhibit complex behaviors. The first model — a network of threshold logic units (binary threshold neurons) — was introduced by McCulloch and Pitts who showed that the control unit of a universal Turing machine can be implemented by such a device [46]. The work

---

[*] Partially supported by M.I.U.R. COFIN, under the project "Linguaggi formali e automi: teoria e applicazioni".

M. Marinaro and R. Tagliaferri (Eds.): WIRN VIETRI 2002, LNCS 2486, pp. 190–216, 2002.
© Springer-Verlag Berlin Heidelberg 2002

of McCulloch and Pitts was heavily influenced by the notion of computability developed by Church and Turing [55] after Goedel's paper on incompleteness.

The behavior of a binary threshold neuron is very simple: it computes a weighted sum of its input lines, outputting 1 if this sum exceeds a fixed threshold, 0 otherwise; some properties of this model can be found in [47]. Other continuous or probabilistic models were introduced and studied, e.g., in [19]. The ideas of the psychologist D.Hebb on the learning process in brain [31] led F.Rosenblatt to develop the first neural model that learn from examples [49]. These works were influenced by the debate on the theme of human-machine comparison. The growing interest in AI [45] led many researchers to abandon this point of view that characterized Cybernetics. Changing in favor of symbolic computation was probably motivated by the success of sequential programming (see, e.g., [4]).

In the same cultural terrain, Hartmanis and Stern introduced the notion of class of problems solvable by time-bounded Turing machines [27]. The classification of problems in terms of their "intrinsic" computational complexity is then reduced to study relations among complexity classes, the aim of the so called "structural complexity".

In the 80's, a new interest in neural networks raised as a consequence of new technological advances (e.g., VLSI) and new interest in non linear systems and parallel or distributed computing. Hopfield's model [35] and backpropagation algorithm [52, 61] became popular in combinatorial optimization and learning. The efficiency in solving learning problems led to an explosive growth of the applications of neural networks in several branches of engineering and science. In the area of computational complexity, Valiant proposed the Probably Approximately Correct (PAC) model of supervised learning [56]. The major novelty of this model is not represented by its probabilistic features (already well known in the area of pattern recognition), but by the precise computational requirements. Finally, results aiming to establish the computational power of feed-forward networks were systematized in the area of parallel computational complexity. A book that emphasizes the computational issues in neural networks is [50].

This paper focuses on the analysis of some relations between computational complexity and neural network theory. The main objectives are:

- to provide results on the computational capabilities of neural networks, by exploring limits or advantages with respect to other conventional models of computation;
- to characterize from a computational point of view the complexity of learning problems arising in neural networks.

In Section 2, we introduce elements of computational complexity. In particular, we recall the complexity classes P and RP of problems solvable in polynomial time on deterministic and probabilistic models of computation, respectively. Moreover, classes containing "intractable" problems, such as NP and co-NP, are considered. The concept of reduction between problems and problem completeness are introduced as powerful tools to compare complexity classes by emphasizing "the more difficult problems in a class".

In Section 3, the model of PRAM (Parallel RAM machines) is described to introduce the parallel complexity classes NC^k of problems solvable by PRAM using polylogarithmic time and a polynomial number of processors.

To capture the computational power of feed-forward neural networks, the classes TC_k^0 of problems solvable via threshold feed-forward networks with a polynomial number of binary neurons arranged in k layers are introduced and compared with the class NC^1. We review separations results among the classes $TC_1^0 \subset TC_2^0 \subset TC_3^0 \subseteq TC_4^0 \subseteq \ldots$, and study the relation between $TC^0 = \bigcup TC_k^0$ and NC^1. In particular, we analyze the possibility of accepting regular languages in TC^0. Under the conjecture $NC^1 \neq TC^0$, a characterization of a subclass of regular languages recognized by constant depth threshold circuits is provided in Section 4.

In Section 5, we consider supervised learning in the context of formal models that can be regarded as variations of the basic model of Probably Approximately Correct (PAC) learning [56]. In supervised learning, a learning algorithm must output an hypothesis that is a good approximation of a boolean function arbitrarily chosen from a given class. The input given to the algorithm is a labeled sample of the target function drawn according to a fixed but unknown probability distribution. A learning algorithm requires two different kinds of resources: data with "sufficient information", measured for instance by the sample size, and "running time" to infer a good hypothesis. As a consequence, we have two criteria of learnability:

– statistical (sample) learnability, where a polynomial bound on the sample size is required;
– polynomial learnability, where a polynomial bound on the running time is imposed.

Here, we analyze the second type of learnability in the basic model (called proper PAC learning) and in some of its variants (agnostic learning, learning with queries, predictability). Some negative results based on complexity theoretic assumptions (such as $P \neq NP$, $NP \neq co\text{-}NP$, RSA cryptosystem is secure) are discussed.

In the last Section, we recall a surprising characterization of NP [5]: NP is the class of languages admitting proofs that can be verified by checking a constant number of bits by a probabilistic algorithm using logarithmically many random bits! We present some consequences of this characterization in the neural area, based on the assumption $P \neq NP$. In particular, we discuss:

– estimation on the error of every polynomial time algorithm that finds approximate solutions of the ground state in a three-dimensional Ising spin glass model,
– limits of the computation of half-spaces in the agnostic PAC model.

2 Structural Complexity: Some Examples

The theory of recursive functions, developed after Goedel's paper on the incompleteness of formal systems [24], leads to separate what is computable from what is not computable. The complexity theory can be seen as a refinement of such theory. Roughly speaking, its aim can be summarized as follows: given a problem and a computational model, to determine how much computational power (in terms of used resources) we need to solve the problem. To be more precise, by using a suitable code, a (*decision*) *problem* can be regarded as a language $L \subseteq \{0,1\}^*$, where $\{0,1\}^*$ is the set of strings on $\{0,1\}$. The size of the instance $x \in \{0,1\}^*$ is the length $|x|$, the answer is 1 if $x \in L$, 0 otherwise. Let A be an algorithm that solves the problem L, and R a resource used by A (Time, Space, ...). If $R_A(x)$ is the amount of resource used by A on input x, the *worst case complexity* of A is the function $R_A(n) = \max_{|x|=n} R_A(x)$.

To study the intrinsic amount of resource for solving a problem, it is useful to introduce the notion of *complexity class* as class of problems solvable by using a given amount of computational resources. An important example is the class P of problems solvable by sequential algorithms with a polynomial bound on the running time. This class is largely independent from the computational model used to describe algorithms (several models of Deterministic Turing Machines, RAM Machines, ...), and a wide range of practical problems is in P. In particular, the notion of polynomial time solvability has been proposed as theoretical counter part of the informal notion of "efficiently solvable problems" (Edmond's thesis).

The problem of defining "feasible" computations is tightly related to the study of the computational complexity of *theorem proving*. We recall that, given $L \subseteq \{0,1\}^*$, a *logical calculus* for L is a computable relation $V : \{0,1\}^* \times \{0,1\}^* \to \{0,1\}$, where $V(x,d) = 1$ means that d is a *proof* of x. V is *correct* if $V(x,d) = 1$ implies that $x \in L$, it is *complete* if for every $x \in L$ there exists a proof d of x, i.e. an element such that $V(x,d) = 1$. NP is the class of languages that admit a complete logical calculus V "easy to compute" (i.e. computable in polynomial time) with "short proves" (i.e. $x \in L$ implies the existence of a proof d of x satisfying $|d| = |x|^{O(1)}$).

Clearly, $P \subseteq NP$, while deciding whether $P \neq NP$ is the most important open problem in complexity theory and it has been recently proposed as one of the seven Millennium Price Problem in Mathematics.

This problem was first proposed by Goedel in a letter to his colleague Von Neumann in 1956 [28]. Quite surprisingly, Goedel expresses the opinion that the problem of theorem proving can not be so hard (i.e. $P = NP!$). Today, it is conjectured that $P \neq NP$, and many problems in NP are considered computationally intractable. However, some of them become tractable by randomized algorithms. To this regard, let RP be the subclass of problems L in NP that admit a logical calculus V such that:

- $x \in L \Rightarrow V(x,d) = 1$ for at least 50% of strings d of length $p(|x|)$, for a suitable polynomial p,
- $x \notin L \Rightarrow V(x,d) = 0$ for all d.

The problem L can be solved by the randomized algorithm that, having in input x, randomly generates a string d of length $p(|x|)$ and then outputs $V(x,d)$.

If the algorithm outputs 1, we are sure that $x \in L$, otherwise an error can take place but with probability less than 50%.

An important tool to prove that a problem does not belong to a given complexity class is *reduction*. Given a set X and a property $p(x)$, a *reduction preserving p* is a reflexive and transitive relation $\angle$ such that, if $p(y) = 1$ and $x \angle y$, then $p(x) = 1$. If there exists a maximum element in X, i.e., an element $a \in X$ such that $x \angle a$ for all $x \in X$, such an element is said to be *complete* for X. It holds:

Proposition 1. *If a is a complete element for X, then $p(a) = 1$ if and only if $p(x) = 1$, for any $x \in X$.*

Consider, for instance, the class NP and the property "L can be solved by a polynomial time algorithm". A well known reduction preserving this property is the "many-one polytime reduction $<_p$": $L_1 <_p L_2$ if and only if there is a polynomial time computable function $f : \{0,1\}^* \rightarrow \{0,1\}^*$ such that $w \in L_1$ if and only if $f(w) \in L_2$. As a consequence of Proposition 1, if we suppose that $P \neq$ NP then complete problems for NP (called NP-complete) are problems in NP not solvable by any polynomial time algorithm.

The first discovered NP-complete problem is SAT the set of satisfiable boolean formulas [20]. (A similar result was independently discovered a year later in Soviet Union [41].) In [39], many combinatorial problems are proved to be NP-complete by reducing them to SAT. Now, many problems originated from computer science, mathematics, operational research, physics, etc., are proved to be NP-complete (see [23] for a compendium).

Another interesting class is co-NP, i.e., languages L whose complement is in NP. Observe that the complement of an NP-complete problem is a problem complete in co-NP; an example is TAUT, i.e., the class of boolean formulas that are tautologies. It is conjectured that NP $\neq$ co-NP. In fact, NP = co-NP would imply the existence of a logical calculus with short proves for tautologies!

3   Parallel Complexity Classes and Neural Networks

According to Edmond's thesis addressed above, P is the class of problems with "efficient sequential algorithms", i.e., requiring polynomial time on RAM Machines. However, there are situations where even linear time can be too much. In this case, parallelism, i.e. the use of synchronized processors, may sometimes reduce running time.

The PRAM (Parallel RAM) is one of the oldest and most widely studied model of parallel computation. A PRAM maintains n processors $P_1, \ldots, P_n$ connected to a common memory with $m > n$ memory location. Every processor is assumed to have constant time access to every memory location. The great computation speed of the PRAM is due to its fast communication capabilities: using the common memory, two processors can communicate in constant time. The main resources used by a PRAM are processors and running time, so that parallel complexity classes are defined in terms of simultaneous time and processors bound. A class of problems considered "efficiently parallelizable" is "Nick's class" $\text{NC} = \bigcup \text{NC}^k$, where NC^k is the class of problems solvable on PRAMs using $O(\log^k n)$ time and a polynomial number of processors on input of size n. Since a PRAM of n^j processors working in $O(\log^k n)$ time can be simulated by a RAM in $O(n^j \log^k n)$, we conclude:

$$\text{NC}^1 \subseteq \text{NC} \subseteq \text{P}.$$

Are there problems in P not efficiently parallelizable? Even in this case we can use reduction. Consider the class P and the property "L can be solved on PRAM using polylogarithmic time and a polynomial number of processors". A well known reduction preserving this property is the L-reduction "$<_L$": $L_1 <_L L_2$ if and only if there is a logarithmic space computable function $f : \{0,1\}^* \rightarrow \{0,1\}^*$ such that $w \in L_1$ if and only if $f(w) \in L_2$. As consequence of Proposition 1, if we suppose that $\text{NC} \neq \text{P}$ then the complete problems for P (called P-complete) are problems in P which are "inherently sequential", not solvable by efficient parallel algorithms.

Another point of view, useful to study low degree complexity classes (for instance, subclasses of NC^1), consists of solving problems by (*uniform*) family of circuits. A problem $L \subseteq \{0,1\}^*$ can be represented by a family of boolean functions $\{f_n\}$, where, for any $x \in \{0,1\}^*$ and $|x| = n$, we have $f_n(x) = 1$ if $x \in L$, 0 otherwise. We say that the family $\{C_n\}$ of boolean circuits solves L if, for any n, C_n computes f_n. Sometimes a notion of uniformity is required: a family $\{C_n\}$ of circuits is called L-uniform if there exists a Turing machine which, given n, constructs C_n in logarithmic space. *Size* (number of gates) and *depth* (length of the longest path from any input to any output gate) are the most used resource measures on circuits. We denote by AC^0 the class of problems solvable by log-space uniform family $\{C_n\}$ of *unbounded fan–in* AND/OR/NOT–circuits of polynomial size and *constant* depth [59].

A model inspired to feed-forward neural networks is that of *threshold circuits*. A *binary threshold neuron* is a device having $x_1, x_2, \ldots, x_n$ binary inputs with $w_1, w_2, \ldots, w_n$, respectively, real weights, and threshold w_0. It computes 1 if and only if $x_1 w_1 + x_2 w_2 + \cdots + x_n w_n \geq w_0$. Stated in other words a neuron computes a linearly separable function f defined as

$$f(x_1, x_2, \ldots, x_n) = \text{hs}\left(\sum_{i=1}^{n} w_i x_i - w_0\right) = \begin{cases} 1 \text{ if } \sum_{i=1}^{n} w_i x_i - w_0 \geq 0 \\ 0 \text{ if } \sum_{i=1}^{n} w_i x_i - w_0 < 0. \end{cases}$$

For any d, we denote by TC_d^0 the class of problems solvable by families of *unbounded fan–in* threshold circuits of polynomial size, polynomial weights, and depth d. Then $\text{TC}^0 = \bigcup_d \text{TC}_d^0$ is the class of problems solvable by families of threshold circuits of polynomial size and *constant* depth [26].

Clearly

$$\text{AC}^0 \subseteq \text{TC}^0,$$

in fact the gates AND, OR, NOT can be simulated by threshold neurons. More-over, $AC^0 \neq TC^0$: the *parity function* $p_n(x_1 \cdots x_n) = x_1 \oplus \cdots \oplus x_n$ requires at least $\frac{\log n}{\log \log n}$ layers to be computed on unbounded fan–in traditional circuits of polynomial size ([36]).

Separation results for the first levels of the hierarchy $\{TC_d^0\}$ are known from the literature (see, e.g., [51]). The parity function, which is not a linearly sep-arable function, is an example of boolean function that belongs to TC_2^0 and cannot be computed in TC_1^0. The *inner product function* $i_n(x_1 \cdots x_n y_1 \cdots y_n) = x_1 \wedge y_2 \oplus \cdots \oplus x_n \wedge y_n$ lies in TC_3^0 but not in TC_2^0.

Another well known relation between threshold and traditional circuits is

$$TC^0 \subseteq NC^1.$$

Establishing whether the inclusion is proper or not can shed light on the real com-putational power of these parallel models. Unfortunately, it is an open problem to decide whether $TC^0 = NC^1$; notice that even the easier problem $TC_3^0 \neq NP$ is still open.

If $TC^0 = NC^1$, the hierarchy $TC_1^0 \subset TC_2^0 \subset TC_3^0 \subseteq TC_4^0 \subseteq \ldots$ would collapse at a certain level [54, Thm. IX.1.6]. This fact is a hardly believed event, thus it is customarily and reasonably assumed that $TC^0 \neq NC^1$.

Surprisingly, several arithmetics problems are in TC^0. Here we take as ex-ample the iterated sum of integers.

Iterated Sum of Integers as Example of Arithmetic Function in TC^0

In what follows $[a]$ denotes the binary representation of the integer a.

Definition 1. *Let $[x_i] = (x_{i,n-1} \cdots x_{i,1} x_{i,0})$ binary integers, for $i \in \{1, \ldots, n\}$. Their iterated sum is the function $S_n : \{0,1\}^{n^2} \rightarrow \{0,1\}^{n+\log n}$ that computes $[s] = [\sum_{i=1}^n x_i]$.*

To prove that iterated sum lies in TC^0, we need the following

Lemma 1. *Let $f : \{0,1\}^n \rightarrow \{0,1\}$ a boolean function in $z_1 \cdots z_n$ such that $f(z_1 \cdots z_n) = \tilde{f}(S)$, where $S = \sum_{i=0}^{n-1} w_i \cdot z_i$ and $f(z_1 \cdots z_n) = 1$ if and only if $S \in [k_i, \tilde{k}_i]$ for $i = 1, \ldots, N$, with N bounded by a polynomial in n. Then $f \in TC_2^0$.*

Proof. (Outline) We begin by proving that f is a sum of polynomially many functions computable by one layer of polynomially many neurons. Let

$$y_{k_j} = \text{hs}(S - k_j) \quad \text{and} \quad \tilde{y}_{k_j} = \text{hs}(\tilde{k}_j - S), \quad \text{for any } j = 1, \ldots, N.$$

Notice that y_{k_j}, or $\tilde{y}_{k_j}$, is computable by a binary neuron with possibly expo-nential weights. It is not difficult to verify that

$$f(z_1 \ldots z_n) = \sum_{j=1}^N (y_{k_j} + \tilde{y}_{k_j}) - N.$$

In fact, if S does not belong to any of the intervals $[k_j, \tilde{k}_j]$, we get $y_{k_j} + \tilde{y}_{k_j} = 1$ for any j and $\sum_{j=1}^{N}(y_{k_j} + \tilde{y}_{k_j}) - N = 0$. Otherwise, if S belongs to $[k_j, \tilde{k}_j]$ for a particular j, we get $y_{k_j} + \tilde{y}_{k_j} = 2$ and $y_{k_i} + \tilde{y}_{k_i} = 1$ for any $i \neq j$, hence $\sum_{j=1}^{N}(y_{k_j} + \tilde{y}_{k_j}) - N = 1$.

It is a well known fact that if a function is computable by threshold circuits of polynomial size, depth d and output gates with polynomially bounded weights, then it is also computable in TC_d^0, for any $d \geq 1$ [25]. Since, by hypothesis, N is bounded by a polynomial in n, $f \in TC_2^0$. □

Theorem 1. *Iterated sum is in* TC_2^0.

Proof. Observe that the k-th bit of $[s]$, where $s = \sum_{i=1}^{n} x_i$, is the k-th bit of the binary representation of

$$s^{(k)} = \sum_{i=1}^{n}\sum_{j=0}^{k-1} 2^j x_{i,j} = \sum_{i=0}^{\log n + k - 1} 2^i s_i^{(k)}.$$

So, to prove the result it is enough to show that $s_{k-1}^{(k)}$ lies in TC_2^0, for $k = 1, \dots, n + \log n$. It holds

$$s_{k-1}^{(k)} = \begin{cases} 1 & \text{if } s^{(k)} \in I_{j,k} = [j2^{k-1}, (j+1)2^{k-1} - 1] \text{ for } j = 1, 3, \dots, 2^{\log n + 1} - 1 \\ 0 & \text{otherwise.} \end{cases}$$

In fact, multiplying j by 2^{k-1} is equivalent to add $k - 1$ zeros before $[j]$ and since j is odd its least significant bit is 1. Moreover, since the right limit of $I_{j,k}$ is $j2^{k-1} + 2^{k-1} - 1 < (j+1)2^{k-1}$, the k-th bit of any integer in $I_{j,k}$ is 1. Finally, by using Lemma 1 and observing that there are polynomially many $I_{j,k}$, we get the result. □

Other problems in TC^0 are: integer product, division, powering and matrix multiplication (in TC_3^0), iterated product of integers (in TC_4^0), etc. (the reader is referred to [26, 34, 60] where he can find a deep study on the exact number of layers in threshold circuits for several tasks).

A breakthrough in parallel complexity has been recently achieved, concerning integer division. Precisely, in [33], author proves that integer division can be computed in uniform TC^0. The notion of uniformity used in this case is even more strict than L-uniformity above recalled: circuit description is required in logarithmic time (DLOGTIME-uniformity).

In the next section we provide examples of "difficult" problems for constant depth threshold circuits, i.e., problems not in TC^0, unless $TC^0 = NC^1$.

4   Regular Languages Not in TC^0, unless $TC^0 = NC^1$

Let us start by defining the class of regular languages. A *finite state automaton* $A = (Q, \Sigma, \delta)$ consists of the finite set Q of states, the input alphabet Σ, and the transition function $\delta : Q \times \Sigma \to Q$ that extends to Σ^* by defining $\hat{\delta} : Q \times \Sigma^* \to Q$ as

$$\hat{\delta}(q, \varepsilon) = q \text{ and } \hat{\delta}(q, x\sigma) = \delta(\hat{\delta}(q, x), \sigma),$$

for each $q \in Q$, $x \in \Sigma^*$ and $\sigma \in \Sigma$. We will safely use δ instead of $\hat{\delta}$.

The automaton A can be seen as a recognizing device by providing an initial state $q_0 \in Q$ and a set $F \subseteq Q$ of final states, then we write $A = (Q, \Sigma, \delta, q_0, F)$. We say A *accepts* $x \in \Sigma^*$ if and only if $\delta(q_0, x) \in F$, otherwise A *rejects* x. The language $L(A)$ accepted by A is the set $L(A) = \{x \in \Sigma^* \mid A \text{ accepts } x\}$.

Definition 2. *A language L is said to be* regular *if and only if it can be recognized by a finite state automaton.*

We denote by Reg the class of regular languages. It is well known that $\text{Reg} \subset \text{NC}^1$ since membership for regular languages is reducible to computing the iterated product of fixed dimension boolean matrices, a problem in NC^1 [21].

An example of regular language in TC^0 is $L_o = \{x \in \{0,1\}^* \mid |x|_1 \text{ is odd }\}$, where $|x|_\sigma$ denotes the number of σ's in x. The automaton accepting L_o is described in Figure 1: the initial state is denoted by an inward arrow, while the final state is double circled. L_o is also an example of regular language in TC_2^0 does not belong to TC_1^0. Observe, in fact, that testing membership for L_o is clearly equivalent to computing parity function which, as recalled in Section 3, belongs to TC_2^0 and not to TC_1^0.

An example of regular language that belongs to TC_3^0, but not to TC_2^0, is given by $L_p = \{x_1 \ldots x_{2n} \mid \bigoplus_{k=1}^{n}(x_{2k-1} \cdot x_{2k}) = 1\}$. The automaton accepting L_p is described in Figure 2.

It is also well known that there are nonregular languages in TC^0, such as, $\{x \mid |x|_0 = |x|_1\}$. To sum up, one can state the following

$$\text{Reg} \subset \text{NC}^1 \text{ and } \text{TC}^0 \not\subset \text{Reg}.$$

In what follows we are going to prove the existence of regular languages that do not belong to TC^0, unless $\text{TC}^0 = \text{NC}^1$.

We need the definition of permutation branching program [6]. Let $\langle S_k, \circ, i \rangle$ be the *symmetric group* of permutations on a set of k elements, and G a subgroup of S_k. A *permutation branching program* of size k and length l on boolean

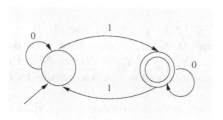

Fig. 1. An automaton for L_o. Such a language is in TC_2^0, but not in TC_1^0

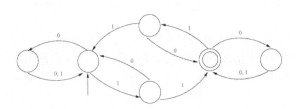

Fig. 2. An automaton for L_p. Such a language is in TC_3^0, but not in TC_2^0

variables $\{x_1, \ldots, x_n\}$ is a sequence $\phi = \langle I_1, I_2, \ldots, I_l \rangle$ of instructions, where

$$I_j = \mathtt{if}\ (x_{i_j} = 1)\ \mathtt{then}\ P_j(1)$$
$$\mathtt{else}\ P_j(0),$$

and $P_j(0), P_j(1) \in G$. Given $\tau \in G$, we say ϕ computes the boolean function $f(x_1, \ldots, x_n)$ via τ if and only if

$$f(x_1, \ldots, x_n) = \begin{cases} 1 & \text{if } P_1(x_{i_1}) \circ \ldots \circ P_l(x_{i_l}) = \tau \\ 0 & \text{if } P_1(x_{i_1}) \circ \ldots \circ P_l(x_{i_l}) = \mathtt{i}. \end{cases}$$

A subgroup G of a group $\mathcal{G}$ is called *normal* if and only if $gG = Gg$, for each $g \in \mathcal{G}$. $\mathcal{G}$ is *simple* whenever it has no other normal subgroups but the trivial ones.

We can state the following

Theorem 2. *Let $\langle \mathcal{G}, \circ, \mathtt{i} \rangle$ be a simple nonabelian group. If f is computed by depth d AND/OR/NOT–circuit, then it is computable via $\tau \in G$ by a permutation branching program ϕ of at most $2^{(2+|\mathcal{G}|)d}$ length.*

Proof. (Outline) First we need the following

Fact: If a function f is computable by ϕ_o of length l via $o \in \mathcal{G}$, then, for any $g \in \mathcal{G}$ and $g \neq \mathtt{i}$, i.e. different from the identity of $\mathcal{G}$, there exist ϕ_g that compute f via $g \in \mathcal{G}$ of at most $2^{|\mathcal{G}|-1}l$ length.

In fact, consider the poset $\langle 2^{\mathcal{G}}, \subseteq, \emptyset \rangle$ and the transformation

$$M(X) = T(X) \cdot T(X) + T(\{\tau\}),$$

where $T(X) = \{g \circ x \circ g^{-1} \mid g \in \mathcal{G}, x \in X\}$ and $A \cdot B = \{a \circ b \mid a \in A, b \in B\}$. It is not difficult to prove that $M(X)$ has a least fixed point $X = M(X) = \mathcal{G}$. Let $X_0 = \emptyset$ and $X_{i+1} = T(X_i) \cdot T(X_i) + T(\{\tau\})$. Note that $X_{|\mathcal{G}|} = \mathcal{G}$. Now, it is enough to prove by induction that f is computable by ϕ_x of length $2^{i-1}l$ via $x \in X_i$.

By hypothesis $\mathcal{G}$ is a simple nonabelian group, then there exist $\tau_1, \tau_2 \in \mathcal{G}$ such that $\tau_1 \circ \tau_2 \neq \tau_2 \circ \tau_1$; we let $\tau_1 \circ \tau_2 \circ \tau_1^{-1} \circ \tau_2^{-1} = \tau \neq \mathtt{i}$. We give an inductive proof on d. Let $f = f_1 \wedge f_2$ (the case $f_1 \vee f_2$ is reducible to that), where f_1, f_2 are computable by depth $d-1$ traditional circuits. By hypothesis there exist ϕ_1, ϕ_2 of at most $2^{(2+|\mathcal{G}|)(d-1)}$ length that compute f_1 and f_2 respectively via $g_1, g_2 \in \mathcal{G}$. By the above fact, there exist $\hat{\phi}_1, \hat{\phi}_3$ that compute f_1 via $\tau_1 \circ \tau_1^{-1}$ and $\hat{\phi}_2, \hat{\phi}_4$ that compute f_2 via $\tau_2 \circ \tau_2^{-1}$ of at most $2^{|\mathcal{G}|} 2^{(2+|\mathcal{G}|)(d-1)}$ length. The composition $\langle \hat{\phi}_1, \hat{\phi}_2, \hat{\phi}_3, \hat{\phi}_4 \rangle$ compute $f = f_1 \wedge f_2$ via $\tau_1 \circ \tau_2 \circ \tau_1^{-1} \circ \tau_2^{-1} = \tau$ with at most $4(2^{|\mathcal{G}|} 2^{(2+|\mathcal{G}|)d}) = 2^{(2+|\mathcal{G}|)d}$ length.   □

Given a group $\langle \mathcal{G}, \circ \rangle$, we can define the *group-like automaton* $\mathfrak{G}$ on $\mathcal{G}$ as $\mathfrak{G} = (\mathcal{G}, \mathcal{G}, \circ, \mathrm{i}, \mathrm{i})$, with i, the identity of $\mathcal{G}$, being both the initial and the unique final state.

It holds the following theorem

Theorem 3. *Let $\langle \mathcal{G}, \circ, \mathrm{i} \rangle$ be a simple nonabelian group and $L_{\mathfrak{G}}$ the language accepted by $\mathfrak{G} = (\mathcal{G}, \mathcal{G}, \circ, \mathrm{i}, \mathrm{i})$, i.e., $L_{\mathfrak{G}} = \{g_1 g_2 \ldots g_n \in \mathcal{G}^* \mid g_1 \circ g_2 \circ \ldots \circ g_n = \mathrm{i}\}$. Then,*

$$L_{\mathfrak{G}} \in \mathrm{TC}^0 \Rightarrow \mathrm{TC}^0 = \mathrm{NC}^1.$$

Proof. It is enough to prove that if $L_{\mathfrak{G}} \in \mathrm{TC}^0 \Rightarrow \mathrm{TC}^0 \subseteq \mathrm{NC}^1$. Let $\{f_n\} \in \mathrm{NC}^1$. By Theorem 2, $\{f_n\}$ is computable by a permutation branching program ϕ via $\tau \in \mathcal{G}$ of length $l = 2^{(2+|\mathcal{G}|)O(\log n)} = O(n^{k|\mathcal{G}|})$, where k is a constant. By definition of permutation branching program, we have

$$f_n(x) = 0 \Leftrightarrow \phi(x) = P_1(x_{i_1}) \circ \ldots \circ P_l(x_{i_l}) = \mathrm{i}. \tag{1}$$

Let $\{g_n\}$ the family of characteristic functions on $L_{\mathfrak{G}}$. By (1) we have

$$f_n(x) = \neg g_n(P_1(x_{i_1}) \ldots P_l(x_{i_l})),$$

By hypothesis $L_{\mathfrak{G}} \in \mathrm{TC}^0$, then $\{g_n\}$ and hence $\{f_n\} \in \mathrm{TC}^0$.   □

This result can be generalized as follows. Given a language $L \subseteq \Sigma^*$, the *syntactic monoid* $\mathcal{M}(L)$ is the quotient monoid $\Sigma^*/\sim_L$, where $\sim_L \subseteq \Sigma^* \times \Sigma^*$ is the congruence defined as: $x \sim_L y$ whenever $vxw \in L$ if and only if $vyw \in L$, for any $v, w \in \Sigma^*$. Clearly, $\mathcal{M}(L_{\mathfrak{G}}) \cong \mathcal{G}$. Given a class $\mathcal{K}$ of algebras, we let the classes: $\mathbf{H}(\mathcal{K})$ of all homomorphic images, and $\mathbf{S}(\mathcal{K})$ of all subalgebras, of algebras in $\mathcal{K}$. It is independently proved in [7] that

Theorem 4. *Let L be a regular language. If there exist a nonabelian simple group in $\mathbf{HS}(\mathcal{M}(L))$ and $L \in \mathrm{TC}^0$, then $\mathrm{TC}^0 = \mathrm{NC}^1$.*

We conclude by giving an example of "difficult" language in the sense of Theorem 4. It is well known that, for any $n \geq 5$, the *alternating group* A_n is simple nonabelian [53]. Moreover, we observe that $A_n \in \mathbf{HS}(S_n)$.

Corollary 1. *Let L_B be the Barrington language accepted by the automaton $B = (S_5, S_5, \circ, \mathrm{i}, \mathrm{i})$. If $L_B \in \mathrm{TC}^0$, then $\mathrm{TC}^0 = \mathrm{NC}^1$.*

The automaton B is quite big and complicated. In [44] we investigate on the parallel complexity of deterministic automata via threshold circuits, and we single out the smallest automaton, in terms of number of states, whose accepted languages (except the trivial ones) are as "difficult" as Barrington language: the 5–state *standard automaton* $St_5 = (\mathbf{Z}_5, \{a, b, c\}, \delta)$ (Figure 3). For any $q \in \mathbf{Z}_5$,

$$\delta(q, a) = q, \quad \delta(q, b) = (q + 1) \ mod \ 5, \text{ and } \delta(q, c) = \begin{cases} 1 & \text{if } q = 0 \\ 0 & \text{if } q = 1 \\ q & \text{otherwise.} \end{cases}$$

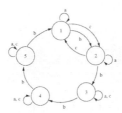

Fig. 3. The 5–state standard automaton St_5. The languages accepted by St_5 (except the trivial ones) are not in TC^0, unless $TC^0 = NC^1$.

5   Learning

Informally, learning is the ability of a system to use information from its environment, adapting its answers to be "correct" in some sense. The main learning paradigms in neural modeling are *supervised* and *not supervised* learning: supervised learning modifies weight connections of the neural model to match the behavior of a "teacher", while the supervised learning modifies weight connections so that the output of the network provides a useful representation of statistics of the environment.

In this paper, we consider supervised learning in the context *of formal models of learning* that are variations of the basic model of *Probably Approximately Correct* (PAC) learning [56]. To specify a formal model of learning, we need to provide:

1. The communication protocol between learner and teacher, stating in particular the types of queries allowed in the interaction.
2. Criteria of successful learning.
3. Quantitative measures of resources used by an efficient learning algorithm.

In the basic model, called *proper* PAC model, positive and negative examples of some unknown target concept, chosen in a known concept class, are presented to the learning algorithm. These examples are drawn randomly according to a give but unknown probability distribution. Using examples, the learning algorithm must, with high probability, output a concept that is a good approximation of the target. Performances are measured in terms of the number of examples needed and time required by the algorithm.

More formally, a learning problem is defined by a *domain* X and a class $F \subseteq 2^X$ of *concepts*. It is often assumed $X = \bigcup X_n$ and $F = \bigcup F_n$, where F_n is the class of concepts on X_n. Here, we will consider $X_n = \{0,1\}^n$ or $X_n = \mathbf{R}^n$.

For computational purposes, we need to represent concepts in some form. In this paper, we consider feed-forward neural networks as representations of concepts: a class C_n of feed-forward neural networks represents the class F_n of concepts if, for every concept $f \in F_n$, there exists a network $c \in C_n$ computing f. For instance, C_n is the class of perceptrons with one hidden layer with 2 neurons and n inputs $x_1, \ldots, x_n$, and F_n is the class of boolean functions computed by networks in C_n. Given a concept f, an example of f is a pair (x, a) where $a = 1$ if $x \in f$, 0 otherwise. A t-sample of f is vector of t examples of f.

A learning algorithm A for a concept class $\langle X_n, F_n \rangle$ represented by C_n can be described by the following protocol:

1. Having in input ε, δ, n, the learner asks the teacher for $t = t(\varepsilon, \delta, n)$ examples.
2. It obtains a t-sample S of a target concept $f \in F_n$; the examples are chosen independently according to a given (but unknown) probability distribution P_n on X_n.
3. The learner call a (possibly randomized) inference procedure which, by having in input the sample S, outputs a representation $c \in C_n$ of an hypothesis $h \in F_n$.

The algorithm is *correct* if, for every $\varepsilon, \delta, n, P_n, f \in F_n$, it outputs with probability at least $1 - \delta$ an hypothesis h that is a ε-approximation of f, i.e. such that $P_n\{x \mid f(x) \neq h(x)\} \leq \varepsilon$.

The algorithm uses two different kinds of resources: sample size and computational time. The least sample size necessary to learn with parameters ε, δ, n represents a_n "information-based" bound. Here "information" means what we must know about the problem to be solved. Methods used in this framework deal with combinatorics and statistics. The computational complexity is related to the running time of the inference procedure. To analyze this parameter, tools from structural complexity are used.

A class $\langle X_n, F_n \rangle$ represented by C_n is said:

- *polynomial-sample learnable* if the *sample-size* $t(\varepsilon, \delta, n)$ is bounded by a polynomial in n, $1/\varepsilon$, $1/\delta$;
- *polynomial-time learnable* if the *running time* of the inference procedure is bounded by a polynomial in n, $1/\varepsilon$, $1/\delta$.

Clearly, polynomial-time learnability implies polynomial-sample learnability, the sample-size being a lower bound to the running time.

The main feature of Valiant's basic model is to provide a rigorous analysis, in terms of structural complexity, of the learnability of classes of concepts. However, its assumptions seem to be weak for certain applications and some efforts have been made to extend the original model. Among variants, we recall:

(i) AGNOSTIC PAC MODEL [29]. The basic model is not suitable for modeling many real world learning problems. First of all, in real learning problems there is no assumption on the target concept; in particular, it is not required that the target belongs to the class of functions computable by the neural architecture used for learning! Second, in the real world, input data are often and somehow corrupted by noise. Finally, in many applications, it is necessary to consider regression problems and not only classification ones as in Valiant's basic model. In the extension proposed by Haussler, the learning problem is described by a (fixed but unknown) probability distribution D on $X \times Y$. It generalizes the basic model, where the probability distribution P on X can be interpreted as the marginal distribution $P(x) = \sum_y D(x, y)$ and the target concept, affected by noise, can be interpreted as $f(x) = argmax_y D(y|x)$. The class of the hypothesis is represented, for instance, by a neural architecture and the goal of the learner is to find, by sampling, the hypothesis h that minimizes the average prediction loss $E_D[L(h(x), y)]$, for a suitable loss function $L : X \times Y \to R^+$.

(ii) PAC LEARNING WITH FIXED DISTRIBUTION. In this framework, a concept class $\langle X_n, F_n \rangle$ represented by C_n is considered as above, but now it comes with a fixed and known probability distribution P_n on X_n. An important case is *PAC learning with uniform distribution.*

(iii) PREDICTION. Given a class of concepts F, a prediction algorithms A (with parameters ε, n) during the learning phase can require random examples of the target f, exactly as in PAC basic model. After learning phase, A receives an element $x \in X_n$ randomly selected according to the same distribution and it "predicts" $A(x) \in \{0, 1\}$: the prediction is incorrect if $f(x) \neq A(x)$. The class F is "predictable" if there exists a prediction algorithm A running in time polynomial in $(n, 1/\varepsilon)$ such that, for every target $f \in F_n$ and distribution probability P_n on X_n, $P_n\{x \mid A(x) \text{ incorrect}\} \leq \varepsilon$ holds true.

(iv) PAC LEARNING WITH QUERIES [3]. In the basic model, the only information the learner can obtain on the target f yielded by the random selected examples. More "complex" types of queries can be considered; among them, we will consider *membership and equivalence queries.* In a *membership query,* the learner sends a given element x to the teacher, obtaining $f(x)$, i.e., the classification of x by the target concept f. In this case, examples are selected by the learner in a possibly adaptive way. In an *equivalence query,* the learner sends a given representation c to the teacher, i.e., a neural network in C. The answer to the query is "yes" if c represents the target concept f, otherwise a counterexample x, an element $x \in X$ for which $f(x) \neq c(x)$, is provided. Observe that a membership query can have several counterexamples, hence the behavior of a teacher is described by an oracle O, which is a function assigning an answer to a query, depending on the target and on the previous events in the learning process.

6 Computational Complexity Aspects in Learning

As we recalled, a learning algorithm requires data with "sufficient information" (measured for instance by the sample size) and "sufficient running time" to infer a good hypothesis. Here, we are mainly interested in the second type of resource. We first briefly recall some concepts and results on the problem of estimating the least sample size necessary to learn with given accuracy and confidence. A good approach to this problem is to consider the notion of uniform convergence of relative frequencies to their probabilities [57].

Polynomial Sample Learnability

Consider concept classes $\langle X_n, F_n \rangle$ and probability distributions P_n on X_n. The probability of a concept f is $P_f = P_n[f(x) = 1]$ and, for a t-sample $S = \{x_1, \ldots, x_t\}$, the relative frequency of the concept f is $v_f(x_1, \ldots, x_t) = \sum f(x_k)/t$. $\langle X_n, F_n \rangle$ is *polynomial uniformly convergent* if there exists a polynomial $p(t, 1/\varepsilon, 1/\delta)$ such that, for all concepts f and all probability distributions P_n, if $t > p(t, 1/\varepsilon, 1/\delta)$, then the probability that $|v_f(x_1, .., x_t) - P_f| > \varepsilon$ does not exceed δ for an independent selection of examples according to P_n. An important combinatorial parameter useful in this context is the *Vapnik-Chervonenkis dimension*. Given a class of concept F on X, a subset $Y \subseteq X$ is *shattered* by F if for every subset $Z \subseteq Y$ there is a concept $f \in F$ such that $Y \cap f^{-1}(1) = Z$. The *Vapnik-Chervonenkis dimension* of F, denoted by, VCdim(F) is the size of the largest shattered subset.

Polynomial uniformly convergence (of relative frequencies to their probabilities) and polynomial sample learnability are strictly related in the context of distribution free PAC learning. In fact:

Proposition 2. *The following statements are equivalent:*

1. $\langle X_n, F_n \rangle$ *is polynomial uniform convergent,*
2. $\langle X_n, F_n \rangle$ *is polynomial sample learnable,*
3. *VCdim(F_n) is bounded by a polynomial in n.*

We point out that by means of the Vapnik-Chervonenkis dimension it is possible to give very precise estimations on the sample size necessary or sufficient to learn. In the case of proper PAC learning, examples of upper and lower bounds are given, respectively, in [18] and in [22]. The Vapnik-Chervonenkis dimension for feed-forward neural network has been estimated; upper and lower bounds are given, respectively, in [11] and [43]. Polynomial uniform convergence and polynomial sample learnability have been studied even for distribution dependence (res., [14], [16]). In this case, the polynomial uniform convergence is more demanding than polynomial sample learnability [14].

Polynomial Time Learnability

Once we have a sample containing sufficient information to learn a reasonable approximation of a concept, the attention is turned to the computational problem of efficiently inferring a good hypothesis from the sample. From the point of view of computational complexity, the problem is to distinguish the classes $\langle\{0,1\}^n, F_n, C_n\rangle$ that admit efficient (i.e., polynomial time) inference procedures from those for which the inference is a computationally difficult goal.

To characterize classes with efficient inference procedures, the key notion is that of hypothesis finder: *a polynomial hypothesis finder* for $\langle\{0,1\}^n, F_n, C_n\rangle$ is a polynomial time randomized algorithm that, having in input a set of labeled examples E of some concept in F_n, outputs with probability $1/2$ a representation $c \in C_n$ consistent with the examples.

From [48]:

Proposition 3. *The concept class* $\langle\{0,1\}^n, F_n, C_n\rangle$ *is properly PAC learnable if:*

1. *VCdim(F_n) is polynomially bounded.*
2. *There is a polynomial hypothesis finder for* $\langle\{0,1\}^n, F_n, C_n\rangle$.

Let, for instance, TC_{1n}^0 denote the class of linearly separable functions on n input. The class $\mathrm{TC}_1^0 = \bigcup_n \mathrm{TC}_{1n}^0$ is properly learnable by networks with a single neuron, since:

1. VCdim$(\mathrm{TC}_{1n}^0) = n + 1$ [58].
2. A formal neuron consistent with the examples of some function in TC_{1n}^0 can by found by solving a Linear Programming problem that admits polynomial time algorithms [38].

Nonlearnability Results from Complexity Theoretic Assumptions

Nonlearnability results can be provided in terms of complexity theoretic assumptions, such as $P \neq$ NP or NP $\neq$ co-NP. In the case of proper PAC learning, nonlearnability results can be expressed by the so called *consistency* problem:

> **Problem:** *Consistency for* $\langle\{0,1\}^n, F_n, C_n\rangle$.
> **Instance:** a set of labeled examples $\langle(x_1, a_1), (x_2, a_2), \ldots, (x_m, a_m)\rangle$, with $x_k \in \{0,1\}^n$, $a_k \in \{0,1\}$.
> **Question:** is there a representation $c \in C_n$ of a concept consistent with the examples, i.e. such that $c(x_k) = a_k$, for any k?

In the area of neural computing, this problem is also known as *loading problem*: "given a network architecture (the class of representation C_n) and given a sample (the set of training examples), find the set of weights (giving a representation $c \in C_n$) so that the network produces correct output on the examples" [37]. The relation between consistency and learnability is contained in the following [48]:

Proposition 4. *If Consistency for $\langle\{0,1\}^n, F_n, C_n\rangle$ is an NP-complete problem, then $\langle\{0,1\}^n, F_n, C_n\rangle$ is not properly learnable (unless* $\mathrm{RP} = \mathrm{NP}$).

This is proved by showing that every learning algorithm A for $\langle\{0,1\}^n, F_n, C_n\rangle$ can be used to obtain a randomized polynomial time algorithm for the corresponding Consistency problem. If such an algorithm A exists, then Consistency for $\langle\{0,1\}^n, F_n, C_n\rangle$ can be solved by a polynomial time randomized algorithm, and since by hypothesis this problem is NP-complete, we can conclude that $\mathrm{NP} = \mathrm{RP}$. The Consistency problem has been proved to be NP-complete for several classes of feed-forward neural networks. This implies that the classes of concepts described by these architectures cannot be properly PAC learned. Among them, there are very simple classes as:

- Conjunction of linearly separable functions [17]
- One hidden layer with k neurons [17, 9] (Figure 4(a))
- 2-Cascade net [42] (Figure 4(b))

The hardness of Consistency problem for these classes has been proved by reduction from other known NP-complete problems. For instance, in [17] it is shown the reduction

SET SPLITTING $<_p$ CONJUNCTION OF LINEARLY SEPARABLE FUNCTIONS.

SET SPLITTING requires, given a set S and a collection $\{I_1, \ldots, I_m\}$ of subsets of S of size 3, to decide if there exists a subset $X \subset S$ such that $I_k \not\subset S$ and $I_k \not\subset S^c$, for any k. Since SET SPLITTING is NP-complete (see, e.g., [23]), the concepts represented by conjunctions of linearly separable functions are not properly PAC-learnable (unless $\mathrm{RP} = \mathrm{NP}$).

Learnability in Extended Models: Membership and Equivalence Queries

Now we consider the problem of properly learn by using membership and equivalence queries. We recall that a learning algorithm A for the class $\langle X_n, F_n\rangle$ represented by C_n is an algorithm that outputs a representation $c \in C_n$ of a concept $f \in F_n$, after adaptively performing at most a polynomial number $p(n)$ of membership or equivalence queries of the kind:

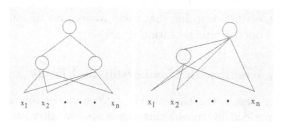

Fig. 4. (a) hidden layer with 2 neurons architecture (b) cascade architecture

- x? (where $x \in X_n$, obtaining the answer $f(x)$),
- r? (where $r \in C_n$, obtaining as answer YES if $r(x) = f(x)$ for any x, otherwise a counterexample b such that $r(b) \neq f(b)$).

As an example of the power of membership queries, we present an algorithm due to Baum [10] for learning the concepts represented by networks with 2 neurons hidden layer. Moreover, we suppose that $X_n = \mathbf{R}^n$, i.e. inputs are in $\mathbf{R}^n$ so that concepts are intersections of halfspaces.

The boundary B of the intersection D between two halfspaces is included in the union of the two separator hyperplanes H_1 and H_2. The algorithm finds, with high probability, a numerical approximation of H_1 and H_2 on the basis of random labeled examples and membership queries. It uses a procedure BOUNDARY(x, y) that, having in input $x \in D$ and $y \notin D$, by a binary search returns (a numerical approximation of) the element z on the intersection between the boundary B and the segment $[x, y]$ (x, y being segment endpoints).

ALGORITHM:

1. Choose a "sufficiently large" set of example $S = \langle (x_1, a_1), \ldots, (x_m, a_m) \rangle$, with $x_k \in \{0, 1\}^n, a_k \in \{0, 1\}$
2. Find $(x, 0), (y, 1) \in S$
3. $z = $ BOUNDARY(x, y)
4. For $k = 1, \ldots, n - 1$ do
   $p = $ small random vector; $v = z + p$
   Membership query v?
   If "answer= 1" then $w_k = $ BOUNDARY(x, v) else $w_k = $ BOUNDARY(x, v)
5. Determine the hyperplane H_1 that contains $\{w_1, \ldots, w_{n-1}\}$
6. Find $(a, 0), (b, 1) \in S$ that are not separated by H_1
7. $z = $ BOUNDARY(x, y)
8. For $k = 1, \ldots n - 1$ do
   $p = $ small random vector; $v = z + p$
   Membership query v?
   If "answer= 1" then $m_k = $ BOUNDARY(a, v) else $w_k = $ BOUNDARY(b, v)
9. Determine the hyperplane H_2 that contains $\{m_1, \ldots, m_{n-1}\}$; return (H_1, H_2)

Since the procedure BOUNDARY returns only a numerical approximation of a point on the boundary, the hyperplanes found by Baum's algorithm are only approximations of the correct planes. To analyze the error, Baum introduces a modified version of PAC learning that takes in account the numerical approximation of target concept representation [10].

Nonlearnability Result with Membership and Equivalence Queries

A nonlearnability result for the model with membership and equivalence queries can be provided by considering the representation problem associated to $\langle \{0, 1\}^n, F_n, C_n \rangle$:

Problem: *Representation for* $\langle \{0,1\}^n, F_n, C_n \rangle$
Instance: a boolean formula $M(x)$ in Disjunctive Form
Question: is there a representation $c \in C_n$ such that $c(x) = M(x)$, for
any x?

From [32]:

Proposition 5. *If Representation for* $\langle \{0,1\}^n, F_n, C_n \rangle$ *is a NP-complete prob-*
lem, then $\langle \{0,1\}^n, F_n, C_n \rangle$ *is not properly learnable (unless* NP $=$ *co-NP).*

Proof. (Outline) The idea is to use a properly learning algorithm A for
$\langle \{0,1\}^n, F_n, C_n \rangle$ to obtain a nondeterministic algorithm NA for the complement
of "Representation for $\langle \{0,1\}^n, F_n, C_n \rangle$". First of all, w.l.o.g., we can suppose:

1. If the concept to be learned is $f \in F_n$, then the last executed instruction is
   a query c? yielding the answer YES.
2. The algorithm can be modified to work with concepts $g \notin F_n$ too. In this
   case A simply counts the number of steps it performs and outputs "FRAUD"
   if the running time $p(n)$ is exceeded, or its action is not defined.

A nondeterministic algorithm NA for the complement of "Representation for
$\langle \{0,1\}^n, F_n, C_n \rangle$" can be obtained by simulating A on the concept represented
by the formula $M(x)$ in input. In particular:

1. When a membership query b? is performed, the result is obtained by simply
   evaluating $M(b)$.
2. When an equivalence query r? is performed, NA first selects nondeterminis-
   tically an example $a \in \{0,1\}^n$, then checks evaluates whether $r(a) = M(a)$.
   If this is true, it ends the computation with REJECT, otherwise it continues
   the computation.
3. When A halts with FRAUD then NA ends the computation with ACCEPT.

Suppose now that there is a representation $c \in C_n$ such that $c(x) = M(x)$
for any x. Then every computation ends with REJECT, as either an example a
in the intermediate equivalence queries is guessed incorrectly (i.e. $r(a) = M(a)$)
or otherwise no counterexample can be found for the final equivalence query.
Suppose on the contrary that $M(x)$ does not represent any concepts in F_n. In this
case the computation of A halts with FRAUD, and hence NA produces the answer
ACCEPT. We conclude that "Representation for $\langle \{0,1\}^n, F_n, C_n \rangle$" is in co-NP
and, since by hypothesis it is NP-complete, we conclude that $NP = $ co-NP. □

Non-predictability Results

While nonlearnability results for a class of concepts by using hypothesis in the
same class can be stated under the assumption NP $\neq$ RP, nonpredictability
results require stronger complexity assumptions used in cryptography. Here we
assume that the *RSA cryptosystem is secure.*

A public key in RSA is a pair $\langle e, N \rangle$ of numbers, where N is the product of two large primes p and q, and e is relatively prime with $\Phi(N) = (p-1)(q-1)$, which is the number of integers less than N relatively prime with N. The corresponding private key is the pair $\langle d, N \rangle$ with $d \cdot e = 1 \pmod{\Phi(N)}$. A message can be viewed as an integer M. Encryption is done by computing $C = M^e \pmod{N}$ and decryption by computing $M = C^d \pmod{N}$. We assume that RSA is secure, i.e. for all $k > 0$ there is no probabilistic polynomial time algorithm that can decrypt messages with probability $O(n^{-k})$, given the message and the public key.

We have seen the multilayer perceptrons are powerful devices. The following result states that this is not always the case [40]:

Theorem 5. *If the* RSA *cryptosystem is secure. Then, for some constant e,* TC_e^0 *is not predictable.*

Proof. (Outline) In [1] it is proved that RSA is not secure if there is a randomized polynomial time algorithm that, on input N, e, and y such that $y = x^e \pmod{N}$, outputs the least significant bit of x. Observe that the least significant bit of x is the parity of $x = y^d \pmod{N}$. If the binary representation of d is $d_{\lceil \log n \rceil} \cdots d_0$, we can compute x as $\prod_{d_k=1} y^{2^k} \pmod{N}$. Since modular iterated multiplication can be computed by a multilayer perceptron with a constant number of hidden layers, we conclude that there is a l-layer perceptron $\Phi(p, q, e)$ that, having in input a binary encoding of

$$\left(y \pmod{N}, \ldots, y^{2^k} \pmod{N}, \ldots, y^{2^{\lceil \log n \rceil}} \pmod{N}, N, e \right),$$

outputs the least significant bit of x.

Suppose that TC_l^0 is predictable by a suitable algorithm A; a polynomial time probabilistic algorithm for computing the parity of x is obtained simulating A with $\varepsilon = 1/4$ on the target concept $\Phi(p, q, e)$ and the uniform distribution on the binary encoding of sequences $\left(y \pmod{N}, \ldots, y^{2^{\lceil \log n \rceil}} \pmod{N}, N, e \right)$ where $y = x^e \pmod{N}$, for $0 \le x < N$. □

7   Some Consequence in Neural Area of a Probabilistic Characterization of NP

NP is the class of languages with "short and easily verifiable proofs". Here, "easily verifiable" means "verifiable by a polynomial time deterministic algorithm". In the 80's, researches were developed on probabilistic algorithms for testing whether d is a proof of x by analyzing only a "small part" of d. To be more precise, consider a relation $V(w, d, r)$, where r is a string of random bits. Given two functions $f(n)$, $g(n)$ and $\langle f(n), g(n) \rangle$-*verifier* for V is an algorithm, running in time polynomial in $|w|$, that computes the relation $V(w, d, r)$ by checking, for every w and r with $|r| = f(|w|)$, only $g(|w|)$ bits in d.

Now, let $PCP(f(n), g(n))$ be the class of languages L for which there exists a relation $V(w, d, r)$ having a $\langle f(n), g(n) \rangle$-verifier such that:

– if $w \in L$ then there exists d such that $V(w, d, r) = 1$, for all r with $|r| = f(|w|)$,

– if $w \notin L$ then for all d, we have that $V(w, d, r) = 0$ for at least 50% of r with $|r| = f(|w|)$.

Observe that, by definition, $NP = PCP(0, n^{O(1)})$. A surprising characterization of NP, given in [5], presents NP as the class of languages admitting proofs that can be verified by checking a constant number of bits by means of a probabilistic algorithm that uses logarithmically many random bits.

Proposition 6. $NP = PCP(O(1), O(\log n))$.

Consequence in Combinatorial Optimization

This yields an interesting consequence in Combinatorial Optimization. Consider the problem Max c-SAT: given a set of clauses with c literals each, find an assignment satisfying the greatest number of clauses. This problem is NP-hard, so there is no polynomial time exact algorithm solving it (unless $P = NP$). What about approximation algorithms for Max c-SAT?

Let us fix an NP-complete problem L and consider the associated relation $V(w, d, r)$ admitting a $\langle c, d \log n \rangle$-verifier. With every word w, associate a c-Conjunctive Form (i.e. a set of c-clauses) F_w as follows:

– Let $d = d_1 d_2 \ldots d_m$, with $d_i \in \{0, 1\}$ and fix a string r of $d \log |w|$ random bits. The verifier answers by checking only c bits, say $d_{k(1)}, d_{k(2)}, \ldots, d_{k(c)}$. On r, define the boolean function $f_r(d_{k(1)}, d_{k(2)}, \ldots, d_{k(c)}) = V(w, d, r)$ and let F_r be a c-Conjunctive Form for f_r, consisting of at most 2^c clauses.

– Let $F_w = \bigcup F_r$.

If $w \in L$, then there exists d such that $V(w, d, r) = 1$ for all r. That implies that all clauses in F_w are satisfied by the assignment d.

If $w \notin L$ then, for all d, we get that $V(w, d, r) = 0$ for at least 50% of r. This implies that, under every assignment d, at least a fraction 2^{-c-1} of clauses in F_w is not satisfied.

Thus, we can conclude that, if $P \neq NP$, every approximation algorithms for Max c-SAT must have relative error at least 2^{-c-1} (otherwise we could use such an algorithm to solve L, a NP-complete problem!).

In principle, this result can be used to give bounds on the error of approximation algorithms for several combinatorial optimization problems [30]. In what follows, we give two examples from neural area. We use as measures of the performances of approximation algorithms the absolute or the relative error: if $A(I)$ is the value found on the instance I by an algorithm A and $Opt(I)$ is the optimum value, the absolute error is $|A(I) - Opt(I)|$ while the relative error is $|A(I) - Opt(I)|/Opt(I)$.

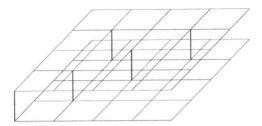

Fig. 5. A tridimensional two levels square greed

Example: Ground State in Spin Glasses

The first example is an application to state solid physics. A spin glass is a dilute magnetic alloy, such as 1% of Mn or Fe embedded in Cu or Au. We consider a simple model, proposed in [8], consisting of an Ising spin glass on a two levels square greed such that, if n is the number of nodes, the number of edges is of order n and vertical edges are at most $\sqrt{n}$. With every node j, a spin variable $\sigma_j \in \{-1, 1\}$ is associated, and with each edge a weight $Y_{ij} \in \{-1, 1\}$, denoting the interactions between nearest neighbor spins. The energy of a spin glass $\sigma = (\sigma_1, \ldots, \sigma_n)$ is given by $H = -\sum Y_{ij}\sigma_j\sigma_j$. We consider the problem of finding a ground state, i.e. a configuration of minimum energy (Ground State Problem) (Figure 5).

With every spin glass we can associate a Hopfield neural network [35] whose Lyapunov function is H. By simulating the Hopfield network, we obtain a polynomial time algorithm that tries to minimize H. Unfortunately, the dynamics of the network reaches a *local minimum*, not the global one as required. This is a general fact: in [8], Barahona proves that the global minimization problem is NP-hard and hence no exact polynomial time algorithm exists.

On the other hand, for planar square greed, the problem is reducible to Minimum Perfect Matching which is a problem solvable in polynomial time [15]. This gives for our problem a polynomial time algorithm with absolute error $O(\sqrt{n})$. The optimality of this result is stated by the following proposition [13]:

Proposition 7. *Consider the Ground State Problem for Ising spin glasses on a two levels square greed such that, if n is the number of nodes, the number of edges is of order n and the vertical edges are at most $\sqrt{n}$. There exists a constant $a > 0$ such that every approximating polynomial time algorithm has absolute error greater than $a\sqrt{n}$ infinitely often.*

This fact is proved by a suitable reduction to Max Cut problem [23], furthermore observing that there exists a constant $b > 0$ such that every approximating algorithm for Max Cut has a relative error at least b infinitely often. In fact, it is possible to exhibit a reduction from c-SAT to Max Cut that, roughly speaking, "preserves" the relative error.

Example: Learning Half-Spaces in the Agnostic PAC Model

In Section 6, we have stated that the class TC_1^0 of linearly separable functions is properly PAC learnable. In the proper model, the target concept is supposed to be a linearly separable function, i.e., an half-space. What happens in the agnostic model, where the learner must try to separate by a plane an arbitrary set of positive and negative examples, not necessarily linearly separable? In this case, the inference procedure tries to find the half-space maximizing the agreement with a given training sample. Unfortunately, there is a lower bound on the relative error holding for every polynomial time approximation algorithm (see, [12]):

Proposition 8. *Every polynomial time approximation algorithm for maximizing the agreement between half-spaces and a given training set presents a relative error greater than 0.009 infinitely often, unless* P = NP.

This fact is proved by a reduction to Max 2-SAT preserving relative error (up to a multiplicative constant). The method works by constructing an approximation algorithm A for Max 2-SAT that uses "maximum agreement with half-spaces" as oracle. The algorithm A works in three phases:

1. (Gadget construction). With every instance I of Max 2-SAT, an instance $f(I)$ of "maximum agreement with half-spaces" is associated.
2. The instance $f(I)$ is given to an arbitrary polynomial time approximation procedure X for "maximum agreement with half-spaces". X returns an half-space P_X.
3. By using P_X, A outputs in polynomial time a feasible solution for the instance I of Max 2-SAT preserving relative error (up to a multiplicative constant).

A good procedure X for "maximum agreement with half-spaces" is turned into a good algorithm for Max 2-SAT. So, a lower bound on the relative error of polynomial time approximation algorithms for Max 2-SAT enables us to obtain lower bounds on the performances of approximation algorithms for "maximum agreement with half-spaces". Different reductions are presented in [2, 12]. Analogous hardness results for nets with k neurons in one hidden layer are proved in [9].

8   Conclusions

In this paper, we discussed some relations between computational complexity and neural network theory. We analyzed computational properties of feedforward networks of binary threshold neurons in the context of parallel complexity classes (TC^0 versus NC^1) and, vice-versa, we pointed out the use of complexity theoretic assumptions to clarify computational aspects in learning and combinatorial optimization. In particular, we discussed some results of interest in neural area, related to a recent probabilistic characterization of NP.

Benefits are related to the rigorous approach to the analysis of computational and learning capabilities of neural networks, by exploring limits or advantages with respect to other conventional models of computation.

Limits are due to the direct applicability of these concepts to great part of applications of neural networks. This is in part given by the intrinsic "asymptotic nature" of complexity classes, while applications do work with precise sizes. Moreover, theoretical results are often based on "worst case analysis" assumptions. As a consequence, the evaluations of computational hardness of problems are often too severe.

References

[1] W. B. ALEXI, B. CHOR, O. GOLDREICH AND C. P. SCHNORR, RSA and Rabin function: Certain parts are as hard as the whole. *SIAM J. Comput.* **17** (1988) 194–209. 209

[2] E. AMALDI AND V. KANN The complexity and approximability of finding maximum feasible subsystems of linear relations. *Theoretical Computer Science* **147** (1995) 181–210. 212

[3] D. ANGLUIN, Queries and Concept Learning. *Machine Learning* **2** (1988) 319–342. 203

[4] M. M. ARBIB, *Brains, Machines and Mathematics* (2nd ed.). Springer Verlag, 1987. 191

[5] S. ARORA, C. LUND, R. MOTWANI, M. SUDAN AND M. SZEGEDY, Proof Verification and Hardness of Approximation. In: *Proc. 33rd Am. IEEE Symp. on Found. Comp. Sci.* (1992) 14–23. 192, 210

[6] D. BARRINGTON, Bounded-width polynomial-size branching programs recognize exactly those languages in NC^1. *J. Comput. Syst. Sci.* **38** (1989) 150–164. 198

[7] D. A. MIX BARRINGTON, K. COMPTON, H. STRAUBING AND D. THÉRIEN, Regular languages in NC^1. *J. Comp. Syst. Sci.* **44** (1992) 478–499. 200

[8] F. BARAHONA, On the computational complexity of Ising spin glass models. *J. of Physics A: Mathematical, nuclear and general* **15** (1982) 3241–3253. 211

[9] P. BARTLETT AND S. BEN-DAVID, Hardness Results for Neural Network Approximation Problems. *Proc. 4th European Conference on Comput. Learning Theory* (1999) 50–62. 206, 212

[10] E. B. BAUM, Neural Nets Algorithms that learn in polynomial time from examples and queries. *IEEE Trans. on Neural Network* **2** (1991) 5–19. 207

[11] E. B. BAUM AND D. HAUSSLER, What size net gives valid generalization? *Neural Computation* **1** (1989) 151–160. 204

[12] S. BEN-DAVID, N. EIRON AND P. M. LONG, On the Difficulty of Approximately Maximizing Agreements. *Proc. 13th Ann. Conference on Comput. Learning Theory* (2000) 266–274. 212

[13] A. BERTONI, P. CAMPADELLI AND G. MOLTENI, On the approximability of energy function in Ising spin glasses. *J. of Physics A: Mathematical, nuclear and general* **27** (1994) 6719–6729. 211

[14] A. BERTONI, P. CAMPADELLI, A. MORPURGO AND S. PANIZZA, Polynomial uniform convergence and polynomial-sample learnability. In: *Proc. 5th Ann. ACM Workshop on Computational Learning Theory* (1992) 265–271. 204

[15] I. BIECHE, R. MAYNARD, R. RAMMAL AND J. P. UHRY, *J. of Physics A: Mathematical, nuclear and general* **13** (1980) 2553–2576. 211

[16] G. BENEDEK AND A. ITAI, Learnability with respect to fixed distributions. *Theoretical Computer Science* **86** (1991) 377–389. 204

[17] A. BLUM AND R. L. RIVEST, Training a 3-node neural network is NP-complete. *Neural Networks* **5** (1992) 117–127. 206

[18] A. BLUMER, A. EHRENFEUCHT, D. HAUSSLER AND M. K. WARMUTH, Learnability and the Vapnik-Chervonenkis Dimension. *J. ACM* **36** (1989) 929–965. 204

[19] E. R. CAIANIELLO, Outline of a theory of thought processes and thinking machines. *J. Theoretical Biology* **1** (1961) 1–27. 191

[20] S. A. COOK, The Complexity of Theorem Proving Procedures. In: *Proc. 3rd Ann. ACM Symposium on Theory of Computing* (1971) 151–158. 194

[21] S. A. COOK, A taxonomy of problems with fast parallel algorithms. *Information and Control* **64** (1985) 2–22. 198

[22] A. EHRENFEUCHT, D. HAUSSLER, M. KEARNS AND L. VALIANT, A general lower bound on the number of examples needed for learning. *Information and Computation* **82** (1989) 247–261. 204

[23] M. R. GAREY AND D. S. JOHNSON, *Computers and intractability. A guide to the theory of NP-completeness.* W. H. Freeman, 1979. 194, 206, 211

[24] K. GOEDEL, Uber Formal Unentscheidbare Satze der *Principia Matematica* und verwandter Systeme I. *Monatshefte fur Matematik und Physik* **38** (1931) 173–198. 192

[25] M. GOLDMANN AND M. KARPINSKI, Simulating Threshold Circuits by Majority Circuits. *SIAM J. Comput.* **98** (1998) 230–246. 197

[26] A. HAJNAL, W. MAASS, P. PUDLÁK, M. SZEGEDY AND G. TURÁN, Threshold circuits of bounded depth. *J. Comput. Sys. Sci.* **46** (1993) 129–154. 195, 197

[27] J. HARTMANIS AND R. E. STEARNS, On the computational complexity of algorithms. *Trans. Am. Math. Soc.* **117** (1965) 285–306. 191

[28] J. HARTMANIS, Goedel, Von Neumann and P $=?NP$ problem. *Bull. of EATCS*, 38, 101-107, 1989. 193

[29] D. HAUSSLER, Decision Theoretic Generalizations of the PAC Model for Neural Net and Other Learning Applications. *Information and Computation* **100** (1992) 78–150. 203

[30] J. HÅSTAD, Some optimal inapproximability results. *Royal Institute of Technology* (1999). 210

[31] D. O. HEBB, *The Organization of Behavior.* Wiley, 1949. 191

[32] T. HEGEDUS, Can complexity theory benefit from learning theory? In: *European Conf. on Machine Learning* (1993) 354–359. 208

[33] W. HESSE, Division is in Uniform TC^0. In: *ICALP: Annual International Colloquium on Automata, Languages and Programming* (2001) 104–114. 197

[34] T. HOFMEISTER, Depth–efficient threshold circuits for arithmetic functions. In: V. ROYCHOWDHURY, K.-Y. SIU AND A. ORLITSKY (eds.), *Theoretical advances in Neural Computation and Learning.* Kluwer Academic, Boston, London, Dordrecht (1994) 37–84. 197

[35] J. HOPFIELD, Neural networks and physical systems with emergent collective computational abilities. In: *Proc. of the National Academy of Science, USA* (1982) 2554–2558. 191, 211

[36] D. JOHNSON, A catalog of complexity classes. In: J. VAN LEEUWEN (eds.), *Handbook of Theoretical Computer Science.* North–Holland (1990) 142–143. 196

[37] J. S. JUDD, *Neural Network Design and the Complexity of Learning.* The MIT Press, 1990. 205

[38] N. KARMARKAR, A new polynomial-time algorithm for linear programming. *Combinatorica* **4** (1984) 373–395. 205

[39] R. M. KARP, Reducibility Among Combinatorial Problems. *Complexity of Computer Computations* (1972) 85–103. 194

[40] M. KEARNS AND L. G. VALIANT, Cryptographic limitations on learning Boolean formulae and finite automata. In: *Proc. of ACM Symp. on Theory of Computing* (1989) 15–17. 209

[41] L. A. LEVIN, Universal Search Problems. *Problemy Peredachi Informatsii* **9** (1973) 265–266. 194

[42] J. H. LIN AND J. S. VITTER, Complexity result on learning with neural nets. *Machine Learning* **6** (1991) 211–230. 206

[43] W. MAASS, Neural nets with superlinear VC dimension. *Neural Computation* **6** (1994) 877–884. 204

[44] C. MEREGHETTI AND B. PALANO, The Parallel Complexity of Deterministic and Probabilistic Automata. *J. Aut., Lang. and Comb.* To be published. 201

[45] M. L. MINSKY, Steps toward artificial intelligence. In: *Proc. IRE* **49** (1961) 8–30. 191

[46] W. S. MCCULLOCH AND W. PITTS, A logical calculus of the ideas immanent in nervous activity. *Bulletin of Mathematical Biophysics* **5** (1943) 115–133. 190

[47] S. MUROGA, *Threshold Logic and its Applications.* Wiley, 1971. 191

[48] L. PITT AND L. G. VALIANT, Computational limitations on learning from examples. *J. ACM* **35** (1988) 965–984. 205

[49] F. ROSENBLATT, *Principles of Neurodynamics.* Spartan Books, 1962. 191

[50] V. ROYCHOWDHURY, K.-Y. SIU AND A. ORLITSKY, *Theoretical advances in Neural Computation and Learning.* Kluwer Academic, Boston, London, Dordrecht, 1994. 191

[51] V. ROYCHOWDHURY, K.-Y. SIU AND A. ORLITSKY, Neural models and spectral methods. In: V. ROYCHOWDHURY, K.-Y. SIU AND A. ORLITSKY (eds.), *Theoretical advances in Neural Computation and Learning.* Kluwer Academic, Boston, London, Dordrecht (1994) 3–36. 196

[52] D. E. RUMELHART, G. E. HINTON AND R. J. WILLIAMS, Learning representations by back-propagating errors. *Nature* **323** (1986) 533–536. 191

[53] W. R. SCOTT, *Group Theory.* Prentice-Hall, 1964. Reprinted by Dover, 1987. 200

[54] H. STRAUBING, *Finite Automata, Formal Logic, and Circuit Complexity.* Birkhäuser, 1994. 196

[55] A. M. TURING, On computable numbers with an application to the Entscheidungs problem. *Proc. London Math. Soc.* 2-42, (1936) 230–265. 191

[56] L. VALIANT, A theory of the learnable. *Communications of the ACM* **27** (1984) 1134–1142. 191, 192, 201

[57] V. N. VAPNIK AND A. Y. CHERVONENKIS, On the uniform convergence of relative frequencies of events to their probabilities. *Theory of Prob. and its Applications* **16** (1971) 264–280. 204

[58] R. S. WENOCUR AND R. M. DUDLEY, Some Special Vapnik-Chervonenkis classes. *Discrete Mathematics* **33** (1981) 313–318. 205

[59] I. WEGENER, *The Complexity of Boolean Functions.* Teubner, Stuttgart, 1987. 195

[60] I. WEGENER, Optimal lower bounds on the depth of polynomial–size threshold circuits for some arithmetic functions. *Information Processing Letters* **46** (1993) 85–87. 197

[61] P. WERBOS, *Beyond Regression: New Tools for Prediction and Analysis in the Behavioral Science*. PhD thesis, Harvard University, 1974. 191

Bayesian Learning Techniques: Application to Neural Networks with Constraints on Weight Space

A. Eleuteri[1], R. Tagliaferri[2], L. Milano[3], F. Acernese[3], and M. De Laurentiis[4]

[1] Dipartimento di Matematica ed Applicazioni "R. Caccioppoli",
Università di Napoli "Federico II", Napoli, and INFN sez. Napoli,
via Cintia, I-80126 Napoli, Italia
eleuteri@na.infn.it
[2] DMI, Università di Salerno
via S. Allende, I-84081 Baronissi (Sa), Italia and INFM unità di Salerno
robtag@unisa.it
[3] Dipartimento di Scienze Fisiche, Università di Napoli "Federico II" and INFN sez.
Napoli, via Cintia, I-80126 Napoli, Italia
[4] Dipartimento di Endocrinologia ed Oncologia Molecolare e Clinica,
Università di Napoli "Federico II", Napoli, Italia
delauren@unina.it

Abstract. In this paper the fundamentals of Bayesian learning techniques are shown, and their application to neural network modeling is illustrated. Furthermore, it is shown how constraints on weight space can easily be embedded in a Bayesian framework. Finally, the application of these techniques to a complex neural network model for survival analysis is used as a significant example.

Keywords: Bayesian learning frameworks, Learning with constraints, Survival analysis.

1 Introduction

The Bayesian approach to learning applied to neural networks (NNs) has been firstly advocated and described in different forms by Buntine and Weigend [1], MacKay [3] and Neal [2]. The main problem in NN modeling is regularization, i.e. the control of model complexity. This strongly depends on the functional form of the model and on cardinality, dimension and noise level of the training data.

In the commonly used maximum likelihood with cross validation (CV) approach to learning, regularization is computationally very expensive and practically usable only for a small number of regularization parameters. Furthermore, the no-free-lunch (NFL) theorems by Wolpert and Macready [8] destroy in some way the presumed "objectivity" of CV techniques (usually used to criticize the subjectivity of the Bayesian approach), by stating that if we do not assume a priori information, then a model chosen by CV performs on average as well

M. Marinaro and R. Tagliaferri (Eds.): WIRN VIETRI 2002, LNCS 2486, pp. 216–232, 2002.

as a random model; this implies that in the limit of using CV to choose one from a large number of models, there is no guarantee of generalization. Furthermore, imposing constraints on the weight space forces the use of constrained optimization techniques, which makes the problem formally more complex due to the introduction of Lagrange multipliers. Finally, the techniques to assess the performances (e.g. confidence intervals) are nearly non-existent.

In a Bayesian context, these difficulties can be avoided in a consistent way. Regularization can be handled by using parameterized priors over the weights of the network, in such a way to include in the model the a priori information about the function we want to realize; when this information is not available, non-informative priors [4] can be used. Furthermore, regularization can be tied to different parts of the model, so that we can extract information on the relevance of our model features [2]. Note that constraints on weight space can be seen as a form of a priori information, and so they should be embedded in the priors. Finally, posterior predictive probabilities of the weights conditioned on the data can be used to make predictions and to easily get confidence intervals around them.

In the next sections we will show the basics of Bayesian modeling techniques from a theoretical and practical viewpoint. Then, a complex example of a NN for Survival Analysis is shown. This has been proved to be a particularly hard problem because constraints on the weight space are required; we show how these can be treated in a consistent way in the Bayesian framework, and how the Metropolis-Hastings algorithm can be modified to sample in an efficient way the posterior distribution on the constrained weight space.

2   Maximum Likelihood vs. Bayesian Modeling

In the conventional maximum likelihood approach to modeling [4], [6], a single parameter vector is found which maximizes a likelihood function:

$$\mathbf{w}_{ML} = \arg \max_{\mathbf{w}} f(\mathbf{w}|\{\mathbf{x}_i\}) \tag{1}$$

where $\mathbf{x}_i$ is the data we want to model.

In contrast, the Bayesian scheme considers a *prior* distribution over parameters which is updated to a *posterior* distribution when we receive data (Bayes's Theorem) [4]:

$$p(\mathbf{w}|\{\mathbf{x}_i\}) = \frac{p(\{\mathbf{x}_i\}|\mathbf{w})p(\mathbf{w})}{\int p(\{\mathbf{x}_i\}|\mathbf{w})p(\mathbf{w})d\mathbf{w}} . \tag{2}$$

It is important to note that when we observe a random phenomenon described by parameters $\mathbf{w}$, maximum-likelihood methods allow *inference* about the parameters from the observations $\mathbf{x}$, while probabilistic modeling gives a description of future observations *conditionally* on the parameters. This is precisely the notion of likelihood, which formally is expressed as:

$$p(\{\mathbf{x}_i\}|\mathbf{w}) \equiv f(\mathbf{w}|\{\mathbf{x}_i\}) \tag{3}$$

that is, the sample density written in the proper order as a function of the unknown parameters depending on the observations.

A Bayesian model is therefore made of a parametric statistical model, described by the likelihood, and a prior distribution on the parameters.

Equation (2) expresses an actualization of the information on the parameters by extracting the information about the parameters themselves contained in the observed data.

Bayesian models can be extended in a hierarchical way [4], [2]. We could, for instance, suppose that the prior distribution is itself parameterized, and define a prior distribution for its parameters (which are then called *hyperparameters*). By using Bayes's Theorem it is then easy (at least in principle!) to express the dependence between parameters and their update.

3   Neural Networks and Bayesian Learning

What we previously said is true whatever the form of model we choose. The case of NNs, however, is representative since usually these models are very complex. In the context of NNs, Bayesian techniques [2], [3] have a number of important features:

1. Regularization can be easily expressed in the Bayesian framework, allowing the use of a large number of regularization coefficients using only the training data. There is no need for validation sets.
2. Strictly connected with regularization is the capability to determine the relevance of input features.
3. Error bars and confidence intervals can be assigned to the predictions of NNs for regression-like tasks.
4. Different models (also with differing architectures) can be compared using only the training data.

While the maximum-likelihood approach to NN training consists in finding a weight vector which maximizes a log likelihood function, in a Bayesian context it consists in sampling the posterior distribution of weights, to obtain a probabilistic model of the data-generating process.

All these features make the Bayesian paradigm attractive; however, there is a drawback: the complexity of certain operations involved in the Bayesian approach requires the evaluation of integrals over high dimensional spaces, which cannot be done using the algorithms commonly used for mono-dimensional integrals since their time complexity is exponential in the dimension of the integration space.

As an example, let us consider the case of the best prediction we can obtain given a new input and the observed data D. It can be written:

$$p(y|\mathbf{x}, D) = \int p(y, \mathbf{w}|\mathbf{x}, D)\mathrm{d}\mathbf{w} = \int p(y|\mathbf{x}, \mathbf{w})p(\mathbf{w}, \boldsymbol{\alpha}|D)\mathrm{d}\mathbf{w}\mathrm{d}\boldsymbol{\alpha} \qquad (4)$$

where $p(y|\mathbf{x}, \mathbf{w})$ is the predictive model of the network. This integral can be seen as the evaluation of the expectation of the function realized by the NN with respect to the posterior distribution of the network weights, which we have expressed as dependent from a vector of hyperparameters. It turns out that except for very simple forms of the posterior and of the network function, the integral is not analytically tractable.

The problem can basically be solved in two ways: approximation of the posterior with a known (and tractable!) distribution or numerical approximation schemes.

3.1 Analytical Approximation: The Laplace Approximation

This method was first applied to NN training by MacKay [3]. He approximates the posterior with a Gaussian centered around the most probable weight vector. By defining the error (or *energy*) function:

$$M(\mathbf{w}) = -\log p(\{\mathbf{x}_i\}|\mathbf{w})p(\mathbf{w}) \tag{5}$$

and expanding (5) in Taylor series around its minimum $\mathbf{w}_{min}$ retaining terms up to second order we get:

$$M(\mathbf{w}) \approx M(\mathbf{w}_{min}) + \frac{1}{2}(\mathbf{w} - \mathbf{w}_{min})^{\mathrm{T}}\nabla\nabla M(\mathbf{w}_{min})(\mathbf{w} - \mathbf{w}_{min}) \tag{6}$$

where $\nabla\nabla M(\mathbf{w}_{min})$ is the Hessian matrix, i.e. the matrix of second derivatives of the error function with respect to the weights. This approximation leads to a Gaussian posterior:

$$p(\mathbf{w}|\{\mathbf{x}_i\}) = \frac{1}{Z_M} \exp(-M(\mathbf{w})) \tag{7}$$

where Z_M is the normalizing constant of a Gaussian density, which can be easily evaluated.

The validity of the Gaussian approximation depends on two factors:

1. cardinality of the training data set,
2. number of modes of the true posterior.

The first one is crucial, because if we have not enough data, then we cannot get a good estimation of the error surface: therefore, it is questionable that we can get a correct approximation. Furthermore, a result by Walker [9] says that a posterior, under very general circumstances, will tend to a Gaussian distribution as the cardinality of the training set goes to infinity. The second factor may seem the most crucial, since if we have many modes, then we can approximate just one of them. However, MacKay [3] argues that this kind of approximation gives good results because it gives a good estimation of the *probability mass* attached to the posterior. Furthermore, it can be shown that in high dimensional spaces the bulk of the mass is not located in the region of high probability density, so that the choice of the mode around which to approximate is not very crucial. The main drawback of this approach, as pointed out in [2], is that the Gaussian approximation may break down when the number of units in the network gets large. However, in practical applications this method has led to good predictive performances.

3.2   Numerical Approximation: Markov Chain Monte Carlo Methods

A straightforward numerical approximation scheme is given by Markov chain Monte Carlo (MCMC) methods, which allow the sampling of the posterior distribution of weights by generating a Markov chain whose limiting distribution is the distribution of interest.

In this way, evaluation of (4) can be done in an efficient way by using the generated sequence to approximate the integral with the following:

$$p(y|\mathbf{x}, D) \approx \frac{1}{N} \sum_{i=1}^{N} p(y|\mathbf{x}, \mathbf{w}_i) \tag{8}$$

which, as N goes to infinity, is guaranteed to converge to the true value of the integral by the Ergodic Theorem [10].

MCMC algorithms differ in the way they generate the chain. For a thorough analysis of these algorithms, see [5] and [10]. In the following, we will concentrate on the Random walk Metropolis-Hastings algorithm, originally used for the simulation of physical systems. Here, we will give a brief description of the algorithm, for an in-depth discussion and examples see [5].

Given a weight vector $\mathbf{w}_k$ at step k, a new candidate state is drawn from a distribution centered around $\mathbf{w}_k$ (the *proposal* distribution). The new state $\mathbf{w}_k^{(n)}$ is accepted if $M(\mathbf{w}_k^{(n)}) < M(\mathbf{w}_k)$, else it is accepted with probability $\exp(M(\mathbf{w}_k) - M(\mathbf{w}_k^{(n)}))$, where $M(\cdot)$ is the energy of the system. The so obtained sequence constitutes a Markov chain which, assuming ergodicity, has a limiting distribution and can be used in the evaluation of (8).

A fundamental feature of the algorithm is that it does not need evaluation of the normalization constant of the target distribution, which in our case would not be analytically possible. Therefore, from now on we will not give expressions for normalizing constants.

4   A Neural Network for Survival Analysis

In this section the basics of survival analysis are described, followed by a brief description of the modeling approaches currently used in literature. Then, a novel NN architecture for survival analysis is described in detail and we show how Bayesian methods can be used to solve some modeling problems related to the task.

4.1   Survival Analysis

Survival analysis [12] is used when we wish to study the occurrence of some event in a population of subjects and the time until the event is of interest. This time is called *survival time* or *failure time*. Examples include: time until failure of a light bulb, time until relapse of cancer, time until pregnancy, time until occurrence of an anomaly in an electronic circuit. Many more examples could be shown from industrial life-testing experiments and clinical follow-up studies.

The time of the event is usually continuous, and we can let it be not completely determined for some subjects. In this case we know only that the subject survived until that time; we say this time is *censored*. The censoring phenomenon defines survival analysis as a *missing data* problem [5], which can be very difficult to solve.

Let T denote an absolutely continuous random variable describing the failure time of a system. If $F_T(t)$ is the cumulative distribution function for T, then we can define the *survival function*:

$$S(t) = P\{T > t\} = 1 - F_T(t) = 1 - \int_0^t f_T(u)\mathrm{d}u \qquad (9)$$

which is the probability that the failure occurs after time t. An important requirement of $S(t)$ is that $S(0) = 1$ (there cannot be a failure before time 0). Also $S(t)$ must be non-increasing as t increases and $\lim_{t\to\infty} S(t) = 0$.

From the definitions of survival and density of failure, we can derive the *hazard function* which gives the probability density of an event occuring around time t, given that it has not occured before t. It can be shown that the hazard has this form [12]:

$$\lambda(t) = \frac{f_T(t)}{S(t)} \ . \qquad (10)$$

Furthermore, since:

$$\frac{\partial \log S(t)}{\partial t} = \frac{1}{S(t)} \frac{\partial S(t)}{\partial t} = -\frac{f_T(t)}{S(t)} \qquad (11)$$

we can write the hazard as:

$$\lambda(t) = -\frac{\partial \log S(t)}{\partial t} \ . \qquad (12)$$

By integrating (12) we get the *cumulative hazard function*:

$$\Lambda(t) \equiv \int_0^t \lambda(u)\mathrm{d}u = -\log S(t) \ . \qquad (13)$$

The survival function can also be defined as dependent on the characteristics of the system whose failure time we want to model:

$$S \equiv S(t, \mathbf{x}) \ . \qquad (14)$$

Note that this function is non-increasing as t increases uniformly w.r.t. $\mathbf{x}$.

4.2   A Neural Network Model

Conventional parametric models are based on strict assumptions on the distributions of failure times and on the form of the influence of the system's characteristics on the survival time, assumptions which usually extremely simplify the experimental evidence. In contrast, semi-parametric models (e.g. Cox's model) do not make assumptions on the distributions of failures, but make instead assumptions on how the system's characteristics influence the survival time; furthermore, these models do not allow for the estimation of survival times.

NNs have been recently used for survival analysis, but most of the efforts have been devoted to extending Cox's model ([14], [17], [19]), or in making piecewise or discrete approximations of the survival or hazard functions ([21], [22], [20]), or ignoring the censoring and treating the problem as a classification one ([15]), which may introduce significant bias into the estimates, as criticized in [16] and [18]. We refer to [16] and [18] for the description of the many limitations which arise in the current use of NNs, limitations due to the use of heuristic approaches which do not take into account the peculiarities of survival data, and/or ignore fundamental issues such as regularization.

In the following we describe a NN architecture for survival analysis which overcomes the described problems. This NN, given a data set of system characteristics and times, provides a model for the survival function (and implicitly, by suitable transforms, of the other functions of interest).

It is well known (see e.g. [6]) that a sigmoid is the appropriate activation function for the output of a NN to be interpretable as a probability. If $V(a) = (1 + \exp(-a))^{-1}$ is such a sigmoid function, by taking into account (9) and using $S(a) = 1 - V(a)$ we can define the activation function of the NN as:

$$y(a) = S(a) = \frac{1}{1 + \exp(a)} \ . \tag{15}$$

In this way, the output can be read as a survival function. Strictly speaking, this definition is *not sufficient*, since we must also enforce the condition that $\forall \mathbf{x}, S(0, \mathbf{x}) = 1$ as we shall see in the following.

Two problems arise in the application of a classical MLP architecture, i.e. the conditions that, for all $\mathbf{x}$:

1. $S(\cdot, \mathbf{x})$ is a non-increasing function of time.
2. $S(0, \mathbf{x}) = 1$,

We address these two problems as follows.

1. We must look at the functional form of the network output. Since it must be a non-increasing function of a, we must ensure that a is a non-decreasing function of t. We have:

$$a = \sum_j w_j^{(2)} g_j(a_j) \ . \tag{16}$$

So, if we suppose that the $g_j(a_j)$ are non-decreasing, then a is non-decreasing if and only if the weights $w_j^{(2)}$ are non-negative. We must now impose that the $g_j(a_j)$ are non-decreasing. Since they are all monotonic non-decreasing functions, then we must impose that their arguments are non-decreasing functions of t. With a similar argument, this can be accomplished if we impose that the weights associated with the time input are non-negative. In short, all the weights on paths connecting the time input to the network output must be non-negative.

2. We set one of the activation functions of the hidden layer to be the $h(t) \equiv -t^{-1}$ function. This node is connected only with the time input. Since the other activation functions are all bounded (and the integration functions for hidden and output nodes is the scalar product), then this ensures us that the following condition

$$\lim_{t \to 0} S(t, \mathbf{x}) = 1 \tag{17}$$

is satisfied uniformly w.r.t. $\mathbf{x}$ if the weight connecting the input t is positive and the weight connecting the unit h to the output is also positive. In this way the expression in (16) goes to negative infinity, so that the output is effectively 1. Note that the weights output by the input t are fed to the remaining hidden units with variable strength weights so that correlations with other input characteristics are taken into account. As we have seen, these weights must also be constrained. In Fig. 1 the architecture of our SNN is shown (the bias connections are not shown).

4.3   Choosing the Likelihood

Let time t be defined as

$$t = \min(c, u) \tag{18}$$

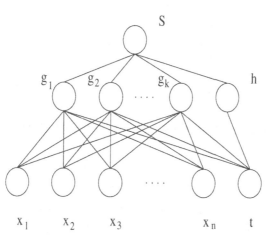

Fig. 1. Architecture of a neural network for survival analysis

where c is a censored time and u is an event time. In this way we can define an indicator variable d such that

$$d = \begin{cases} 1 & \text{if } t \text{ is an event time} \\ 0 & \text{if } t \text{ is a censored time} \end{cases} . \tag{19}$$

In this way, the likelihood of an event at time t can be written [12]:

$$l(d|t, \mathbf{x}) = S(t, \mathbf{x})^{1-d} f_T(t, \mathbf{x})^d . \tag{20}$$

By assuming the independence of time-characteristics pairs $(t_k, \mathbf{x}_k)$, we can write the likelihood for a set of observations $\{(t_k, \mathbf{x}_k)\}_k$ as:

$$L = \prod_k l(d_k|t_k, \mathbf{x}_k) . \tag{21}$$

From this an error criterion suitable for network training can be defined (after some math):

$$E = -\log L = \sum_k -d_k \log \left(-\frac{\partial S(t_k, \mathbf{x}_k)}{\partial t} \right) + \sum_k (d_k - 1) \log S(t_k, \mathbf{x}_k) \tag{22}$$

where $\frac{\partial S(t_k, \mathbf{x}_k)}{\partial t}$ is the time component of the Jacobian of the NN which can be evaluated by using an efficient backpropagation procedure:

$$J_t \equiv \frac{\partial y}{\partial t} = \sum_j \frac{\partial y}{\partial a} \frac{\partial a}{\partial a_j} \frac{\partial a_j}{\partial t} = \sum_j \frac{\partial y}{\partial a} g'(a_j) w_j^{(2)} w_{jt}^{(1)} \tag{23}$$

and the result follows from the application of the chain rule and from the definition in (16).

It will be useful to put the error criterion in (22) in exponential form:

$$p(D|\mathbf{w}) = \frac{1}{Z_E} \exp(-E(D|\mathbf{w})) \tag{24}$$

where Z_E is a normalizing constant and D is the target data. This is our *noise model*.

4.4   Choosing the Prior Distribution

The prior over weights should reflect any knowledge we have about the mapping we want to build. Furthermore, it must take into account the fact that we have both constrained and unconstrained weights. Assuming the a priori independence of the weights (as it is natural), we can give a Gaussian prior to unconstrained weights, and an exponential prior to the constrained ones; in this way we favor smooth mappings with small weights. In order to not violate basic scaling laws of the weights [2], we must assign them to different groups, depending on their position in the network and the role they have. Under these assumptions, we propose the following parameterized priors:

$$p(\mathbf{w}^{(u)}|\boldsymbol{\alpha}^{(u)}) = \prod_{k=1}^{G_u} \left(\frac{\alpha_k^{(u)}}{2\pi}\right)^{W_k/2} \exp\left(-\frac{\alpha_k^{(u)}}{2} \sum_{i=1}^{W_k} w_k^{(i)\,2}\right) \tag{25}$$

$$p(\mathbf{w}^{(c)}|\boldsymbol{\alpha}^{(c)}) = \prod_{k=1}^{G_c} \alpha_k^{(c)\,W_k} \exp\left(-\alpha_k^{(c)} \sum_{i=1}^{W_k} w_k^{(i)}\right) \mathcal{I}(\mathbf{w}^{(c)}) \tag{26}$$

where $\mathbf{w}^{(u)}$ and $\mathbf{w}^{(c)}$ are the sets of unconstrained and constrained weights, respectively, $\boldsymbol{\alpha}^{(u)}$ and $\boldsymbol{\alpha}^{(c)}$ are the vectors of the corresponding prior parameters (inverse variances and inverse means), respectively, $\mathcal{I}(\cdot)$ is the indicator function, W_k is the number of weights in the k−th weights group and G_u and G_c denote the number of unconstrained and constrained weights groups, respectively.

The complete prior will be the product of the two priors, and it is useful to put it in exponential form:

$$p(\{\mathbf{w}^{(u)}, \mathbf{w}^{(c)}\}|\boldsymbol{\alpha}^{(u)}, \boldsymbol{\alpha}^{(c)}) = \frac{1}{Z_R} \exp(-R(\{\mathbf{w}^{(u)}, \mathbf{w}^{(c)}\}|\boldsymbol{\alpha}^{(u)}, \boldsymbol{\alpha}^{(c)})) \tag{27}$$

where Z_R is a normalizing constant and R is the following function:

$$R(\{\mathbf{w}^{(u)}, \mathbf{w}^{(c)}\}|\boldsymbol{\alpha}^{(u)}, \boldsymbol{\alpha}^{(c)}) = \sum_{k=1}^{G_u} \frac{\alpha_k^{(i)}}{2} \sum_{i=1}^{W_k} w_k^{(i)\,2} + \sum_{k=1}^{G_c} \alpha_k^{(i)} \sum_{i=1}^{W_k} w_k^{(i)} - \log \mathcal{I}(\mathbf{w}^{(c)}) + C \tag{28}$$

where C is an expression independent of the weights.

4.5   Evaluation of the Posterior

With the expressions for the prior and the noise model, we can evaluate the posterior:

$$p(\mathbf{w}|D) = \frac{1}{Z_M} \exp(-M(\mathbf{w}|D)) \tag{29}$$

where Z_M is a normalizing constant and M is the energy function which has the following expression:

$$M(\mathbf{w}|D) = E(D|\mathbf{w}) + R(\mathbf{w}|\boldsymbol{\alpha}) \tag{30}$$

where we have used a shorthand notation to express weights and hyperparameters. We have not shown the dependency of the function from the hyperparameters since they can be considered as *nuisance parameters* which must be integrated out when we are going to make a prediction on new data (see (4)).

Sampling of the posterior $p(\mathbf{w}, \boldsymbol{\alpha}|D)$ can be done by using the *Gibbs sampling* algorithm. In the first step, the hyperparameters are kept constant and the weights are sampled from $p(\mathbf{w}|\boldsymbol{\alpha}, D)$ using the Metropolis-Hastings algorithm.

In the second step, the weights are kept constant and the hyperparameters are sampled from the following distribution:

$$p(\boldsymbol{\alpha}|\mathbf{w}, D) = \frac{p(D, \mathbf{w}, \boldsymbol{\alpha})}{p(D, \mathbf{w})} = \frac{p(\mathbf{w}|\boldsymbol{\alpha})p(\boldsymbol{\alpha})}{p(\mathbf{w})}. \tag{31}$$

The sampling can be done in an efficient way if, for each group of weights, the prior over the parameters $p(\mathbf{w}|\boldsymbol{\alpha})$ is chosen so that the prior over the hyperparameters $p(\boldsymbol{\alpha})$ is *conjugate* [4] to the posterior $p(\boldsymbol{\alpha}|\mathbf{w}, D)$. For the chosen priors in (25) and (26), it can be shown that the natural conjugate prior is the gamma distribution.

In fact, for each group of constrained weights we have (to not clutter the notation we have not expressed the groups of the weights or hyperparameters):

$$p_c(\alpha|\mathbf{w}) \propto p_c(\mathbf{w}|\alpha)p_c(\alpha) \propto \alpha^W \exp(-\alpha r(\mathbf{w}))\alpha^{\nu_c-1}\exp(-\mu_c\alpha) = \tag{32}$$
$$= \alpha^{(W+\nu_c)-1}\exp(-(r(\mathbf{w}) + \mu_c)\alpha).$$

where $r(\mathbf{w}) = \sum_i w_i$, W is the number of weights in the group and ν_c4 and μ_c are the parameters of the prior over hyperparameters.

Similarly, for each group of unconstrained weights we have:

$$p_u(\alpha|\mathbf{w}) \propto p_u(\mathbf{w}|\alpha)p_u(\alpha) \tag{33}$$
$$\propto \alpha^{W/2}\exp(-\alpha r(\mathbf{w}))\alpha^{\nu_u-1}\exp(-\mu_u\alpha) = \tag{34}$$
$$= \alpha^{(W/2+\nu_u)-1}\exp(-(r(\mathbf{w}) + \mu_u)\alpha).$$

where $r(\mathbf{w}) = \frac{1}{2}\sum_i w_i^2$, W is the number of weights in the group and ν_u and μ_u are the parameters of the prior over hyperparameters.

4.6   A Modified Metropolis-Hastings Algorithm

Using the Metropolis-Hastings algorithm to train the SNN model can give high rejection rates, due to the constraints in weight space. In fact, the proposal distribution with a fixed variance can take as candidate states not-admissible weight vectors which should in principle be excluded a priori. A naive solution would be to scale the variance by the distance from the origin of the current weight vector (since some of its components must be non-negative). However, this strategy would violate the reversibility of the chain, since the algorithm would use different scalings depending on the positions before and after the acceptance step. In general, we cannot use information which depends on the current values of the weights.

How can we solve the problem? We have devised a simple effective strategy, which consists in making the proposal distribution non-isotropic and its variance scaled by the current value of the hyperparameters. The variance gives us the information on the possible magnitude of the weights. It can be shown that this strategy does not violate the reversibility of the chain, since the hyperparameters are kept constant between the Metropolis-Hastings and Gibbs steps of the sampling process.

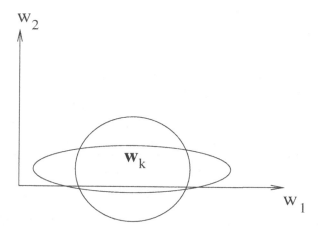

Fig. 2. How the modified Metropolis-Hastings algorithm works

In Fig. 2 a bidimensional example is shown, in which the variable w_2 is constrained. As can be seen, a spherical distribution would intersect half of its volume with the non-admissible part of the space. In contrast, by scaling the variance of the distribution by the magnitude of the weights, we get an ellipse which does not constrain the movement in the admissible part of the space but reduces its movement toward prohibited zones. In the next section we will show some examples of the application of this technique.

4.7 Training of the SNN Model on Synthetic Data

In this section we show the results of training the SNN model on a set of synthetic data with the described techniques.

A data set of 2000 samples was generated by inversion sampling from the following time distribution:

$$T \sim f_T(t) = t \exp\left(-\frac{t^2}{2}\right)$$

and then by simulating the following censoring time random variable:

$$C \sim U(0, \max T)$$

where $\max T$ is the maximum value obtained in the simulation process of the time distribution. The event times were then obtained by evaluating:

$$d = \min(t, c)$$

where t and c are time and censoring time samples. A maximum fraction of censored times was fixed at 20% of the length of the data set.

The data set was then randomly split in training and testing sets with 1000 samples each, by taking care to hold the same fraction of censored times in each set.

To show the performance of the SNN model, two experiments were performed, with the standard and with the modified Metropolis-Hastings algorithms. One hundred chains were started from different and dispersed positions, and 3000 samples were generated for each chain, with the first 500 discarded. A Gibbs sampling phase was executed every 50 Metropolis-Hastings steps. In Table 1 the rejection rates for the first eight chains are shown. As can be seen, the scaling is indeed successful in reducing the rejection rate. To assess the significativity of the differing rates, a Kolmogorov-Smirnov test on the distributions of rejections was made, and it showed that they are indeed different.

Table 1. Rejection rates of sampling with and without scaling

No scaling	Scaling
0.43	0.13
0.23	0.14
0.26	0.18
0.42	0.21
0.25	0.13
0.21	0.12
0.30	0.11
0.29	0.17

Finally, to assess the convergence of the chains, the *estimated potential scale reduction* diagnostic statistic [7], [5] was evaluated on the energies of the chains. Gelman and Rubin suggest to monitor the value of the statistic and accepting a group of chains if it is less than 1.05 or 1.1. The value in the case of the energies generated with the modified Metropolis-Hastings is 0.99, while for the energies generated with the standard algorithm is 1.72, showing that, according to the above criterion, in the first case we can assume convergence, while in the second case we cannot.

In Figs. 3–6 example energies sequences and performances of the SNN model are shown. It is visually clear that in the case of the standard Metropolis-Hastings convergence has not been fully reached. Please note that only the last 1500 samples from each chain have been used in the test.

The output of the model has been compared with the non-parametric Kaplan-Meier (KM) estimator [12], which is the standard method used in prognostic studies to analyze survival data. However, this estimator is noisy, as can be seen from the different performances on the test data and on the complete data set; furthermore, it does not allow for predictions being a purely descriptive method, while the SNN model is predictive.

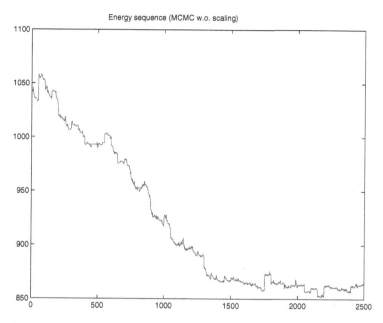

Fig. 3. An energy sequence from a chain trained with Metropolis-Hastings without scaling

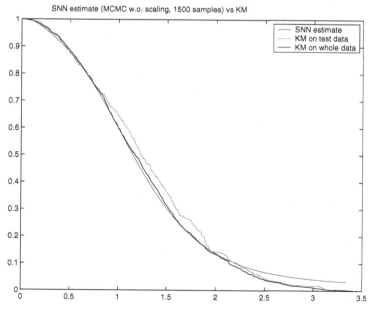

Fig. 4. Performance of the SNN model trained with Metropolis-Hastings without scaling

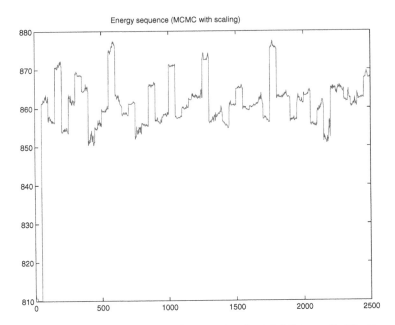

Fig. 5. An energy sequence from a chain trained with Metropolis-Hastings with scaling

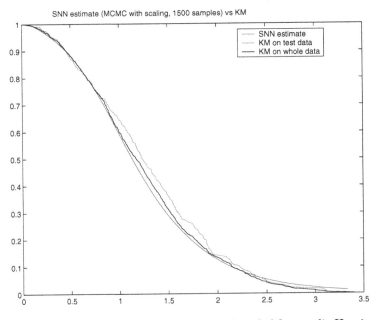

Fig. 6. Performance of the SNN model trained with Metropolis-Hastings with scaling

Finally, the SNN model trained with the modified Metropolis-Hastings algorthm has a better tail behavior than the other SNN model because this last one has not yet reached the convergence.

5   Conclusions

In this paper a general overview of Bayesian learning for NNs has been done, in particular with reference to the problem of training networks in constrained weight spaces, which is a much more difficult problem than training in an uncostrained weight space, typical of regression and classification tasks.

As an example of the relevance of this problem, a novel and complex NN model for Survival Analysis has been shown which overcomes the problems of other NN approaches to this kind of problems. To train this model a modified Metropolis-Hastings algorithm has been developed which can significantly lower the rejection rates and thus help speed up convergence of training.

The results of training the SNN model on synthetic data can be directly compared with the KM estimation of the survival curve, which is the standard method currently used in survival analysis. Finally, our model also allows for robust predictions due to the Bayesian approach to training and regularization.

We plan to do further tests on real-world data, which will show how this model can effectively be used to aid users in a decision making process.

Acknowledgments

This paper has been partially supported by AIRC and MIUR COFIN 2000.

References

[1] W. L. Buntine, A. S. Weigend. Bayesian back-propagation. Complex Systems **5(6)** (1991) 603–643   216
[2] R. M. Neal. Bayesian Learning for Neural Networks. Springer, New York (1996) 216, 217, 218, 219, 224
[3] D. J. C. MacKay. A practical Bayesian framework for backpropagation networks. Neural Computation **4(3)** (1992) 448–472   216, 218, 219
[4] C. P. Robert. The Bayesian Choice, Second Edition. Springer, New York (2001) 217, 218, 226
[5] C. P. Robert, G. Casella. Markov Chain Monte Carlo Methods. Springer, New York (1999)   220, 221, 228
[6] C. M. Bishop. Neural Networks for Pattern Recognition. Clarendon Press, Oxford (1996)   217, 222
[7] A. Gelman, D. B. Rubin. Inference from iterative simulation using multiple sequences (with discussion). Statist. sci. **7** (1992) 457–511   228
[8] D. H. Wolpert, W. G. Macready. No free lunch theorems for search. Technical Report SFI-TR-95-02-010, The Santa Fe Institute (1995)   216
[9] A. M. Walker. On the asymptotic behaviour of posterior distributions. Journal of the Royal Statistical Society B **49(3)** (1969) 80–88   219

[10] S. P. Meyn, R. L. Tweedie. Markov Chains and Stochastic Stability. Springer-Verlag, London (1993) 220

[11] S. Duane, A. D. Kennedy, B. J. Pendleton, D. Roweth. Hybrid Monte Carlo. Physics Letters B **195(2)** (1987) 216–222

[12] F. E. Harrell jr. Survival and Risk Analysis - Technical Report. Duke University Medical Center (1993) 220, 221, 224, 228

[13] K. Liestøl, P. K. Andersen, U. Andersen. Survival analysis and neural nets. Statistics in medicine **13** (1994) 1189–1200

[14] D. Faraggi, R. Simon. A neural network model for survival data. Statistics in medicine **14** (1995) 73–82 222

[15] H. B. Burke et al. Artificial Neural Networks Improve the Accuracy of Cancer Survival Prediction. Cancer **79(4)** (1997) 857–862 222

[16] B. D. Ripley, R. M. Ripley. Neural Networks as Statistical Methods in Survival Analysis. Artificial Neural Networks: Prospects for Medicine (R. Dybowsky and V. Gant eds.), Landes Biosciences Publishers (1998) 222

[17] B. Bakker, T. Heskes. A neural-Bayesian approach to survival analysis. Proceedings IEE Artificial Neural Networks (1999) 832–837 222

[18] G. Schwarzer, W. Vach, M. Schumacher. On the misuses of artificial neural networks for prognostic and diagnostic classification in oncology. Statistics in medicine **19** (2000) 541–561 222

[19] P. J. G. Lisboa, H. Wong. Are neural networks best used to help logistic regression? An example from breast cancer survival analysis. IEEE Transactions on Neural Networks (2001) 2472–2477 222

[20] H. Wong, P. Harris, P. J. G. Lisboa, S. P. J. Kirby, R. Swindell. Dealing with Censorship in Neural Network Models. IEEE Transactions on Neural Networks (1999) 3702–3706 222

[21] R. M. Neal. Survival Analysis Using a Bayesian Neural Network. Joint Statistical Meetings report, Atlanta (2001) 222

[22] E. Biganzoli, P. Boracchi, E. Marubini. A general framework for neural network models on censored survival data. Neural Networks **15** (2002) 209–218 222

A Short Review of Statistical Learning Theory

Massimiliano Pontil

Dipartimento di Ingegneria dell'Informazione,
Via Roma 56, 53100 Siena, Italy
pontil@dii.unisi.it

Abstract. Statistical learning theory has emerged in the last few years as a solid and elegant framework for studying the problem of learning from examples. Unlike previous "classical" learning techniques, this theory completely characterizes the necessary and sufficient conditions for a learning algorithm to be consistent. The key quantity is the *capacity* of the set of hypotheses employed in the learning algorithm and the goal is to control this capacity depending on the given examples. Structural risk minimization (SRM) is the main theoretical algorithm which implements this idea. SRM is inspired and closely related to regularization theory. For practical purposes, however, SRM is a very hard problem and impossible to implement when dealing with a large number of examples. Techniques such as support vector machines and older regularization networks are a viable solution to implement the idea of capacity control. The paper also discusses how these techniques can be formulated as a variational problem in a Hilbert space and show how SRM can be extended in order to implement both classical regularization networks and support vector machines.

Keywords: Statistical learning theory, Structural risk minimization, Regularization

1 Introduction

We begin by introducing the problem of learning from examples and the statistical framework in which this problem is studied.

1.1 Learning from Examples

Learning theory studies the problem of recovering the input-output mapping between two random variables, $\mathbf{x} \in X$ and $y \in Y$, that are related by a probabilist relationship. In the following we assume for simplicity $Y \subset \mathbb{R}^n$ and $Y \subset \mathbb{R}$. We say that the relationship is probabilistic because generally an element of set X does not determine uniquely an element of set Y, but rather a probability distribution on Y. This can be formalized assuming that a probability distribution $P(\mathbf{x}, y)$ is defined over the set $X \times Y$. The probability distribution $P(\mathbf{x}, y)$ is *unknown* and we are only provided with a finite set examples, that is with a data set

M. Marinaro and R. Tagliaferri (Eds.): WIRN VIETRI 2002, LNCS 2486, pp. 233–242, 2002.
© Springer-Verlag Berlin Heidelberg 2002

$$D_l \equiv \{(\mathbf{x}_i, y_i) \in X \times Y\}_{i=1}^l,$$

called the *training set*, obtained by sampling l times the set $X \times Y$ according to $P(\mathbf{x}, y)$. The problem of learning consists of, given the data set D_l, providing an *estimator*, that is a function $f : X \to Y$, that can be used, given any value of $\mathbf{x} \in X$, to predict a value $y \in Y$. When Y is a continuous subset of $\mathbb{R}$, the problem is known as *regression*. In the case that $Y = \{-1, 1\}$ we have the binary classification problem.

In statistical learning theory the standard way to solve the learning problem consists in defining a *risk functional*, which measures the average amount of error associated with an estimator, and then to look for the estimator, among the allowed ones (see below), with the lowest risk. If $V(y, f(\mathbf{x}))$ is the loss function measuring the error we make when we predict y by $f(\mathbf{x})$, then the average error is the so called *expected risk*:

$$I[f] \equiv \int V(y, f(\mathbf{x})) P(\mathbf{x}, y) \, d\mathbf{x} dy \tag{1}$$

We assume that the expected risk is defined on a "large" class of functions $\mathcal{F}$, called *hypothesis space*, and we denote by f_0 the function which minimizes the expected risk in $\mathcal{F}$:

$$f_0(\mathbf{x}) = \arg \min_{\mathcal{F}} I[f]. \tag{2}$$

In the case of classification $\mathcal{F}$ is a set of functions from X to $\{-1, 1\}$ which are called indicator functions and the loss function is simply $V(y, f(\mathbf{x})) = \theta(y f(\mathbf{x}))$, where $\theta(\xi)$ is equal to 1 is $\xi > 0$ and zero otherwise (Heavyside function).

The function f_0 is our ideal estimator, and it is often called the *target* function. Under minor assumptions we can assume that f_0 is unique. Unfortunately this function cannot be found in practice, because the probability distribution $P(\mathbf{x}, y)$ that defines the expected risk is unknown, and only a sample of it, the data set D_l, is available. To overcome this limitation we need an *induction principle* that we can use to "learn" from the limited number of training data we have.

Statistical learning theory builds on the so-called *empirical risk minimization (ERM)* induction principle. The ERM method consists of using the data set D_l to build a stochastic approximation to the expected risk, which is usually called the *empirical risk*, and is defined as:

$$I_{\mathrm{emp}}[f; l] = \frac{1}{l} \sum_{i=1}^l V(y_i, f(\mathbf{x}_i)). \tag{3}$$

We denote by $\hat{f}_l$ the minimizer of the empirical risk in $\mathcal{F}$. An important problem of the theory is whether the minimum of the empirical risk is close in probability to the expected risk of $\hat{f}_l$, that is whether the inequality:

$$I[\hat{f}_l] < I_{\text{emp}}[\hat{f}_l; l] + \epsilon \tag{4}$$

holds with high probability η and for a small value of ϵ[1]. If this is the case, then we can use the the function $\hat{f}_l$ to predict the value y of a new input vector $\mathbf{x}$ with high confidence.

It is clear that if $\mathcal{F}$ is very "large", then we can always find $\hat{f}_l \in \mathcal{F}$ with small, possibly zero, empirical error. However, this does not guarantee that the expected risk of $\hat{f}_l$ is also small. Intuitively this means that the hypothesis space $\mathcal{F}$ has great flexibility or *capacity* to fit well the training data.

In the case of classification the concept of capacity is very simple: The capacity or VC-dimension [22] of a set of indicator functions is the maximum number h of vectors $\mathbf{x}_1, \ldots, \mathbf{x}_h$ that can be separated into two classes in all 2^h possible ways using functions of the set. If, for any number N, it is possible to find N points that can be separated in all the 2^N possible ways, we will say that the VC-dimension of the set is infinite.

The concept of capacity can be extended as well to the case of regression, that is to the case where $\mathcal{F}$ is a set of real value functions - see [1]. However, this extension requires some technicalities which are not necessary for the purpose of this short review. Here we just want to analyze the bound (4) in the case of classification in order to outline the idea of structural risk minimization.

2   Structural Risk Minimization

It is possible to derive equations that relate ϵ above to the capacity h, the number of examples l and the probability η. From a qualitative point of view, all these results basically say that, for a fixed value of η, ϵ is an increasing function of h and a decreasing function of l. Moreover, for all practical purposes ϵ can be treated as a function of $\frac{h}{l}$ only.

Vapnik and Chervonenkis [22] have shown that for the classification problem the following bound holds with high probability:

$$I[\hat{f}_l] < I_{epm}[\hat{f}_l] + O(\sqrt{\frac{h}{l} \ln \frac{l}{h}}) \tag{5}$$

Notice that the inequality (5) is meaningful in practice only if the VC-dimension is finite and less than l. Since the space $\mathcal{F}$ is usually very large (i.e. all functions in L_2), one typically considers smaller hypothesis spaces $\mathcal{H}$. Of course, all the definitions and analysis above still hold, where we replace f_0 with the minimizer of the expected risk in $\mathcal{H}$, $\hat{f}_l$ with the minimizer of the empirical

---

[1] Since we are solving a minimization problem, we expect the minimum of the empirical risk to be small, possibly zero. Then the question whether also the inequality:

$$I_{\text{emp}}[\hat{f}_l; l] < I[\hat{f}_l] + \epsilon$$

holds is not important.

risk in $\mathcal{H}$, and h with the VC-dimension of $\mathcal{H}$. Moreover, inequality (5) suggests a method for achieving good generalization: not only minimize the empirical risk, but instead minimize a combination of the empirical risk and the *complexity of the hypothesis space* measured by the second term in the r.h.s. of inequality (5). This observation leads us to the method of *Structural Risk Minimization (SRM)*.

The idea of SRM is to define a nested sequence of hypothesis spaces $H_1 \subset H_2 \subset \ldots \subset H_{n(l)}$ with $n(l)$ a non-decreasing integer function of l where each hypothesis space H_i has VC-dimension finite and larger than that of all previous sets, i.e. if h_i is the VC-dimension of space H_i, then $h_1 \leq h_2 \leq \ldots \leq h_{n(l)}$. For example H_i could be the set of polynomials of degree i, or a set of splines with i nodes, or some more complicated nonlinear parameterization. For each element H_i of the structure the solution of the learning problem is:

$$\hat{f}_{i,l} = \arg \min_{f \in H_i} I_{\text{emp}}[f; l]. \tag{6}$$

Because of the way we defined our structure it is clear that the larger i is the smaller the empirical error of $\hat{f}_{i,l}$ is (since we have greater "flexibility" to fit our training data), but the larger the VC-dimension part (second term) of the r.h.s. of (5) is. Using such a nested sequence of more and more complex hypothesis spaces, the SRM learning technique consists of choosing the space $H_{n^*(l)}$ for which the right hand side of inequality (5) is minimized.

The method of SRM can be applied in the same way to the regression case. This only requires to extend the concept of capacity to real valued loss functions - see [7] for a discussion.

3 Regularization

Unfortunately, the implementation of SRM method is computationally expensive for many practical applications and impossible in the case where the training set is large, say $l > 10^4$. Various algorithms which approximatively implement the idea of SRM have been proposed. In the case of regression, SRM is strictly related to the approach of regularization theory which was developed in the mathematical framework of Functional Analysis[2] - see [19, 3, 23] and references therein. Like SRM, this approach consists on imposing additional constraints to the ERM method in order to restrict the hypothesis space. Unlike the SRM formulation, however, regularization theory directly looks for a minimum of the following functional:

$$H[f] = \frac{1}{l} \sum_{i=1}^{l} V(y_i, f(\mathbf{x}_i)) + \lambda \Omega(f), \tag{7}$$

where $\Omega(f)$ is a smoothness functional of f, called stabilizer, such that lower values of the functional correspond to smoother functions, and λ a fixed positive

---

[2] Historically, regularization theory was proposed before SRM, which, in fact, was inspired by it.

real number, called regularization parameter, which somehow controls the trade off between the two terms. The regression case with $V(y, f(\mathbf{x})) = (y - f(\mathbf{x}))^2$ corresponds to the well known standard regularization, which has been proposed in the context of learning by Girosi and Poggio [15].

3.1 Reproducing Kernel Hilbert Spaces

We now consider an important example of Hypothesis space. We chose $\mathcal{F}$ to be a reproducing kernel Hilbert spaces (RKHS) and $\Omega(f)$ the norm of f in the RKHS. This is equivalent to assume that the function f underlying the data can be represented as:

$$f(\mathbf{x}) = \sum_{n=1}^{\infty} a_n \phi_n(\mathbf{x}), \tag{8}$$

where $\{\phi_n(\mathbf{x})\}_{n=1}^{\infty}$ is a set of given, linearly independent basis functions[3], and c_n are the parameters that we want to learn from the given examples D_l. The stabilizer $\Omega(f)$ is defined as follows:

$$\Omega(f) = \sum_{n=1}^{\infty} \frac{a_n^2}{\lambda_n}, \tag{9}$$

where $\{\lambda_n\}_{n=1}^{\infty}$ is a decreasing, positive sequence, whose series is finite.

An important feature of this scheme (see, e.g., [8]) is that the minimizer of functional (7) has, independently on the loss function V, the same general form

$$f(\mathbf{x}) = \sum_{i=1}^{l} c_i K(\mathbf{x}, \mathbf{x}_i), \tag{10}$$

where we have defined the symmetric kernel[4] K as follows:

$$K(\mathbf{x}, \mathbf{x}_i) = \sum_{n=1}^{\infty} \lambda_n \phi_n(\mathbf{x}) \phi_n(\mathbf{x}_i).$$

Notice that Equation (10) establishes a representation of the function f as a linear combination of kernels centered in each data point.

3.2 Learning Algorithm in RKHS, Support Vector Machines and Regularization Networks

The coefficients c_i in Equation (10) are generally the solution of a system of non-linear equations. Only in the particular case where the cost function is quadratic,

---

[3] In the classification case we will assume that our indicator functions can be written as sign($f(\mathbf{x})$), with $f(\mathbf{x})$ given by Equation (8).

[4] The kernel K can be seen as the kernel of a RKHS - see [2] for a review.

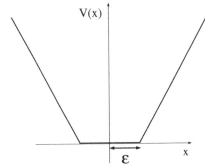

Fig. 1. The ϵ−insensitivity loss function

that is $V(y, f(\mathbf{x})) = (y - f(\mathbf{x}))^2$, the coefficients c_i are found by solving a linear system[5].

Learning techniques based on the minimization of functionals of the form of H in (7) can be justified for a few choices of the loss function V using a slight extension of the tools and results of Vapnik's statistical learning theory [7]. Important cases are standard regularization and Support Vector Machines, a learning technique which was proposed for both classification [4] and regression [20]:

– Standard (L_2) Regularization (SR)

$$V(y_i, f(\mathbf{x}_i)) = (y_i - f(\mathbf{x}_i))^2 \tag{11}$$

– Support Vector Machines Regression (SVMR)

$$V(y_i, f(\mathbf{x}_i)) = |y_i - f(\mathbf{x}_i)|_\epsilon^\sigma, \tag{12}$$

– Support Vector Machines Classification (SVMC)

$$V(y_i, f(\mathbf{x}_i)) = \theta(1 - y_i f(\mathbf{x}_i))(1 - y_i f(\mathbf{x}_i))^\sigma, \tag{13}$$

where $\theta(\cdot)$ is the Heaviside function and the function $|\cdot|_\epsilon$, called epsilon-insensitive loss, is defined as follows (see Figure 1):

$$V(x) \equiv |x|_\epsilon \equiv \begin{cases} 0 & \text{if } |x| < \epsilon \\ |x| - \epsilon & \text{otherwise.} \end{cases} \tag{14}$$

$$V(y, f(\mathbf{x})) = V^\sigma(y f(\mathbf{x})) = |1 - y f(\mathbf{x})|_+^\sigma. \tag{15}$$

We can also consider loss functions which are a positive power of the previous scale-insensitive loss functions, i.e. $|x|_\epsilon^\sigma$, or $|1 - y f(\mathbf{x})|_+^\sigma$, with $\sigma > 0$. This is especially interesting in the case of classification. In Figure 2 we plot some of the possible loss functions for different choices of the parameter σ. Note that when $\sigma < 1$ the loss is not convex anymore.

---

[5] This is why standard regularization is simpler to implement than other techniques.

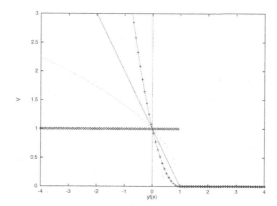

Fig. 2. Hard margin loss (line with diamond-shaped points), soft margin loss (solid line), nonlinear soft margin with $\sigma = 2$ (line with crosses), and $\sigma = \frac{1}{2}$ (dotted line)

The parameter σ is typically set to 1 or 2. In this case it can be shown that the coefficients c_i are the solution of a quadratic programming (QP) problem[6] Algorithms solving these QP-problems are discussed in [13, 14].

A remarkable feature of the SVM technique is that the loss functions (12) and (13) determine quite different properties of the solution which is, unlike in the case of standard regularization, sparse in the c_n (see [8]). With this we mean that only a (typically) small fraction of the coefficients c_i are nonzero. In order to gain an intuition about this phenomenon let us consider the regression case: note that the epsilon-insensitive loss assigns zero cost to errors smaller then ϵ. In other words, for the cost function $|\cdot|_\epsilon$ any function closer than ϵ to the data points is a perfect interpolant. We can think to the parameter ϵ as the resolution at which we want to look the data. For this reason we expect that the larger ϵ is, the more sparse the representation will be.

Data point $\mathbf{x}_i$ associated with the nonzero coefficients in Equation (10) are called support vectors. The interpretation of the support vectors is more intuitive in the case of classification. In this case the function in Equation (8) can be seen as a boundary surface in the input space X in the sense that points such that $f(\mathbf{x}) > 0$ (resp. $f(\mathbf{x}) < 0$) are classified in the class 1 (resp. -1). The support vectors are those data points that lie near the boundary surface. More precisely let us assume for the moment that the training set is separable, that is $f(\mathbf{x}_i) = y_i,\ \forall\, i = 1, \ldots, l$ (this is always possible for an appropriate choice of the basis functions ϕ_n). Then it can be shown that the support vectors are the nearest points to the boundary surface, where the distance is measured in the RKHS and it is given by:

---

[6] If $\sigma = 2$, the regularization parameter appears in the objective function of the QP-problem. If $\sigma = 1$, it appear in the "box constraints" as $c_i \leq \frac{1}{2\lambda}$.

$$d = \frac{1}{\Omega(f)},$$

where $\Omega(f)$ is the norm of f in the RKHS (Equation (9)). If the training set is not separable the support vectors are either the data points at a distance less that d from the boundary or the points which are misclassified. In both cases if all the data points which are not support vectors were discarded from the training set the minimum of functional (7) and the solution (8) would be unchanged. In this context, an interesting perspective on SVM is to consider its information compression properties. The support vectors represent in this sense the most informative data points and compress the information contained in the training set: for the purpose of, say, classification of future vectors only the support vectors need to be stored, while all other training examples can be discarded[7]. This is a key property of SVM and might explain why this technique works well in many practical applications.

A similar analysis holds for the regression case but a clear geometric interpretation is still missing. It is interesting to observe that the SVM technique was first proposed for classification problems and then extended to the regression problem. It was also shown in [17] that SVM for classification are a special case of SVM for regression as soon as the parameter ϵ is large enough. For the technical discussion see [17].

4   Discussion

There are still many open problems concerning structural risk minimization, regularization theory and SVM and our understanding of them is still improving. We refer the reader to [7] for a more detailed overview of these important concepts.

It is also interesting to observe that SVM's and regularization can be interpreted as the MAP solution of a Bayesian model where the regularization functional is the minus log-likelihood of the posterior probability of the examples. In this context, the regularization term is the result of assuming a zero mean Gaussian prior on the coefficient a_n in Equation 9. Likewise, the empirical error is the minus log likelihood of the output noise on the $i.i.d$ input examples. For a detailed discussion see [7]. [16] discusses the model of the noise underlying the epsilon insensitive loss function. Finally, it is also interesting to note that SVM regression technique can be related to other function and signal approximation techniques (see, e.g., [8]). In particular sparse representations from overcomplete dictionaries can be studied with appropriate kernel functions.

---

[7] There is in fact a relation between the compression factor expressed as the ratio of data points to support vectors and the probability expected risk of the SVM (see [21]). More in general, Vapnik, in comparing the empirical risk minimization principle with the Minimum Description Length principle [18], derives a bound on the generalization error as a function of the compression coefficient.

Acknowledgment

Most of the material paper is taken from the introduction of the author Ph.D. Thesis entitled "Study and application of statistical learning theory", University of Genova, December 1998. The author would like to thank Alessandro Verri, Tomaso Poggio, Theodoros Evgeniou, and Sayan Mukherjee for useful discussions.

References

[1] N. Alon, S. Ben-David, N. Cesa-Bianchi, and D. Haussler: 1993, 'Scale-sensitive dimensions, uniform convergence, and learnability'. *Symposium on Foundations of Computer Science.* 235

[2] N. Aronszajn. Theory of reproducing kernels. *Trans. Amer. Math. Soc.*, 686:337–404, 1950. 237

[3] M. Bertero. Regularization methods for linear inverse problems. In C. G. Talenti, editor, *Inverse Problems*. Springer-Verlag, Berlin, 1986. 236

[4] C. Cortes, and V. Vapnik: 1995, 'Support Vector Networks'. *Machine Learning* **20**, 1–25. 238

[5] L. Devroye, L. Györfi, and G. Lugosi: 1996, *A Probabilistic Theory of Pattern Recognition*, No. 31 in Applications of mathematics. New York: Springer.

[6] T. Evgeniou, M. Pontil, C. Papageorgiou, and T. Poggio: 2000, 'Image representations for object detection using kernel classifiers'. In: *Proceedings ACCV*. Taiwan, p. (to appear).

[7] T. Evgeniou, M. Pontil, and T. Poggio: 1999, 'Regularization Networks and Support Vector Machines'. Advances in Computational Mathematics 13, pp 1–50, 2000. 236, 238, 240

[8] F. Girosi. An equivalence between sparse approximation and Support Vector Machines. *Neural Computation*, 10(6):1455–1480, 1998. 237, 239, 240

[9] F. Girosi, M. Jones, and T. Poggio: 1995, 'Regularization theory and neural networks architectures'. *Neural Computation* **7**, 219–269.

[10] T. Jaakkola, and D. Haussler: 1998, 'Probabilistic Kernel Regression Models'. In: *Proc. of Neural Information Processing Conference.*

[11] M. Kearns, and R. Shapire: 1994, 'Efficient distribution-free learning of probabilistic concepts.'. *Journal of Computer and Systems Sciences* **48**(3), 464–497.

[12] V. A. Morozov: 1984, *Methods for solving incorrectly posed problems*. Berlin, Springer-Verlag.

[13] E. Osuna, R. Freund, and F. Girosi: 1997, 'An Improved Training Algorithm for Support Vector Machines'. In: *IEEE Workshop on Neural Networks and Signal Processing*. Amelia Island, FL. 239

[14] J. C. Platt. Sequential minimal imization: A fast algorithm for training support vector machines. Technical Report MST-TR-98-14, Microsoft Research, April 1998. 239

[15] T. Poggio and F. Girosi. Networks for approximation and learning. *Proceedings of the IEEE*, 78(9), September 1990. 237

[16] M. Pontil, S. Mukherjee, and F. Girosi. On the noise model of support vector machine regression. A. I. Memo, MIT Artificial Intelligence Laboratory, 1998. 240

[17] M. Pontil, R. Rifkin, and T. Evgeniou. From regression to classification in support vector machines. A.I. Memo 1649, MIT Artificial Intelligence Lab., 1998. 240

[18] J. Rissanen. Modeling by shortest data description. *Automatica*, 14:465–471, 1978. 240

[19] A.N. Tikhonov, and V.Y. Arsenin: 1977, *Solutions of Ill-posed Problems*. Washington, D.C.: W.H. Winston. 236

[20] V.N. Vapnik. *The Nature of Statistical Learning Theory*. Springer, New York, 1995. 238

[21] V.N. Vapnik: 1998, *Statistical Learning Theory*. New York: Wiley. 240

[22] V.N. Vapnik, and A.Y. Chervonenkis: 1971, 'On the Uniform Convergence of Relative Frequencies of events to their probabilities'. *Th. Prob. and its Applications* **17**(2), 264–280. 235

[23] G. Wahba: 1990, *Splines Models for Observational Data*. Philadelphia: Series in Applied Mathematics, Vol. 59, SIAM. 236

Increasing the Biological Inspiration of Neural Networks

Domenico Parisi

Institute for Cognitive Sciences and Technologies, National Research Council
15 Viale Marx, 00137 Rome, Italy
parisi@ip.rm.cnr.it

Abstract. We describe three extensions of current neural network models in the direction of increasing their biological inspiration. Unlike "classical" connectionism, Artificial Life does not study single disembodied neural networks living in a void but it studies evolving populations of neural networks with a physical body and a genotype and living in a physical environment. Another extension of current models is in the direction of richer, recurrent network structures which allow the networks to self-generate their own input, including linguistic input, in order to reproduce typically human "mental life" phenomena. A third extension is the attempt to reproduce the noncognitive aspects of behavior (emotion, motivation, global psychological states, behavioral style, psychogical disorders, etc.) by incorporating other aspects of the nervous system in neural networks (e.g., sub-cortical structures, neuro-modulators, etc.) and by reproducing the interactions of the nervous system with the rest of the body and not only with the external environment.

Keywords: Artificial life, Mental life

1   Introduction

Neural networks are interesting models of behavior and cognitive capacities because they are biologically inspired models. A crucial reason for choosing neural networks against symbol-manipulation models is that, unlike symbol manipulation models, neural networks incorporate a number of properties of biological systems, in particular of nervous systems, that appear to be important not only to better understand the behavior and cognitive capacities of natural organisms, including humans, but also to construct more useful technologies. Neural networks process information in parallel rather than in sequence, they are intrinsically quantitative in nature, they allow the simultaneous satisfaction of multiple constraints, they deal adequately with incomplete or disturbed input, they degrade gracefully when internally "lesioned", and they are not "designed" by the researcher/engineer but the researcher/engineer limits him/herself to deciding the conditions under which the system autonomously finds solutions to problems by self-organizing (learning). These biologically inspired properties of neural networks are what makes them attractive as models of the behavior of real organisms and as the basis of new kinds of technological artifacts and solutions.

M. Marinaro and R. Tagliaferri (Eds.): WIRN VIETRI 2002, LNCS 2486, pp. 243–252, 2002.
© Springer-Verlag Berlin Heidelberg 2002

Like all models in science, neural networks simplify with respect to reality. The nervous system is an extremely complicated portion of reality, as can be gathered from any neuroscience textbook, and a typical artificial neural network captures of the actual nervous system only an extremely limited number of very fundamental properties. This is not a criticism of neural networks since, as we have said, all models in science simplify with respect to reality and models allow us to better understand reality just because they simplify reality. The real problem is to incorporate in a model those aspects of reality which are critical for understanding the phenomena of interest while leaving other aspects out.

Research using very simplified neural networks has been able to illuminate many important phenomena of behavior and cognition and to suggest useful practical applications of neural networks. However, it is plausible that by including other aspects of biological reality, aspects which typical neural networks leave out, neural network models can help us understand other phenomena of behavior and cognition and to contruct more useful technologies. In this chapter we describe some extensions of neural network research in the direction of increasing the biological inspiration of neural network models.

2   Neural Networks in an Artificial Life Perspective

Artificial Life tries to understand all phenomena of the living world by constructing artificial systems that reproduce living phenomena [1]. Behavior and cognition are properties of biological organisms and therefore they are among the phenomena of the living world. Since neural networks are artificial systems (computer simulations) that try to reproduce behavior and cognition, neural networks are by definition part of Artificial Life. However, explicitly viewing neural networks in the perspective of Artificial Life introduces a number of important changes in research using neural networks and makes Artificial Life Neural Networks (ALNNs) [2] rather different from "classical" neural networks [3].

Unlike "classical" neural networks, ALNNs:
- have a physical body - live in and interact with a physical environment
- have a genotype associated with them - are members of biologically evolving populations of neural networks.

What is simulated in ALNN simulations is not a single nervous system (neural network) but a population of organisms that are all individually different from one another, each individual has a body (which sometimes is not simulated but is a physical robot [4]) with specific physical properties (e.g., size, shape, spatial disposition of sensory and motor organs, type of information encoded in the sensory organs, degrees of freedom of the motor organs, etc.), each individual is born, develops, possibly reproduces, and dies, each individual inherits from its parents a genotype which, together with the environment and the individual's experience in the environment, determines how the individual develops and its adult behavior.

What are the implications of using ALNNs rather than "classical" neural networks?

By being embodied in a physical body and by controlling this body ALNNs are, primarily, sensory-motor systems. What is encoded in their input and output units cannot be arbitrarily decided by the researcher but the input units necessarily encode sensory information which is physically caused by some current event or property of the external environment, and the output units encode some movement of the organism's body or body part. This has important implications for the internal representations of neural networks. What neural networks basically do is transform activation patterns into other activation patterns. An input activation pattern is progressively transformed in the network's successive layers of internal units until an output activation patterns is generated. Two principles govern these transformations: categorization and discrimination. Categorization is making different inputs which must be responded to with the same output progressively more similar. Discrimination is making similar inputs that must be responded to with different outputs more different. Therefore, in neural networks it is the output that dictates the nature of internal representations (internal activation patterns). Since ALNNs are systems for mapping sensory inputs into motor outputs, ALNNs suggest an action-based theory of knowledge: the network's "knowledge", i.e., the network's architecture and its connection weights that allow the network to respond to the input with the appropriate output, determines internal representations that reflect the properties (similarity space) of motor outputs rather than the properties (similarity space) of sensory inputs. In an ALNN it is the sensory input that causes the internal representations but it is the motor output which dictates the form of these representations [5].

Another implication of having a body is that the body is part of the environment with which the neural networks interacts. ALNNs interact with the body-external environment but they also interact with the rest of the organism's body, i.e., with the body-internal environment. The neural network receives information from inside the body and it causes changes in the internal state of the body.

A very important property of ALNNs is that they are ecological networks, i.e., they live in and interact with a physical environment which is part of what is simulated [6]. In "classical" networks it is the researcher who decides what is the input to a neural network and who judges the network's output (in supervised learning models). On the other hand, ALNNs receive their inputs from the environment and their performance is "judged" by the environment in which they happen to live. The fact that ALNNs have a body and live in a physical environment has the crucial consequence that, unlike "classical" neural networks, ALNNs have some control on their input. "Classical" networks are restricted to responding as effectively as possible to the input that happens to arrive from outside (from the researcher). In contrast, ALNNs can to some extent choose their own input. With their motor output ALNNs change either the physical relation of their body/body part to the external environment (by locomoting, turning the eyes or the head, reaching and touching objects, etc.) or the external environment itself (by manipulating objects, displacing them, changing their properties, putting them together or pulling them apart, etc.). This has the consequence that ALNNs with their behavior can influence the future inputs that they will receive from the environment. Hence, ALNNs are not restricted to learning to respond better to whatever input arrives from outside but they can learn to behave in such a way that they are exposed to useful input, i.e., input which is more informative, easier to be responded to, allowing the network to learn more, etc.

Controlling one's own input is a critical property of biological organisms. To understand their behavior it not sufficient to understand and simulate the sequence of causes and effects which takes place from input to output inside the neural network but it is also crucial to understand and simulate the sequence of causes and effects which takes place from output to input outside the neural network in the external environment (or inside the organism's body but outside its nervous system). In particular human intelligence seems to rely very much on controlling one's inputs and it is reasonable to think that more "intelligent" technologies could be realized if we were able to incorporate this trait of biological organisms in our technologies. Furthermore, humans tend to adapt to their environment by modifying the environment rather than modifying themselves, and this active adaptation can only be studied if the simulations include an environment that can be modified. This may have important technological implications if we allow our technological artefacts, for example robots but also software agents, to choose between learning/evolving, i.e., modifying themselves to perform better in a given environment, and modifying the external environment to make the environment easier for them to live in.

ALNNs are not only embodied and situated but they are also evolutionary. ALNNs are accompanied by a genotype which is inherited by each individual ALNN from its parents and which determines some of the properties of the individual, for example its network architecture. Genotypes are not fixed and decided by the researcher but they are the result of a process of evolution which takes place in the successive generations of the population of which the individual is a member [7]. Evolutionary change is due to selective reproduction, sexual recombination of portions of the genotypes of the two parents (mother and father), and random mutations. Any aspect of an individual can be encoded in the genotype and therefore can evolve: the network architecture, the network's connection weights (or constraints on weights; e.g., if a weight is excitatory or inhibitory), the individual's learning parameters (e.g., learning rate and momentum in backpropagation learning), what is encoded and how in the individual's input and output units, etc.

Evolutionary neural networks allow the researcher to study the interaction and cooperation between two types of adaptations: adaptation at the individual level (learning) and adaptation at the population level (evolution). For example, evolution may cooperate with learning if evolution is entrusted with the task of finding the best network architectures and learning with the task of finding the best connection weights for those architectures. Network architecture may be a critical variable in a neural network's performance. Nonmodular architectures run the risk of neural intereference if the organism must accomplish two or more different tasks. If one and the same connection between two units is used in two or more tasks, the connection may receive conflicting messages during learning. It may be asked to increase its weight value in order to accomplish one task and to decrease this value to accomplish another task. This risk is avoided by modular networks where each module includes connections that are dedicated to only one task [8]. Furthermore, possessing the appropriate modular architecture may help neural networks to identify and exploit the structure which is implicit in a task. However, modular architecture should not be designed (hardwired) by the researcher but it should emerge as part of the process of acquiring the ability to accomplish the task. There exist learning algorithms that allow a single network to develop the appropriate network architecture together with the appropriate connection weights but evolutionary (genetic) algorithms seem to be more generally useful to identify useful network architectures.

Most work using "classical" neural networks is based on simple architectures where the only modularity is represented by the successive layers of internal units. In contrast, the nervous system clearly is a highly modularized system with various internal distinctions and sub-distinctions: e.g., brain stem, sub-cortical, cortical; frontal, temporal, parietal, occipital lobes; the two cortical emispheres; the various sub-regions within a cortical lobe, etc. It is highly probable that the exceptional performances of the human brain are due not only to the high number of its neurons but also to the brain's very complex modularity. The use of genetic algorithms for developing appropriate network architectures across successive generations, while the connection weights for these architectures are found by each individual during its life on the basis of the individual's experience in the environment (learning), allows research using ALNNs to explore the possibilites offered by this two-level adaptation process which appears to be specifically appropriate for keeping track of changes in the environment at two temporal scales: long term changes for evolution, short term changes for learning.

As we have said, any aspect of an ALNN, and of its body, can be encoded in the genotype and can evolve. In "classical" neural networks what is encoded in the network's input and output units, and how it is encoded, is normally decided by the researcher. In ALNNs it is not necessarily so. Even if the environment in which an ALNN lives is decided by the researcher (but, as we have seen, the network can modify the environment), which of the physico-chemical properties, events, and processes that make up the environment is encoded in the neural network's input units, and how, remains to be decided and can emerge as part of the evolutionary adaptation of a population of ALNNs to their environment. And the same applies to what is encoded in the networks' output units, and how. If what is encoded in the input and output units, and how it is encoded, is specified in the genotype, evolution can find the best input and output encodings rather than leaving this decision to the researcher. For example, it may turn out that since input and output encodings co-evolve, they must be mutually appropriate, that is, co-adapted, and there is no absolute best input or output encoding but what is the best input encoding depends on the the output encoding, and viceversa.

Another aspect of change which can be explored using ALNNs is development or ontogeny, that is, changes (developmental stages, critical periods, etc.) that occur during the life of an individual and that are under the influence of the individual's genotype. All the changes that occur in an individual during the individual's life depend both on the individual's genotype and on the particular experiences of the individual in the particular environment. However, changes that are mainly attributable to the genotype tend to be called maturation, those that are mainly attributable to experience are called learning, and those in which both the genotype and individual experience have a significant role can be called development. Genotypes are not entirely "executed" (decoded) at birth but they may encode a "developmental program" which specifies what develops at what age. Developmental programs represent adaptive solutions to living in a particular environment, even when they simply specify which environmental input to process at successive ages.

3   Mental Life

"Classical" neural networks tend to have a simple feedforward architecture. Input arrives from outside and activation is propagated through one or more successive layers of internal units until an output is generated. Humans possess nervous systems with a rich and complex structure of recurrent or feedback connections which allow the network to self-generate its own input and to respond to this self-generated input rather than to input arriving from outside, i.e., from the external environment and from the rest of the organism's body. This is the basis of mental life, i.e., of mental images, memory recollections, thoughts, reasonings, predictions, planning, and also dreams and allucinations. The neural network self-generates its own sensory input and it generates motor output which is not physically executed and therefore has no causal effect on the external environment but may result in self-generated sensory input. For example, a visual (mental) image is the self-generation inside the neural network of an internal representation which is similar to the internal representation produced in other occasions by some visual input from the external environment. Mental life in humans is strongly influenced and made more powerful by the use of language. Language begins in humans as the production of phono-articulatory movements that result in sounds or the arrival of sounds produced by other individuals. In both cases the different sounds are correlated with specific experiences of the organism and with the internal representations produced by these experiences. This correlation gives meaning to the sounds that are produced or received by the organism and allows to organism to work with the sounds as substitutes of the experiences. Much of mental life is internal self-generation of linguistic (meaningful) sounds and the organism's responses to these self-generated linguistic sounds.

A crucial aspect of mental life is the ability to generate predictions of future input. A prediction is an activation pattern in some sub-set of the neural network's internal units which matches some future or possible input from the external world and which is then fed back with recurrent connections to the neural network for further processing. Predictions are of two types: predictions of events (inputs) that happen independently from the organism's behavior (e.g., wheather forecasts) and predictions of inputs resulting from some planned but not yet executed action on the part of the organism (e.g., predicting that if I drop a glass, the glass will break). The first type of predictions may be important because they allow the organism to prepare to future input. But it is the second type of predictions, predictions of the results of one's own actions, that may boost the intelligence and effectiveness of an organism's behavior. As we know, ecological neural networks tend to influence their own input by modifying with their (motor) output either the physical relation of the organism's body/body part to the external environment or the external environment itself. A neural network can plan a movement but before physically executing the movement it can generate a prediction of the future input that it will receive from the external environment when the movement will be actually executed. These predictions may explain automaticity of behavior (movements are generated in response to the predicted input resulting from movements rather than in response to the actual input) and, at another level, they can be subject to evalutations on the part of the neural network in order to decide whether to actually execute a movement or sequence of movements or refrain from doing so. This of course is the basis of reflective action, planning, and the adoption of decisions.

4   Noncognitive Aspects of Behavior

Almost all work which is dedicated to the construction of artificial systems is restricted to the reproduction of the cognitive aspects of behavior and leaves completely out its many important noncognitive aspects. Cognitive aspects refer to what an organism can do or is able to do, to its skills, abilities, knowledge, intelligence, whereas noncognitive aspects include motivations and emotions, and many other behavioral phenomena in real organisms. One reason for this preference for the cognitive aspects of behavior is that the construction of "intelligent" artificial systems tends to have a practical, technological or engineering, orientation, and there is the idea that what we need practically are artificial systems with abilities and intelligence unencumbered by motivational and emotional aspects that can only limit and interfere with their performance and their intelligence. Of course, if one is interested in understanding and explaining the behavior of real organisms, i.e., if one has purely scientific goals, this preference is completely unjustified, but even if one has practical and technological goals it is not clear that ignoring the noncognitive aspects of behavior is always a wise choice.

What are the noncognitive aspects of behavior? This is a very preliminary list.

Organisms sleep and they are awake. When they are awake, organisms can have various levels of alertness: very alert, normally active, tired, drowsy, etc. Furthermore, pathology tells us that organisms can be in various peculiar states that are called coma, vegetative state, and lock-in syndrome.

Organisms respond to stimuli in various ways: very quickly and automatically (reflexes), in ways that do not imply that they are aware of the stimuli and even of their responses to the stimuli, in conscious ways, reflectively, after pondering various alternatives, etc. Pathology shows that implicit (nonconscious) processing of the input can be spared while explicit (conscious) processing may be gone (blindsight, neglect).

Organisms can be in various emotional states which influence their behavior and their learning. They can be in various motivational states which dictate which input they attend to and which input they (at least consciously) ignore, and therefore what they do. These motivational states can have various levels of intensity and they can conflict with each other if two motivational states are both active at the same time and both are intense - with important emotional consequences. Again, various pathological behaviors, i.e., behaviors that cause suffering and behavioral ineffectivess in the individual, may be exhibited by organisms because of problems associated with motivation and emotion (e.g., pathological fear and anxiety, pathological lack of motivation and behavior in depression) [9] [10].

Organisms have different personalities and styles of behavior that result from different noncognitive characteristics of their behavior rather than from different levels of cognitive effectiveness (intelligence, ability). Intelligence may be considered a quantitative measure and individuals (or artificial systems) which have more intelligence are automatically preferred to less intelligent individuals. In contrast, different individuals (and artificial systems) with different personalities and styles of behavior can be appropriate for different tasks and situations. Organisms can be male or female and this biological difference can be reflected in differences in behavior.

Noncognitive aspects of behavior tend to be ignored in neural network research because current neural network models capture only some very limited aspects of the nervous system and they almost completely ignore the rest of the body and the interactions between the nervous system and the rest of the body. Inputs can be responded to with motor responses by completely by-passing the brain (through the interneurons in the spinal chord), by going through subcortical circuits (implicit processing) in the brain, or by calling on the more complex processing capacities of cortical circuits (explicit processing). These distinctions are ignored in current neural network models. Furthermore, current neural network models can be interpreted as reproducing the action of only two kinds of neurotransmitters, glutamate for excitatory synapses and GABA (gamma-aminobutyric acid) for inihibitory synapses, but in the brain there are many other neurotransmitters and neuromodulators which play a critical role especially with respect to the noncognitive aspects of behavior [11]. Neuropeptides may be produced by the same neurons that produce glutamate and GABA but they have a different, modulatory, influence on synapses since, while glutamate and GABA have rapid and rapidly disappearing action, neuropeptides tend to have slower and more persistent action. But aside from neurotransmitters and neuromodulators produced and acting in the brain's cortex, there are many other chemical substances (neuroamines: serotonin, dopamine, epinephrine, norepinephrine, etc.) which are produced for example in the brain stem (the part of the brain at the point of junction with the spinal chord) and which affect both sub-cortical (thalamus, hypothalamus, hyppocampus, amigdala) and cortical structures. It is these molecules, in addition to the hormones produced by the body's endocrine system and transported to the brain through the blood circulatory system, that have effects very different from those of cortical neurotransmitters (more diffuse, aspecific, slow acting, generally nonconducive to permanent learning, etc.) and which are responsible for many emotional and motivational aspects of behavior. These effects are similar to those of psychological drugs and this may explain similarities and differences between the action of psychological drugs and psychotherapy.

5   Conclusion

We have described three extensions of neural network models which increase their biological inspiration by adding more biological "facts" and constraints to these models. Research using neural networks in an Artificial Life perspective, that is, networks with a body, an environment, and a genotype, has already produced many interesting results under the name of adaptive behavior, evolutionary robotics, and Artificial Life. Little work has been done on mental life and higher level cognition in artificial organisms and almost nothing on the noncognitive aspects of behavior. However, there appear to be no intrinsic obstacles to extending neural network models in these directions, by adding recurrent circuits to neural network architectures, simulating the structure and functioning of noncortical portions of the nervous system, and reproducing the interactions of the nervous system with the rest of the body rather than with the external environment. This will allow a better match between artificial systems that are constructed by us and real organisms and will perhaps provide new ideas for better technologies and applications.

References

[1] Langton, C. G. (eds): Artificial Life: An Overview. MIT Press, Cambridge, Mass, (1995). 244
[2] Parisi, D.: Neural Networks and Artificial Life. In:G. Parisi, D. Amit (eds.): Frontiers of Life. Academic Press, San Diego, Cal. (in press). 244
[3] Rumelhart, D. E., McClelland, J. L.: Parallel Distributed Processing. Explorations in the Microstructure of Cognition. Volume 1. Foundations. MIT Press, Cambridge, Mass, (1986). 244
[4] Nolfi, S., Floreano, D.: Evolutionary Robotics. MIT Press, Cambridge, Mass, (2001). 244

[5] Di Ferdinando, A., Parisi, D.: Internal representations of sensory input reflect the motor output with which organisms respond to the input. In: Carsetti, A. (ed.): Seeing and Thinking. Kluwer,Amsterdam (in press). 245

[6] Parisi, D., Cecconi, F., Nolfi, S.: Econets: Neural Networks that Learn in an Environment. Network 149-168 (1990). 245

[7] Holland, J. H.: Adaptation in Natural and Artificial Systems. MIT Press, Cambridge, Mass, (1992). 246

[8] Di Ferdinando, A., Calabretta, R., Parisi, D.: Evolving Modular Architectures for Neural Networks. In: French, R., J. P. Sougn(eds.): Connectionist Models of Learning, Development, and Evolution. Springer-Verlag, Berlin Heidelberg New York, (2001). 247

[9] Grossberg, S.: How Allucinations May Arise from Brain Mechanisms of Learning, Attention, and Volition. Journal of the International Neuropsychological Society (in press). 250

[10] Grossberg, S.: The Imbalanced Brain: From Normal Behavior to Schizophrenia. Biological Psychiatry (in press). 250

[11] LeDoux, J.: Synaptic Self. How Our Brains Become What We Are. Viking Press, New York (2002). 250

Author Index

Lecture Notes in Computer Science

For information about Vols. 1–2414
please contact your bookseller or Springer-Verlag